The TABLE BOOK

FROM THE EDITORS OF POPULAR WOODWORKING

POPULAR WOODWORKING BOOKS
CINCINNATI, OHIO
www.popularwoodworking.com

Read This Important Safety Notice

To prevent accidents, keep safety in mind while you work. Use the safety guards installed on power equipment; they are for your protection.

When working on power equipment, keep fingers away from saw blades, wear safety goggles to prevent injuries from flying wood chips and sawdust, wear hearing protection and consider installing a dust vacuum to reduce the amount of airborne sawdust in your woodshop.

Don't wear loose clothing, such as neckties or shirts with loose sleeves, or jewelry, such as rings, necklaces or bracelets, when working on power equipment. Tie back long hair to prevent it from getting caught in your equipment.

People who are sensitive to certain chemicals should check the chemical content of any product before using it.

Due to the variability of local conditions, construction materials, skill levels, etc., neither the author nor Popular Woodworking Books assumes any responsibility for any accidents, injuries, damages or other losses incurred resulting from the material presented in this book.

The authors and editors who compiled this book have tried to make the contents as accurate and correct as possible. Plans, illustrations, photographs and text have been carefully checked. All instructions, plans and projects should be carefully read, studied and understood before beginning construction.

Prices listed for supplies and equipment were current at the time of publication and are subject to change.

THE TABLE BOOK. Copyright © 2010 by Popular Woodworking. Printed and bound in China. All rights reserved. No part of this book may be reproduced in any form or by any electronic or mechanical means including information storage and retrieval systems without permission in writing from the publisher, except by a reviewer, who may quote brief passages in a review. Published by Popular Woodworking Books, an imprint of F+W Media, Inc., 4700 East Galbraith Road, Cincinnati, Ohio, 45236. (800) 289-0963 First edition.

Distributed in Canada by Fraser Direct
100 Armstrong Avenue
Georgetown, Ontario L7G 5S4
Canada

Distributed in the U.K. and Europe by David & Charles
Brunel House
Newton Abbot
Devon TQ12 4PU
England
Tel: (+44) 1626 323200
Fax: (+44) 1626 323319
E-mail: postmaster@davidandcharles.co.uk

Distributed in Australia by Capricorn Link
P.O. Box 704
Windsor, NSW 2756
Australia

 Visit our Web site at www.popularwoodworking.com.

Other fine Popular Woodworking Books are available from your local bookstore or direct from the publisher.

14   13   12   11   10   5   4   3   2   1

Library of Congress Cataloging-in-Publication Data

The table book / from the editors of Popular woodworking. -- 1st ed.
    p. cm.
  ISBN 978-1-4403-0427-9 (pbk. : alk. paper)
  1. Tables. 2. Woodwork. I. Popular woodworking.
  TT197.5.T3T332 2010
  684'.08--dc22
                    2010006834

ACQUISITIONS EDITOR: David Thiel
SENIOR EDITOR: Jim Stack
DESIGNER: Brian Roeth
PRODUCTION COORDINATOR: Mark Griffin
PHOTOGRAPHERS: Staff of Popular Woodworking
ILLUSTRATORS: Staff of Popular Woodworking

Metric Conversion Chart

TO CONVERT	TO	MULTIPLY BY
Inches	Centimeters	2.54
Centimeters	Inches	0.4
Feet	Centimeters	30.5
Centimeters	Feet	0.03
Yards	Meters	0.9
Meters	Yards	1.1

About the Authors

STEVE SHANESY, publisher of *Popular Woodworking Magazine*, is a native of Troy, Ohio, and has more than 20 years experience in cabinet shops. Steve graduated from Ohio University with a BS in journalism and from Los Angeles Trade Technical College with a certificate in cabinetmaking and millwork. He worked as foreman at AE Furniture Manufacturing in Los Angeles —the city's premier commercial and residential furniture maker.

CHRISTOPHER SCHWARZ, executive editor for *Popular Woodworking Magazine*, is a long-time amateur woodworker and professional journalist. He built his first workbench at age 8 and spent weekends helping his father build two houses on the family's farm outside Hackett, Ark. — using mostly hand tools. He has journalism degrees from Northwestern University and The Ohio State University and worked as a magazine and newspaper journalist before joining Popular Woodworking in 1996. Despite his early experience on the farm, Chris remains a hand-tool enthusiast.

ROBERT W. LANG, senior editor for *Popular Woodworking Magazine*, grew up in northeastern Ohio and has been a professional woodworker since the early 1970s. He learned woodworking repairing wooden boats on Lake Erie and in a large commercial shop in Cleveland. Along the way he studied industrial design at The Ohio State University. His experience includes building custom furniture and cabinets as well as managing and engineering large architectural millwork projects. He is the author of several "Shop Drawings" books about furniture and interiors of the Arts & Crafts Movement of the early 1900s.

GLEN HUEY, senior editor for *Popular Woodworking Magazine*, is long-time professional woodworker, author, DVD host and woodworking teacher. Glen joined the staff of *Popular Woodworking* in 2006.

MALCOLM HUEY, father of Glen Huey. He taught Glen all he knows about woodworking. Well, almost everything.

DAVID THIEL has been a woodworker (both professionally and for fun) for more that 30 years. He spent 10 years as a senior editor for *Popular Woodworking Magazine* and is now the executive editor for *Popular Woodworking* books. David also appeared as the host of DIY Network's Tools & Techniques series for more than 100 episodes.

JIM STACK, senior editor for *Popular Woodworking* books, is a flat-lander derelict who grew up in south central Nebraska. He graduated from the Berklee College of Music in Boston with a Bachelor's degree in music composition. After moving to Cincinnati, he worked in local cabinet- and furniture-making shops for almost 20 years. He now builds guitars and other contraptions as the mood strikes him. Jim joined F+W Media in 1999.

JOHN HUTCHINSON lives in Ohio and is an architect who loves to design and build mildly eccentric furniture.

JIM STUARD is a former editor for *Popular Woodworking Magazine*. He now hosts a website devoted to fly fishing and does woodworking when he can.

Table of Contents

122

TWO TUB TABLES

128

PRAIRIE-STYLE COFFEE TABLE

136

BUTLER TRAY TABLE

146

PLYWOOD NESTING TABLES

150

GREAT DANISH MODERN TABLE

154

MALOOF-STYLE TABLE

160

GAME TABLE

166

NAKASHIMA-INSPIRED TABLE

172

FEDERAL INLAY TABLE

182

BALTIMORE CARD TABLE

192

CREOLE TABLE

202

DRAW-LEAF GAME TABLE

212

ASIAN BEDSIDE TABLE

218

QUEEN ANNE SIDE TABLE

230

SHAKER DROP-LEAF TABLE

238

MODERN OCCASIONAL TABLE

244

QUEEN ANNE DINING TABLE

254

SHAKER TRESTLE TABLE

260

GREEK KEY DESK

Introduction

The invention of the table is a great idea. The first person to realize that stuff could be put at their fingertips, rather than having to bend over to retrieve it, probably had a sore back and knew there had to be a better way. Also, sitting on the ground to eat was getting old, but that's about the chair, not a table. Hmm, which came first — the chair or the table?

To keep it simple, this book is about the table. We've compiled 35 projects from *Popular Woodworking* magazine and *Popular Woodworking* books. Each project is unique, all are functional and each one serves a specific need or desire on the part of the original designer. Does a table need fancy curved legs (or in the case of a couple projects — no legs at all) or to be made of wood? Nope, but once a need is fulfilled, it's the nature of creative people to be, well, creative.

There's something for everyone in this book. But, to be fair, most of the projects require intermediate to advanced woodworking skills. The first project is a portable writing desk like Thomas Jefferson might have used. Back then, when folks traveled, they took their packed luggage and a laptop writing desk. They wrote letters, journals and stories as they traveled. When they got to where they were going, they would probably encounter a Queen Anne dining table, maybe a Shaker trestle table or a Shaker drop-leaf table.

Nowadays, we still eat at a table, we put our overnight stuff on a small table by our bed and toss magazines on a coffee table. All these are projects in this book.

Oh, let's don't forget game tables. We've a few for you to choose from. There's a checkers/chess table, a Porringer side table that could be used to play cards and it'll hold your drinks without them getting in the way.

We've got round tables, square tables, rectangular tables, glass-topped tables. There's tables with no legs, one table with one leg (well, it has one big foot), a table with three legs, several with four legs, one with five legs and one with 6 (it could be made with up to 20) legs. A couple of tables are U-shaped, one has a continuous leg (really, it has no beginning and no end) and one table that is made from strips of wood using only butt-joint joinery.

You'll have the opportunity to learn how to work with veneers and inlays, how to make Cabriole and tapered legs and how to make a table out of a slab of wood. Some tables have drawers and one has a lower shelf so you can stash stuff out of the quickly when surprise guests show up at your door.

Start with the first project, start in the middle or work your way backwards through the book, it doesn't matter. Each project is unique and stands on its own two (or three or whatever) feet.

Writing letters longhand is one of life's simple pleasures, as is building this traditional lap desk.

Portable Writing Desk

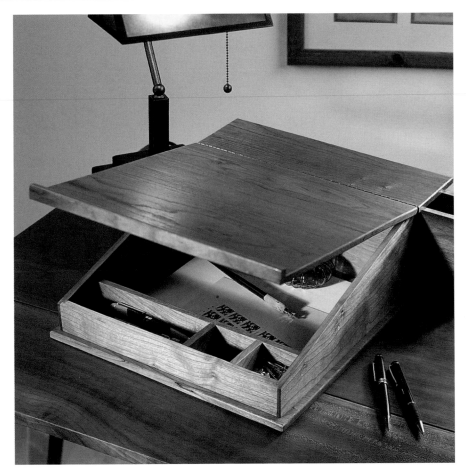

BY DAVID THIEL

The portable writing desk was an integral part of 18th- and 19th-century life, when writing was the only form of long-distance communication. As people spread across the globe in the 19th century, correspondence by mail became much more popular, and so did the writing desk.

The portable desks needed to be sturdy and lightweight, hold stationery and writing utensils, and have a place for people to write easily. The desk seen here will do all of the above, plus hold paper clips, rubber bands and more in the simple side drawer.

While you might not abandon your laptop computer for this more traditional item, it is an excellent place to write holiday cards, thank-you notes and personal correspondence. Though we all like the immediacy of email, a hand-written letter always is a welcome surprise.

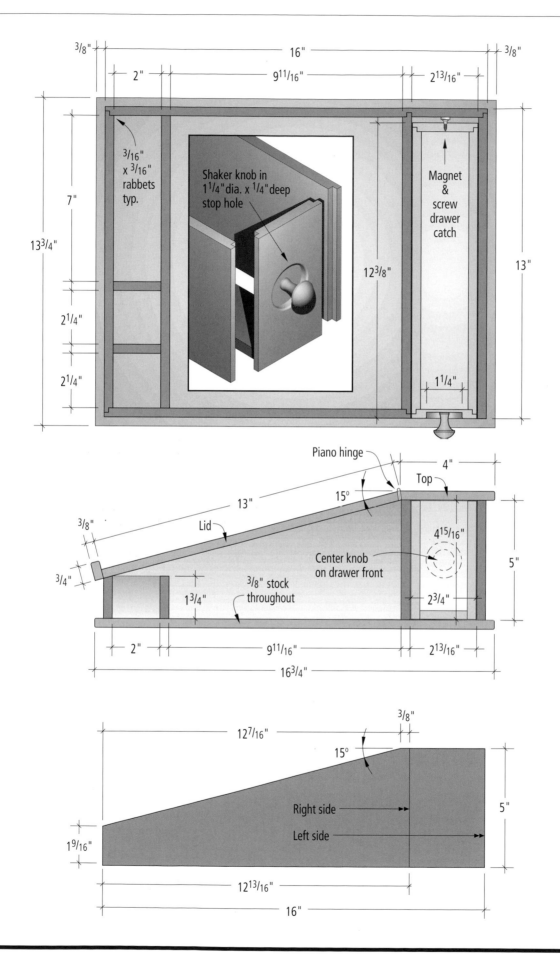

PORTABLE WRITING DESK • INCHES (MILLIMETERS)

QUANTITY	PART	STOCK	THICKNESS	(mm)	WIDTH	(mm)	LENGTH	(mm)	COMMENTS
1	Top	Cherry	3/8	10	4	102	13 3/4	349	
1	Lid	Cherry	3/8	10	13	330	13 3/4	349	
1	Bottom	Cherry	3/8	10	16 3/4	425	13 3/4	349	
1	Left side	Cherry	3/8	10	5	127	16	406	3/16" × 3/16" rabbet BE
1	Right side	Cherry	3/8	10	5	127	12 13/16	325	3/16" × 3/16" rabbet BE
1	Back	Cherry	3/8	10	5	127	12 13/16	325	3/16" × 3/16" rabbet OE
1	Front	Cherry	3/8	10	1 3/4	44	12 13/16	325	3/16" × 3/16" rabbet BE
1	Back divider	Cherry	3/8	10	5	127	12 13/16	325	3/16" × 3/16" rabbet BE
1	Front divider	Cherry	3/8	10	1 3/4	44	12 1/4	311	
2	Interior dividers	Cherry	3/8	10	1 3/4	44	2	51	
1	Lid lip	Cherry	3/8	10	3/4	19	13 3/4	349	
2	Drawer sides	Cherry	3/8	10	5	127	1	25	3/16" × 3/16" rabbet BE
2	Drawer front and back	Cherry	3/8	10	5	127	2	51	3/16" × 3/16" rabbet BE
1	Drawer bottom	Cherry	3/8	10	2	51	11 5/8	295	
1	Drawer knob	Cherry	3/4 dia.	19			5/8	16	

BE=both ends, OE=one end

LEFT: To avoid making mistakes once you're at the machine, mark each of the pieces as either inside or outside, as well as the ends that will need rabbet cuts.

PHOTOS BELOW: Cut rabbets in multiple passes on the saw. The first pass, with the piece pushed against the fence, defines the shoulder of the rabbet (top). The second pass (lower), with the piece moved away from the fence, clears the rest of the waste. A combination blade will leave ridges in the rabbet; a few more passes over the blade will remove those.

After carefully laying out the angle locations on both sides, use the band saw and cut about 1/16" wide of the line to allow for accurate trimming.

To clean up the band saw cuts and ensure they're identical, clamp the two sides together and use a bench plane to clean them up simultaneously.

With the front piece clamped between the sides (without glue) transfer the angle from the side to the front piece. Do the same on both ends, then use a straightedge or rule to connect the lines on the front and back. This defines the waste that needs to be removed. A block plane makes quick work of this angle.

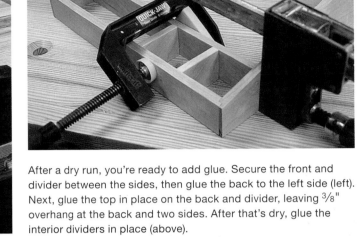

After a dry run, you're ready to add glue. Secure the front and divider between the sides, then glue the back to the left side (left). Next, glue the top in place on the back and divider, leaving ⅜" overhang at the back and two sides. After that's dry, glue the interior dividers in place (above).

ABOVE LEFT: Bevel the lid to match the angle formed by the sides and the front edge of the top. Lay the lid in place and transfer the angle to the lid from the top using a ruler. Then use your block plane to bevel the edge of the top.

ABOVE RIGHT: Because wood moves with changes in humidity, the bottom needs to expand from front to back — without breaking the box. This is solved by screwing the bottom to the box through elongated screw holes.

LEFT: Make the drawer using the same rabbet joints as the desk. The two sides fit between the front and back, while the bottom is glued in place between the four pieces.

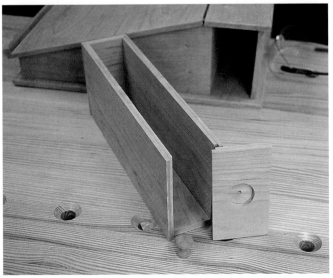

While this is one of the most traditional furniture forms, building one of these small tables is not all that complicated.

PROJECT
2

Classic Shaker Candle Stand

BY MALCOLM HUEY

Built by members of the Mount Lebanon community in New York during the first half of the 19th century, this recognizable Shaker form is actually their stylish interpretation of earlier forms. The legs are a derivation of a Sheraton design. The Shakers referred to the leg design as "umbrella" or "spider feet." I first found this table in John Kassay's *The Book of Shaker Furniture*. The original shown in the book is part of the J.J.G. McCue collection, and resides in the Museum of Fine Arts in Boston. A very similar cherry table is also in the collection of the Metropolitan Museum of Art in New York City.

Forgiving Form

While I've included detailed patterns for both the pedestal and the legs on this table, the form is actually forgiving. If your turning ends up a little thinner in one area, or the legs end up a hair thinner at the bottom, it's okay. It's a nice-looking project that will allow you to practice your skills and end up with a great-looking table.

Everything about the table connects to the pedestal, so let's begin there. I've included a pattern that gives the diameter of the pedestal all along its length. While the turning skills required for the piece aren't taxing, it's not something to attempt your first time at the lathe. Some basic knowledge of turning is required.

Start with a 12/4 maple turning blank that is about 20" long. Turn the entire piece to round, finishing out at about 2⁷⁄₈" in diameter. That's the largest diameter dimension used on the pattern, but if you end up with less than that, adjust the rest of the dimensions to match that difference. Turn the rest of the pedestal according to the pattern, leaving a 1"-diameter × ¾"-long stub on both ends.

When you're done with the pedestal, the next step is to cut the three sliding dovetail grooves for the legs on the base of the pedestal. The legs are oriented at 120° around the base of the pedestal. You need to mark the locations accurately, but to cut the grooves I've borrowed from a few different books to make a router jig that makes it nearly foolproof. The jig is made from shop scraps and holds the two stubs of the pedestal in place and uses a screw to hold the pedestal oriented correctly to cut each groove. Use two different bits to cut the grooves. Start with a ½" straight bit to remove most of the wood, then follow up with an 8° dovetail bit. Stop the groove at the shoulder, 3½" up from the base of the pedestal.

The next step is to rough out the legs by milling three pieces to ⁷⁄₈" × 4" × 15". Then use the provided scaled pattern to lay out the shape of the legs in pencil on the pieces. Make sure the grain runs the length of the leg, or your legs could snap. Determine the location of the dovetail pin on each leg and cut the corner from the leg blank at that point. Before shaping the rest of the leg, it's easier to cut the dovetail pin first.

Set up your dovetail bit in a router table. Attach an auxiliary fence to allow you to hold the leg upright against the fence. Run a test piece on some scrap to see if your offset is correct. You want the fit to be tight at this point. You'll hand-fit each joint later. When the test piece fits to your satisfaction, run each side of the leg past the bit, shaping the pins.

With this important joint complete on all three leg pieces, head for the band saw and rough cut the legs to shape. Then use a spindle sander (or spokeshave) and shape the legs to finished size. On the original Shaker piece, the legs are also tapered slightly in thickness down to the feet. You can achieve this authentic look with a bench plane.

The next step is to fit each leg to the pedestal. I re-use part of my router jig as a stop on my bench to hold the pedestal in place while I carefully pare away material with a chisel until each leg slides in place with a snug fit.

Once satisfied, trim the lower stub off the pedestal, finish sand the legs and post, and glue the legs in place. You now have a table base.

If your joint is well-made, you shouldn't need any clamping pressure. The Shakers used metal plates across the base of the pedestal to hold the legs in place, but our glues are more reliable. Allow the glue to cure and move on to the top.

CLASSIC SHAKER CANDLE STAND • INCHES (MILLIMETERS)

QUANTITY	PART	STOCK	THICKNESS	(mm)	WIDTH	(mm)	LENGTH	(mm)	COMMENTS
1	top	maple	$3/4$	19	20	508	20	508	oversized for cutting out top
1	mounting plate	maple	$3/4$	19	5	127	$13^3/4$	349	
3	legs	maple	$7/8$	22	$19^9/16$	497	$14^5/8$	371	
1	pedestal	maple	$3^1/2$	89	$3^1/2$	89	24	610	blank size before turning
4	wood screws	steel	No. 9	4.5			$1^1/4$	32	

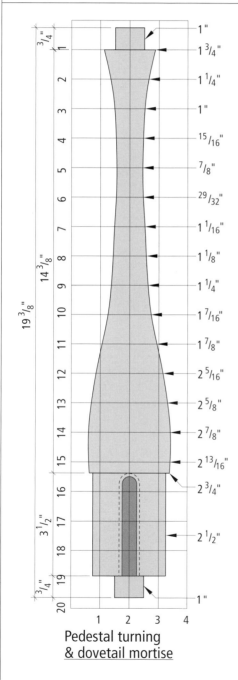

Pedestal turning & dovetail mortise

Turning the pedestal is a great way to practice your lathe skills. While there is a pattern to follow, the lines are fluid enough to allow for personalization, slight miscalculations or both.

The dovetailing jig makes it easy to place the leg, run the groove, then rotate the leg to the next position.

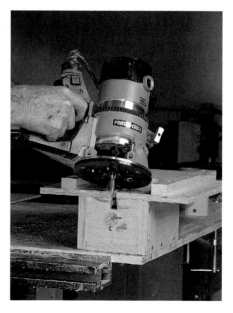

Note the screw in the diagram (opposite page) and photo (below) that's used to hold the pedestal in the appropriate position.

The last two parts are the easiest to make. If you can find a piece of maple that is 20" wide, use it for the top. That's what the Shakers did, and it looks great. If you can't find a board that wide, look for a thicker piece, cut it in half along the width on your band saw and make the top bookmatched. While you're scrounging for wood, grab a piece that's 5" × 13¾" to use as the mounting plate.

To shape the top, I use a circle-cutting jig that mounts to my router. With the center of the jig attached to the underside of the top, cut the 19⅞"-diameter shape using a spiral bit, making the cut in three or four passes. When the top is round, chuck a ½" roundover bit in your router and round over the bottom edge of the top. Then do the same to the

top edge with a ¹⁄₁₆" roundover bit (or break the edge with sandpaper).

To keep the mounting like the original, both ends of the plate taper to ¼" thick within the first 3⅜" of each end. I think the safest way to do this is to use a band saw to cut the taper, then use a sander to clean up the surface.

With the plate tapered, cut a ³⁄₁₆" roundover on all four edges and drill a 1"-diameter hole in the center of the plate. Then drill a few more mounting holes for attaching the top. Now is the time to finish sand the piece.

To attach the base to the mounting plate, cut a saw kerf across the width of the top stub on the pedestal, running the kerf with the grain. Slip the mounting plate over the top of the stub, then add

glue and drive a wedge into the saw kerf to lock the plate in place. When the glue is dry, cut the tenon and stub flush to the top of the mounting plate.

All that's left is to attach the top and add the finish. I use a water-based aniline dye made by Moser that's available from Woodworker's Supply (see supplier's list on page 270). In my shop we traditionally dilute the dye more than the manufacturer recommends. Be sure to make some sample boards to find a color that you like. Next, follow that with a couple coats of orange shellac. I level that with 360-grit sandpaper and then apply a brown glazing stain over the shellac. After I allow that to dry overnight, a few coats of lacquer finish the job.

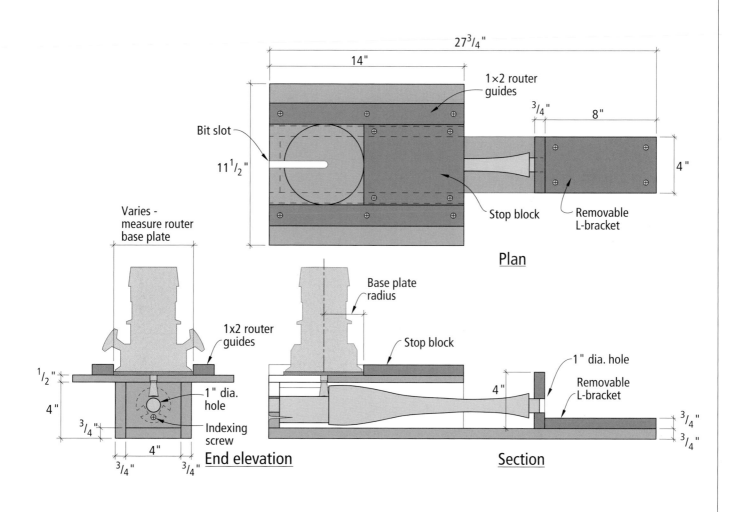

Plan

End elevation

Section

To cut the mating pins for the sliding dovetails, a router table works best. By using an auxiliary fence clamped above the table, first one side of the leg is run (left), then the leg is turned around and the opposite side is run (right).

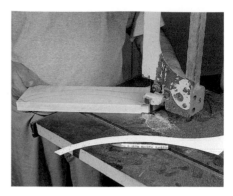

The leg shape is created by making a full-size template from the included scaled pattern, then transferring that to the leg blanks. A band saw makes quick work of the roughed-out shapes.

A spindle sander makes what could be a daunting task reasonably painless. By using double-sided tape to hold the legs together, all three can be sanded at the same time, reducing work and ensuring uniform shapes.

10"

Dashed lines -
final shape

5/8"

3/8"

135°

15"

2"

2"

Leg pattern

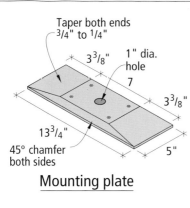

Taper both ends
$^3/_4$" to $^1/_4$"

$3^3/_8$"

1" dia. hole

7

$3^3/_8$"

$13^3/_4$"

45° chamfer both sides

5"

Mounting plate

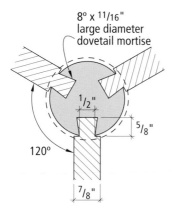

8° x $^{11}/_{16}$" large diameter dovetail mortise

$^1/_2$"

$^5/_8$"

120°

$^7/_8$"

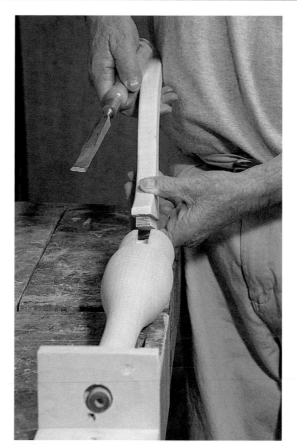

No matter how accurate your machining, there needs to be some hand-work to make the legs fit just right. Don't make the joint too tight, just snug.

A circle-cutting jig attached to my router lets me make a true circle. Take increasingly deeper passes around the perimeter of the top to complete the cut.

It's a good idea to drill clearance holes in the mounting plate before gluing it to the base.

A small project that's big on details.

Thorsen House Side Table

BY DAVID THIEL

I've always appreciated the look of furniture designed by architects Charles and Henry Greene. Though often equated with the Arts & Crafts movement at the beginning of thc 20th century, their furniture designs reflect an Asian influence that softens the often hard lines of Arts & Crafts furniture. While looking for a piece to build, I was talking with Robert W. Lang, senior editor for *Popular Woodworking* and author of the just-published *Shop Drawings for Greene & Greene Furniture* (Fox Chapel). He suggested adapting a small side table originally made for the Thorsen House in Berkeley, Calif.

The cutouts on the aprons quickly won me over, but I did make a couple modifications that lightened the look of the table. Rather than a full-width shelf captured between two straight stretchers, I opted to make the stretcher with a top-and-bottom cloud-lift design and make the shelf only half the width of the original. I also added some ¹⁄₁₆" quirk details to the corners of the legs and the edges of the aprons, stretchers and the shelf. These "rabbets" add a simple shadow line to a very pleasant design.

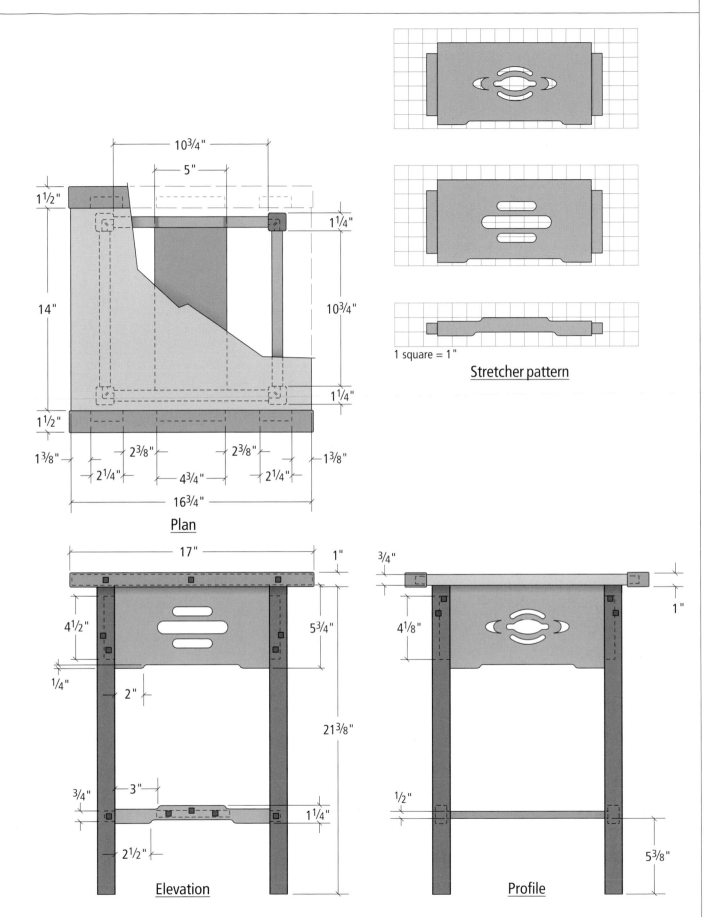

1 square = 1"

Stretcher pattern

Plan

Elevation

Profile

THORSEN HOUSE SIDE TABLE • INCHES (MILLIMETERS)

QUANTITY	PART	STOCK	THICKNESS	(mm)	WIDTH	(mm)	LENGTH	(mm)	COMMENTS
1	top	mahogany	$3/4$	19	$16^3/4$	425	$15^1/2$	394	$3/4$" TBE
2	breadboard ends	mahogany	1	25	$1^1/2$	38	17	432	
4	aprons	mahogany	$3/4$	19	$5^3/4$	146	$12^1/4$	311	$3/4$" TBE
4	legs	mahogany	$1^1/4$	32	$1^1/4$	32	$21^1/4$	540	
2	stretchers	mahogany	$3/4$	19	$1^1/4$	32	$12^1/4$	311	$3/4$" TBE
1	shelf	mahogany	$1/2$	13	$1^3/4$	45	$11^1/4$	286	
32	pegs	Ebony	$3/8$	10	$3/8$	10	$1/4$	6	

TBE = tenon both ends

Start With the Lumber

Selecting your lumber for this table is an important step. Because it's such a small piece, wild grain will dramatically change the overall appearance. You want to look for mahogany that is as straight grained as possible. This will become even more critical if you're bookmatching the top piece. And because of the high cost of mahogany, I definitely recommend bookmatching. It allows you to buy 8/4 material and resaw for the top, aprons and stretchers,

while still allowing enough thickness to yield the legs and breadboards.

Start by selecting the best wood for the top piece. Pay careful attention to the grain orientation as the piece is almost square and it's easy to get the direction reversed, which will yield a funny-looking top. Resaw the top pieces, then surface and join the two boards, trimming to allow the best grain match possible. Now glue the two (hopefully no more) pieces together to form the top.

A $3/8$" mortising chisel makes quick work of the apron mortises on each leg. One of the stretcher mortises is visible on the leg at the bottom of the photo.

While the glue is drying, select the next-best sections of your wood for the aprons and stretchers. Resaw the necessary pieces from your 8/4 material to yield the balance of your pieces. Then surface-plane, joint and saw the stock to final thickness, width and length.

Mortise & Tenon Joinery

The joinery for the table should start at your mortiser. I chose a ³⁄₈" mortising chisel for all the mortises on this piece. Mark the locations of the mortises on the legs, paying careful attention to the location for the lower stretchers. There are only two stretchers and they will require mortises on only one inside face of each leg. Orient the legs so those faces are on the inside.

The mortises for the aprons are ⁷⁄₈" deep and 4½" long. They are centered on

the legs and start ¾" down from the top of the legs. The two apron mortises will intersect one another in the leg, so be careful while cutting the second mortise to avoid damaging the rather thin interior corner left by the two mortises. The stretcher mortises are ¾" long and start 5⅛" up from the bottom of the legs.

While you're at the mortiser, lay out and cut the ⁷⁄₈"-deep mortises in the breadboard ends. The middle mortise is 4¾" long and centered on each breadboard. The two outer mortises are 2¼"

long and start 1⅜" in from each end. All the breadboard mortises are centered in the thickness of the breadboards.

Remove the top from the clamps and trim it to finished size. I used the table saw to cut the tenons on all the pieces, but you may choose to use a router. In fact, I was a little lazy on the saw and opted to leave the ⅛" blade in rather than switch to a dado to run the tenons. There's also a little logic behind my laziness. By making repeat cuts on the cheek of the tenon my blade leaves slight ridges on the surface. If test fitting my tenon achieves a fit that is too snug, I'm able to come back with a rabbeting plane and trim the tenon to fit. Then, miter the ends of the tenons to fit the legs.

Cloud Lifts and Quirks

With the tenons cut it's time to add some of the details. Each of the aprons and the two stretchers have what have been coined "cloud lift" designs. This shaped offset is formed on the lower edge of each apron and on both the top and bottom of the two stretchers. The offset is ¼". The location of the offsets can be determined from the scaled patterns for the aprons and stretchers. The transition isn't a radius, though you could do it that way if you prefer. Rather, the transition can be drawn using ¼" radii, but should then be softened to make the transition

The cloud lifts are subtle curves, not radii. Make a template (bottom) of the curve you like, then transfer that curve to your aprons and stretchers.

The tenons are created on the saw by first defining the shoulders both on the thickness (left) and then the width (right) of each tenon. I then made repeat cuts on the tenon, nibbling away the waste.

To avoid too much filing and sanding, cut as close as you can on the band saw. I cut in close to the line around the curves first (left), then come back and use the cutting edge of the blade to nibble away the waste up to the line (right).

The quirk detail is created on the legs using the table saw. Essentially, you're creating a $1/16" \times 1/16"$ rabbet on each corner of the leg.

The bearing guide shown on this trim router allows the bit to follow the curves of the cloud lifts. You could also install a bearing-guided bit in a router table to make the quirk detail.

more subtle. I made a few test pieces before I was satisfied with the curve, then used that test piece to mark the cloud-lift transitions on the actual pieces. With your pieces marked, head to the band saw and make your cloud-lift cuts. Use a file and sandpaper to clean up the shapes on all the pieces.

To add a little trick for the eye I cut a $1/16"$ rabbet (or quirk) on the long edges of the legs using the table saw (see photo below), and also on the four long edges of the small shelf. To add the same detail to the lower edge of the aprons and all the edges of the stretchers, I set up a trim router with a bearing guide and a straight bit. The guide allows the bit to follow the cloud lifts without difficulty.

Patterns & Ebony

Before assembly, use your scroll saw or fretsaw to cut out the patterns on the aprons. Enlarge the scaled patterns to full size, then attach them to the aprons using adhesive spray. Cut the patterns and use sandpaper and small files to clean them up.

One last step is to make the square holes for the ebony accent pegs. I again used my $3/8"$ mortising chisel to make these $3/8"$-deep holes. The locations of the dual pegs on the legs are $1/4"$ in from either side and the pegs are $5/8"$ apart

ABOVE: Use glue only on the center mortise and tenon of the breadboards. The outer tenons are allowed to move freely to compensate for wood movement.

LEFT: To make the pegs, carefully rip the accent wood to slightly larger than the mortise size. Round the ends of the "stick" using sandpaper, then carefully trim off the 1/4"-tall pegs on the band saw. Sand the peg sides at a slight angle (smaller at the bottom) and glue them in place just proud of the leg's surface.

from one another. The pegs at the tops of the legs start ¾" down from the top of the leg. The lower pattern starts 3⅛" down from the top. The pegs on the stretchers and breadboards are evenly spaced as shown.

Assembly

Finish sand all the pieces of the table base and assemble the frame. Start with the sides that have the stretchers. Then glue the last two aprons between the two frames. Before gluing up the top, use a ⅛"- radius router bit to soften the long edges of the top and all the edges of the breadboard pieces. Finally, glue on the breadboards. Screw the shelf in place through two holes in the stretchers that will receive the ebony pegs.

The pegs are next (see photo above). I used ebony, but you could also use walnut.

I Used my biscuit jointer to cut slots on the inside of the aprons to match the Z-shaped metal mirror fasteners. I then screwed these to the top.

The last step is the finish. A coat of boiled linseed oil will leave a lighter finish, allowing the mahogany to darken with age, or you can speed the process by using a stain. A top coat of lacquer and you have a table with unique details that make it stand out.

This table can be built in a few hours
or a leisurely weekend.

Round Taboret

BY DAVE GRIESMANN

Recently my wife put in a request for a
small round-top table for our entry way.
I did some checking around the internet
and eventually saw an Arts & Crafts table
that fit the general description, but our
house has more contemporary furniture.
I thought about it for a while, changed
a few features as well as the material
(no oak in this one) and came up with
a design that required minimal lumber
and a chance to use my new trim router.

I knew I wanted to paint the base and
have a natural finish on top. I got lucky
and found some maple boards at a local
home improvement center. Then I headed over to the racks with the pine and
found what I needed. I cut the maple
and pine boards into 22" lengths and
edge-glued them together to make two
22" × 22" blanks for my top and sub-top.
The butt joint is one of the simplest of
all woodworking joints, but when working with material that is already at its
finished thickness, it can be a challenge
to hold the edges of the pieces level with
each other.

A simple way to solve this problem
is to add biscuits to the edge joints; they
make it easy to align the pieces during
glue-up. Use three biscuits at each joint,
do a little sanding after the glue dries
and you're done.

If you look at the illustration on the
facing page you can see that the legs of
the table slant in from the floor to the
top. To accomplish this I set my miter
saw to cut at an 88° angle and cut the
ends of my 3"-wide boards. I slid the
boards down 24" and made another cut

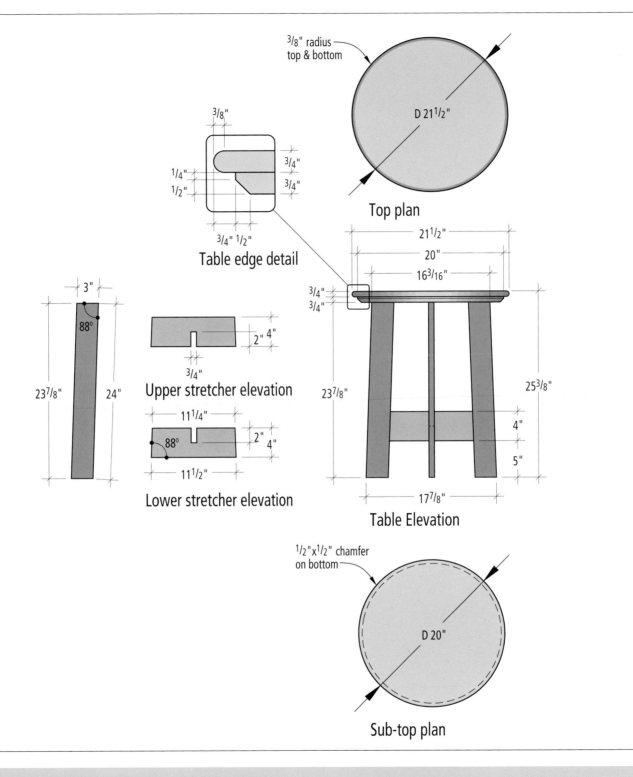

3/8" radius
top & bottom

D 21¹/₂"

Top plan

Table edge detail

3/8"
3/4"
1/4"
1/2"
3/4"
3/4" 1/2"

Upper stretcher elevation

3"
88°
23⁷/₈" 24"

2" 4"
3/4"

Lower stretcher elevation

11¹/₄"
88°
2" 4"
11¹/₂"

Table Elevation

21¹/₂"
20"
16³/₁₆"
3/4"
3/4"
23⁷/₈"
25³/₈"
4"
5"
17⁷/₈"

1/2"x1/2" chamfer
on bottom

D 20"

Sub-top plan

ROUND TABORET • INCHES (MILLIMETERS)

QUANTITY	PART	STOCK	THICKNESS	(mm)	WIDTH	(mm)	LENGTH	(mm)	COMMENTS
1	top	maple	3/4	19	21³/₄ D	552			
1	sub base	pine	3/4	19	20 D	508			
2	stretchers	pine	3/4	19	3¹/₂	89	11¹/₂	292	
4	legs	pine	3/4	19	3	76	24	610	

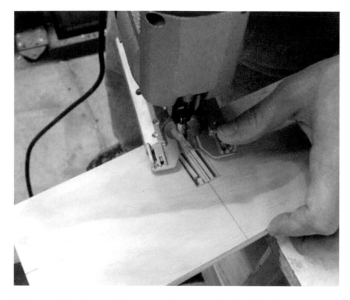

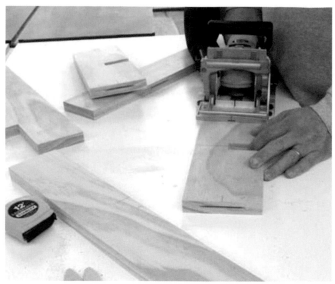

When cutting the half-lap notches, cut to the inside of the pencil lines, then nibble away the waste with successive cuts. A rasp and file will smooth the rough edges.

Biscuits attach the legs to the stretchers. While the slot in the stretcher is centered on the end, the slot in the leg is centered 7" up from the bottom.

Clamping on a angle can cause the clamps to slip, messing up the procedure. A couple of scrap blocks cut at a complementary angle bring the clamping surface back to 90°.

at the same angle. These two cuts give me my four finished leg lengths and the legs slanted perfectly.

Next are the two stretchers. Keeping my saw set at 88°, I cut one end of a 4"-wide board, then flip it over (end-for-end, keeping the same edge against the miter saw fence) and measure 11½" from the tip of the miter cut and make another cut at 88°. The two cuts should be at opposite angles to each other like a picture frame part. Cut the other stretcher.

The two stretchers have a half-lap joint at the center so they will interlock.

To create this joint, lay out and mark a ¾" × 2" notch at the center of both stretchers — with one notch at the top edge of one stretcher and the other at the bottom edge of the other stretcher.

I then clamp one of the stretchers to my bench and use my jig saw to cut out the sides of the notch (leaving the pencil marks) and start cross cutting to remove the waste in between. Then I use my files and rasp to fine tune the joint to a snug fit.

Attach legs attach to the ends of the stretchers using biscuits. Mark and cut the biscuit slots on both ends of the two

stretchers. Make the matching slots on the legs centered 7" up from the inside bottom of each leg.

To clamp the legs, I cut out four blocks that were 90° on one side and 88° on the other. I used these blocks to counter the slant of the legs, which gave me two parallel sides to clamp.

Starting with the sub-top, I used a tape measure and drew an × from corner to corner on the underside of the piece. This located the center point.

I then used a long piece of scrap and drilled a hole at one end to accept the

Using a ½" high, 45-degree chamfer bit in my trim router, I cut the bevel profile on the underside of my sub-top. This isn't a requirement for any building reason, but refines the underside of the table.

To finish the edge of the top I used a ³/₁₆"-roundover bit on both the top and bottom edges. A little hand sanding will blend the radius to the top and edge, removing the slight "edge" left by the router.

The legs are attached to the sub base using dowels whose locations are determined from below (left). Then holes are drilled and the dowels are put in place from above.

tip of a pencil and measured in 10" in on center and drilled another hole for a nail. I used this home-made compass to draw the circle.

I clamped the sub-top to my bench and cut out the circle leaving the line inside my cut. Switching between my files, rasps and sander I smoothed up the edge of the top, then added a chamfer to the bottom edge.

I adjusted the compass to 10¾" to draw a 21½" diameter top, cut it out and

added a roundover profile to the edge.

I unclamped the legs and sanded them with 120 grit and assembled the two halves. I centered the legs on the sub-top, marked the leg locations, marked an × at each leg location by drawing lines from corner to corner of the traced marks and drilled a small hole through the sub-top at each leg location.

I placed the sub-top on top of the legs and drilled ⅜" holes through the sub-top into the center of each leg about

½" deep. Then I cut a ⅜" dowel cut into four pieces, applied glue in the holes and the dowels and tapped them into each leg. After the glue dried I cut the dowels flush and sanded the sub-top. I drilled through the sub-top and attached it to the top using four 1¼" × No.8 screws.

I applied several coats of wipe-on polyurethane to the maple top. Using flat black latex paint, I painted the sub-top and legs. Finally, apply a coat of paste wax on the top.

Building this project will give you insights into mitered joinery and a multifaceted column base.

PROJECT
5

Marble-top Art Deco Table

BY GLEN HUEY

Created in the likeness of a piece designed by French designer Maurice Dufrene in the 1930s, this round Art Deco side table has it all. A marble slab is inset into a bold, round top, a strong center column creates shadows in the light and an understated ring-shaped base is slightly elevated.

The top is created much like a wagon wheel, using segments to produce the circular element. Other parts are turned on the lathe, and the column has a straightforward design that shouts Art Deco. If you are a student of this style of furniture, you will absolutely have to build this table.

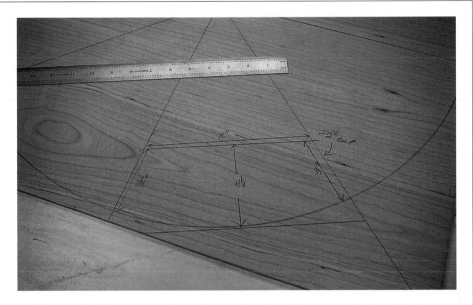

1 To start this piece, you need to determine the size of the segmented top. Create a full-size drawing of the round top and divide the circumference into eight sections. The eight sections determine the 22½° cut for each end of the sections. Lay back 3¼" from the intersection of the circle and the section dividing line to ensure space for the biscuit joinery. From that back line, measure out to just past the apex of the circle. To copy my piece, the result is a 4¼"-wide piece that is 11¼" on the long side.

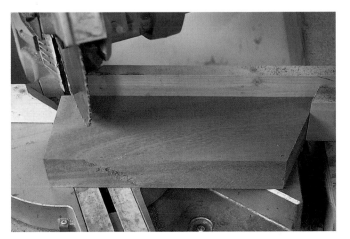

2 Mill your segment pieces to size and cut the 22½° cuts on each end to form a pie-shaped piece. Repeat the cuts on all eight pieces.

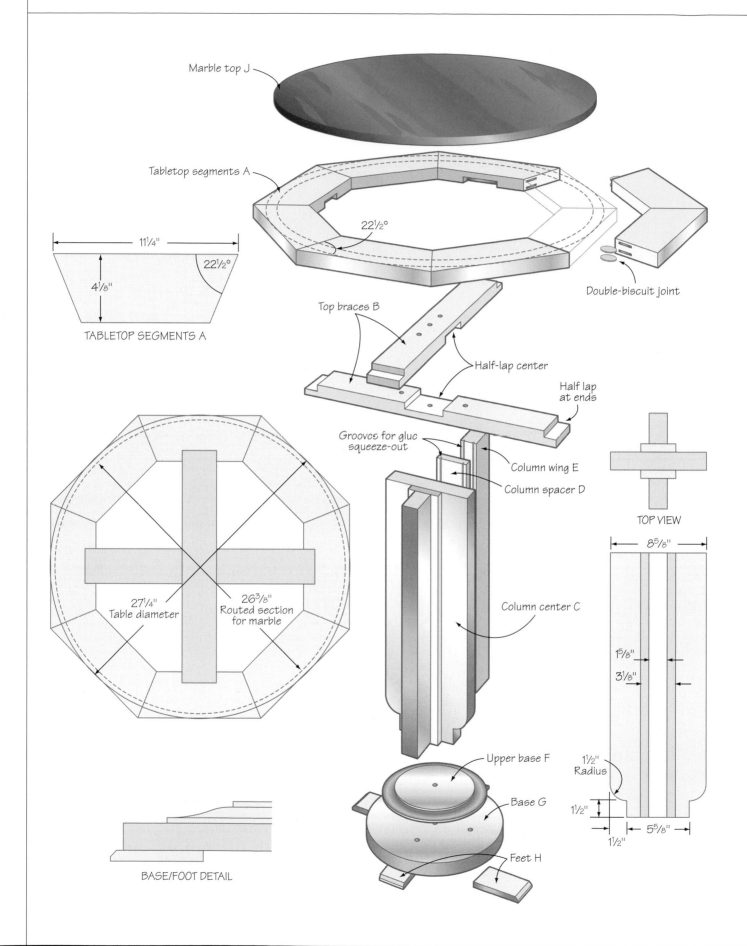

Marble top J

Tabletop segments A

22½°

Double-biscuit joint

11¼"

22½°

4⅛"

TABLETOP SEGMENTS A

Top braces B

Half-lap center

Half lap at ends

Grooves for glue squeeze-out

Column wing E

Column spacer D

27¼"
Table diameter

26⅜"
Routed section
for marble

Column center C

TOP VIEW

8⅝"

1⅝"

3⅛"

1½"
Radius

Upper base F

Base G

1½"

BASE/FOOT DETAIL

Feet H

5⅝"

1½"

MARBLE-TOP ART DECO TABLE • INCHES (MILLIMETERS)

REFERENCE	QUANTITY	PART	STOCK	THICKNESS	(mm)	WIDTH	(mm)	LENGTH	(mm)	COMMENTS
A	8	tabletop segments	mahogany	1³⁄₄	(45)	4¹⁄₄	(108)	11¹⁄₄	(285)	22¹⁄₂° cut BE
B	2	top braces	mahogany	1¹⁄₂	(38)	3¹⁄₈	(79)	20⁷⁄₈	(530)	¹⁄₂" (13) lapped center
C	1	column center	mahogany	1⁵⁄₈	(41)	8⁵⁄₈	(219)	23³⁄₄	(603)	
D	2	column spacers	mahogany	³⁄₄	(19)	3¹⁄₈	(79)	23³⁄₄	(603)	
E	2	column wings	mahogany	1³⁄₄	(45)	2³⁄₄	(70)	23³⁄₄	(603)	
F	1	upper base	mahogany	1	(25)	9⁵⁄₈	(245)	9⁵⁄₈	(245)	lathe-turned
G	1	base	mahogany	1¹⁄₄	(32)	13⁵⁄₈	(346)	13⁵⁄₈	(346)	lathe-turned
H	4	feet	mahogany	¹⁄₂	(13)	1⁵⁄₈	(41)	4¹⁄₄	(108)	
J	1	top	marble	³⁄₄	(19)	26³⁄₈	(670)	round		

Note: BE = both ends.

HARDWARE

8   No. 8 x 1¹⁄₄" (32mm) Slotted-head wood screws

5   No. 8 x 2" (51mm) Square-drive deck screws

5   ⁵⁄₁₆" x 4" (8mm x 102mm) Lag screw with washers

12   No. 7 x ³⁄₄" (19mm) Slotted-head wood screws

Glue

#20 Biscuits

³⁄₁₆" (5mm) Dowel pin

¹⁄₄" (6mm) Spacer

³⁄₁₆" x 1" (5mm × 25mm) Dowel

Aniline dye stain

Lacquer, sealer and finish

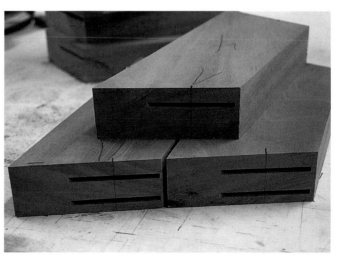

3 Clamp the pieces with a band clamp. If your measurements were correct, the fit is tight. If you are off a bit, you can make small changes to the angle cuts on individual pieces to arrive at a tight fit. When ready, mark the location for the biscuit slot.

4 On the segments, transfer the layout line for the biscuit slots to both faces of the piece and cut one slot referenced to the top and one to the bottom, creating twin slots on each end.

5 Glue the ends with the biscuits in place and clamp with a band clamp until dry.

6 Cut the top braces to size and create the half-lap center joint.

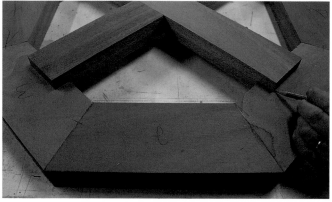

7 Assemble the top braces and mark all four ends with an X. Separate the two and cut a 3/4" × 1" rabbet on the ends of each brace. Cut only the X-marked ends, so that when joined the braces have the cuts on the same face.

8 Set the brace assembly in place on the underside of the joined top and mark the ends. Remove the necessary areas with a router or chisels. It helps to keep the brace in the same position to match the cuts, so mark one end with the top section location.

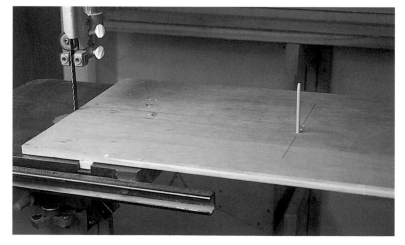

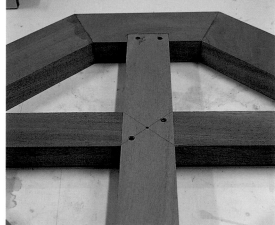

9 Prepare your band saw to cut the top section to round. Attach a cleat that fits into the saw guide to a piece of plywood. Square a line from the blade and mark 13⅛", or half the diameter of the finished top. Drill a 3/16" hole for a short dowel pin.

10 Before you attach the brace assembly to the top, locate a center in the brace and drill a 3/16" hole. Secure the brace with glue and 1¼" screws in the center, then attach the assembly to the top in the same manner.

11 Lay the top section on the pin in the plywood platform with a flat area at the blade. It will be a tight fit. Turn the saw on and slowly rotate the top section, cutting to a circle.

12 Once cut, sand all surfaces of the now round top. Round over both the top and bottom exterior edges with a 3/16" roundover bit.

13 Set up the plunge router with the circle-cutting jig. Place the 3/16" dowel pin in place, then add a 1/4" spacer to the pin. Set the router to cut 1/4" deep, and the outside cutting edge of the bit (3/4" straight) to be exactly 5/16" from the outside edge of the top. Hook the circle-cutting jig over the pin and plunge-cut the first pass on the top. With the outer edge defined, move to the extreme inside cut and repeat the process, each time moving toward the outer edge. This process allows the router base to rest on the existing material with each pass, and on the top's outer rim on the final passing cut. Also, notice how I lock the top in place with the plywood pieces. It will need to be secured.

15 Next, mill the pieces for the column. Make the 1 1/2"-radius cut at both edges of the column center and one edge of each of the column wings. It is easy to create a simple jig and use a router and pattern bit to complete this step.

14 When the cutting is complete, clean up the recessed top with a scraper.

35

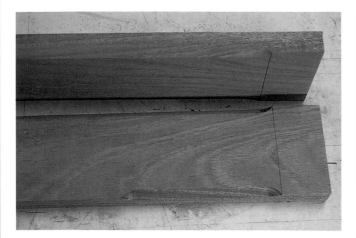

16 Use a chamfer bit and router on both edges of the two column spacers. Stay short of the ends for appearance.

17 At the table saw, cut a shallow groove on the back sides of the spacers and wings. Make the cut on both edges. This will become a reservoir to prevent glue squeeze-out during the assembly of the column.

18 Attach the wings to the center of the spacers with glue and 1¼" screws. Use just enough glue to work; a slight excess should be caught in the grooves from the previous step, but too much will still result in squeeze-out.

19 This is how the wing/spacer unit attaches to the column center. Because we are joining face grain, the connection is made with glue only.

20 Make the connection in two steps: One side, then the other when the first is dry.

21 Insert a short dowel into the base and slide the upper base onto the pin. Mark a line around the upper base onto the base. Remount the base on the lathe and cut a shallow groove just inside the marked line. This is another glue reservoir.

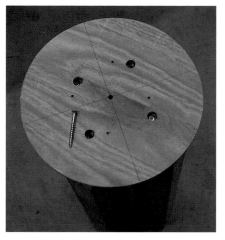

22 Mill and turn the upper base to profile and the base to size. With the base on the lathe, mark the exact center. Drill a 3/16" hole at center of the base and at the intersection of the lines used to mount the face plate onto the upper base (this is the bottom side).

23 Attach the upper base to the column with 2" screws, making sure the heads are countersunk.

24 Spread glue onto the bottom side of the upper base and inside the groove cut into the top of the base. Using the dowel pin, attach the two and clamp until dry.

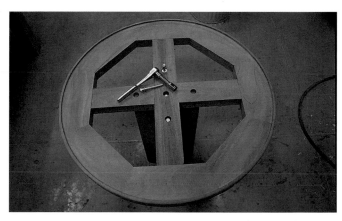

25 **ABOVE LEFT:** Mill the feet to size, cut a chamfer on the ends, then cut the blank into two equal pieces. Locate the feet directly in alignment with the column edges and attach with glue and 3/4" screws. Countersink the heads.

26 **ABOVE RIGHT:** Predrill the top and column for the 5/16" lag screws. Drill a 7/8" countersunk hole in the top so that the washer and the lag-screw head will be recessed. Finish the hole with a 5/16" bit. Set the top in place on the legs and mark the hole locations. Predrill the column with a 1/4" bit. Attach the top to the column with the lag screws.

27 **LEFT:** The finish I selected for this piece is a water-based aniline dye stain with a lacquer top coat. All that is left is to order the marble insert for the top and set it in place to finish the project.

This Greene & Greene Garden Bench looks great on your patio or in your living room.

PROJECT
6

Greene & Greene Garden Table

BY JIM STUARD

A reader from Claremont, California, Everett Vinzant, liked our Greene & Greene Garden Bench so much he decided to build a coffee table to go with it. He sent us a photo of it, and we decided it was such a good idea we tweaked his nice design and built this table. We call this project "Revenge of the Cloud Lifts" because it's loaded with this undulating signature Arts & Crafts detail. Because there are so many cloud lifts, this is a good project to use template routing on a router table to make them all.

Making Templates

Begin by cutting the parts out according to the cutting list. Then make your plywood templates, scaling from the patterns. Mark a center line across each template. This will help you line up the parts for routing. Finish each template by adding two handles to the templates in the locations shown.

Roughing the Parts

Mark a center line across parts B, C, D, F, G, K and on two top slats (J). Mark a center line down the middle and across parts E and K. These get a four-hole cutout. Make four copies of the small four-hole cutout and one of the larger four-hole patterns. Cut the patterns to within ½" of the holes. Using spray adhesive, attach the small patterns on the end

uprights (E) and the large pattern on the center slat (K) lining up the cross hairs on the pattern with the cross hairs on the parts. Drill ¼" clearance holes in each hole and cut out the squares with a scroll saw. You can't quite cut all of the holes on the center slat but come close and clean up the rest with a chisel.

Routing the Parts

Mount a ⅜" pattern bit into a router table and set the depth of the bearing to run against the template while cutting the part. After routing the cloud lifts, cut all of the biscuit joints for the base and top. Use a biscuit joiner to cut slots for No. 0 biscuits, which are perfect for joining the base and top parts.

The easiest way to lay out the biscuit joints is to dry-clamp the end assembly together and mark the centers of the ends on the apron pieces and legs. The aprons have a ¼" setback from the outside of the legs, so cut the biscuit slots on the apron assembly first. Then, using a ¼" spacer, set up the biscuit joiner to cut the offset on the legs. Use No. 20 biscuits on the short aprons (C) and No. 0 face-frame biscuits (or dowels) on the end dividers and uprights (D and E). Before assembly, rout a ¼" radius on the legs and the ends of the apron parts that contact the legs. Rout the rest of the assembly after gluing up. One last step before assembly is to drill screw pockets into the upper aprons for attaching the top. Glue up the end assembly.

After drying, mark the location of the base stretcher on each end assembly. Take the long aprons and base stretcher and dry clamp the entire base together. The base stretcher should be press fit between the end assemblies. Repeat the same process of cutting No. 20 biscuit slots on the long aprons and end assemblies. Dowel the base stretcher into each end assembly using two ⅜" dowels. After doweling the stretcher, lay out and scroll saw the profile on the ends of the top stretchers using the patterns. Let the top stretchers into the base using half-lap joints according to the diagram. Then glue the entire base together and screw the stretchers into the top edge of the base.

Wood Words

Pierce Cut: Raising the table saw's blade through a part and lowering it when done. In solid lumber, this works only when making a rip cut. Man-made materials (such as MDF and plywood) can be ripped or crosscut.

Climb Cut: Slowly routing backwards from the cutting direction of a router bit. This will give a smoother cut in figured woods and when routing across end grain.

Begin cutting out the ½" Baltic birch templates by drilling holes at the proper corners. Raise the blade on the table saw into the middle of the stock to make the straight cuts. Band saw the rest and clean up the cloud lifts using a disc sander.

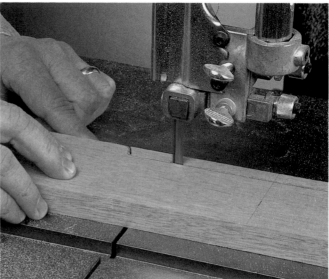

Use the center lines to index the template on what will be the back of each piece (it will eventually have nails driven into it) and draw the appropriate cloud lift or reverse cloud lift. Cutting close to the line, rough out these pieces on the band saw.

Pattern routing the parts is easy using the templates. Nail the appropriate template to a roughed out part, using the index lines for reference. Begin routing with the bit cutting against the wood. When you come to a cloud lift, use a climb cut so you don't burn the rounded corner.

Lay out a ⅝"-deep by ¾"-wide notch into the top stretcher and the base. The notch is 2¾" in from the stretcher end and 8" in from the joint where the apron meets the leg. Notice the clearance holes drilled into the top edge of the base and stretcher.

Begin the top assembly by routing a ¼" radius on the top long edge of all the slats. Using ¼" spacers, clamp the slats together without glue. Dry clamp the ends in place and mark for biscuit joints. Cut the biscuit slots and glue this top sub-assembly together. When dry, place the long top frame pieces against the sub-assembly and mark the inside corner where the short frame meets the long frame. Rout a ¼" radius on the inside edge of the long frame piece between the corner marks. With a rasp, finish the radius where it tapers on the ends. Mark and cut biscuit slots, then glue up the top. After drying, cut a profile on each corner using the pattern for the top stretchers. Rout a ¼" radius on the outside edge of the top.

After sanding, center the base on the underside of the top and attach it to the top using 1½" screws in the screw pockets and 1¾" screws in the top stretchers. No finish is required. If you leave the table unfinished outdoors, it will turn a beautiful silver color.

GREENE & GREENE GARDEN TABLE • INCHES (MILLIMETERS)

REFERENCE	QUANTITY	PART	STOCK	THICKNESS	(mm)	WIDTH	(mm)	LENGTH	(mm)	COMMENTS
A	4	legs	mahogany	2	51	2	51	17$\frac{1}{4}$	438	
B	2	long aprons	mahogany	$\frac{3}{4}$	19	3	76	32	813	
C	1	short aprons	mahogany	$\frac{3}{4}$	19	3	76	14	356	
D	1	end divider	mahogany	$\frac{3}{4}$	19	3	76	14	356	
E	1	end uprights	mahogany	$\frac{3}{4}$	19	2	51	3$\frac{1}{4}$	83	
F	1	base stretcher	mahogany	$\frac{3}{4}$	19	3	76	34	864	
G	1	top stretchers	mahogany	$\frac{3}{4}$	19	1$\frac{1}{4}$	32	23	584	
H	1	top frame long	mahogany	$\frac{3}{4}$	19	2$\frac{1}{4}$	57	48	325	
I	1	top frame short	mahogany	$\frac{3}{4}$	19	2$\frac{1}{2}$	64	19	483	
J	2	top slats	mahogany	$\frac{3}{4}$	19	2$\frac{1}{2}$	64	43	1092	
K	1	center slat	mahogany	$\frac{3}{4}$	19	3	76	43	1092	

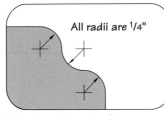

All radii are $\frac{1}{4}$"

Full-size detail of corner profile

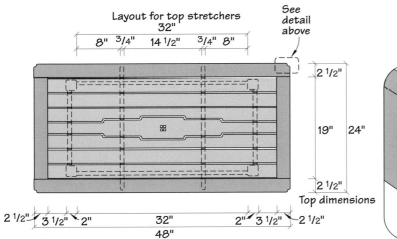

Layout for top stretchers
32"

8" $\frac{3}{4}$" 14 $\frac{1}{2}$" $\frac{3}{4}$" 8"

See detail above

2 $\frac{1}{2}$"

19"   24"

2 $\frac{1}{2}$"

Top dimensions

2 $\frac{1}{2}$" 3 $\frac{1}{2}$" 2" 32" 2" 3 $\frac{1}{2}$" 2 $\frac{1}{2}$"
48"

Plan

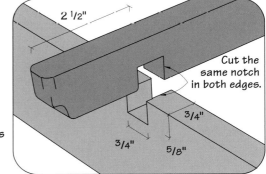

2 $\frac{1}{2}$"

Cut the same notch in both edges.

$\frac{3}{4}$"

$\frac{3}{4}$" $\frac{5}{8}$"

Detail of top stretcher

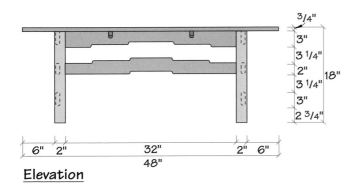

$\frac{3}{4}$"
3"
3 $\frac{1}{4}$"
2"   18"
3 $\frac{1}{4}$"
3"
2 $\frac{3}{4}$"

6" 2" 32" 2" 6"
48"

Elevation

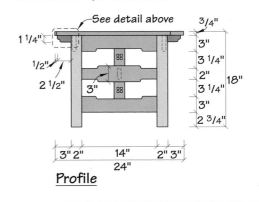

See detail above

1 $\frac{1}{4}$"

$\frac{1}{2}$"

2 $\frac{1}{2}$"

3"

$\frac{3}{4}$"
3"
3 $\frac{1}{4}$"
2"   18"
3 $\frac{1}{4}$"
3"
2 $\frac{3}{4}$"

3" 2" 14" 2" 3"
24"

Profile

Full-Size diagram of both four-hole cutouts,
the double radius on the top stretcher and top, the layout
for all of the cloud lifts on the table and a scale
diagram of the jig used for routing the cloud lifts.

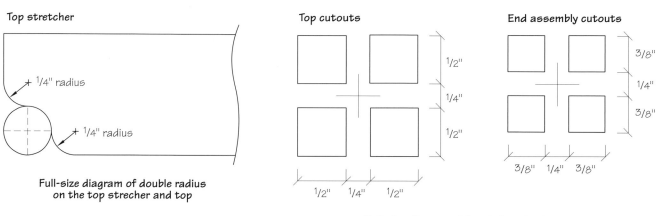

Top stretcher

1/4" radius

1/4" radius

Full-size diagram of double radius
on the top strecher and top

Top cutouts

1/2"

1/4"

1/2"

1/2"   1/4"   1/2"

End assembly cutouts

3/8"

1/4"

3/8"

3/8"   1/4"   3/8"

Full-size diagram of four hole cutouts
in the top and end assemblies

Full-size diagram of the cloud lifts. Use this to lay out the
individual cloud lifts on the jig above. Each square equals 1".

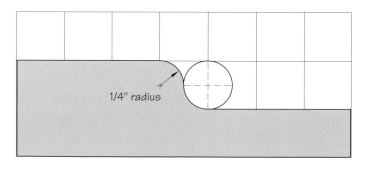

1/4" radius

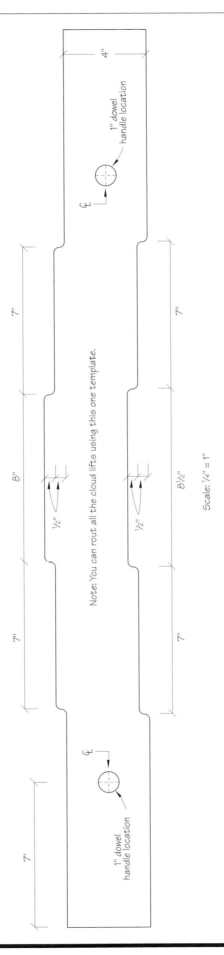

1" dowel
handle location

7"

8"

7"

1" dowel
handle location

Note: You can rout all the cloud lifts using this one template.

1/2"

1/2"

7"

8 1/2"

7"

4"

1" dowel
handle location

Scale: 1/4" = 1"

Before developing the rectilinear Craftsman style, Gustav Stickley experimented with curvaceous Art Nouveau designs.

PROJECT
7

Gustav Stickley Poppy Table

BY ROBERT W. LANG

In 1898, Gustav Stickley took a working vacation. With more than 20 years of experience as a furniture maker, he was ready to change direction, and he headed across the Atlantic Ocean for inspiration. The Arts & Crafts movement was strong in England, while in France the latest thing was L'Art Nouveau.

FACING PAGE: Fresh look from an old design. This small tea table was originally made more than 100 years ago by Gustav Stickley. His sense of proportion and design was not limited to straight lines.

In 1900 Stickley debuted several new designs marketed as "New Furniture" by the Tobey company of Chicago. This table was one of the most striking of those pieces, heavily influenced by Art Nouveau and a far cry from the rectilinear designs of the Craftsman style furniture he would become best known for.

There is a hint of things to come, however. The edges of the top, shelf and legs are all sinuous curves, but the surfaces are essentially flat, and the corners are just barely broken. It also presents an interesting engineering problem. Beneath the carved surfaces and waving edges, the table is based on a pentagon,

so the angles between the stretchers, shelf and five legs are at 72˚, not 90°.

This "Poppy Table" has been on my to-do list for a long time, and when I came across some good photos from an auction, I decided that the time was right to go ahead.

Engineering First

When I began working on the design, my first concern was the shape of the pieces. I soon realized that this project would also be a structural challenge. In the original, face-grain plugs are visible on the outside of the legs, centered on the shelf. Usually this means a screw is

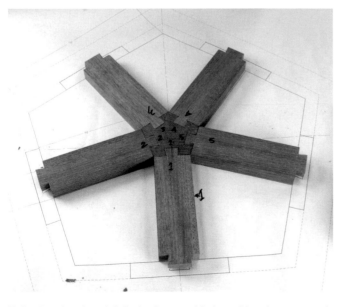

Following the plan. A full-size layout aids in making the parts and the joints accurately. As the table was assembled, I compared the actual pieces to the lines on the drawing.

The hub is the keystone. All of the structural parts of the table radiate from this small piece, so it needs to be precise. This shooting jig lets me trim it down in tiny increments.

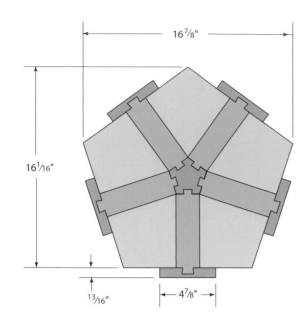

16 7/8"

16 1/16"

13/16"

4 7/8"

PLAN BELOW TOP

2"

HUB PLAN

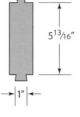

3/4"

5 13/16"

1"

STRETCHER

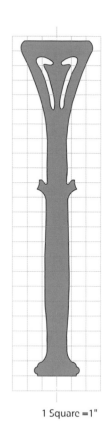

1 Square = 1"

LEG PATTERN

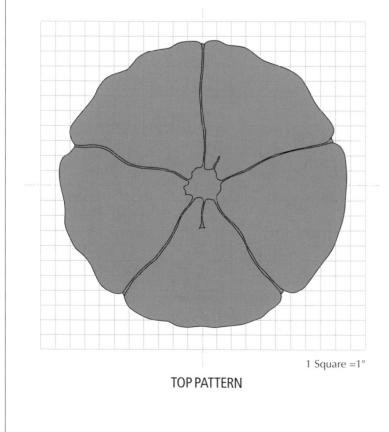

1 Square = 1"

TOP PATTERN

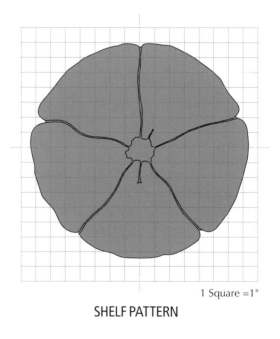

1 Square = 1"

SHELF PATTERN

GUSTAV STICKLEY POPPY TABLE • INCHES (MILLIMETERS)

QUANTITY	PART	STOCK	THICKNESS	(mm)	WIDTH	(mm)	LENGTH	(mm)	COMMENTS
1	top	mahogany	$^{13}/_{16}$	21	$21^{13}/_{16}$	554	$22^{5}/_{16}$	567	
1	shelf	mahogany	$^{13}/_{16}$	21	$16^{1}/_{16}$	408	$16^{7}/_{8}$	429	
5	legs	mahogany	$^{13}/_{16}$	21	5	127	$22^{5}/_{8}$	575	
1	hub	mahogany	$^{13}/_{16}$	21	$3^{1}/_{16}$	78	$3^{1}/_{4}$	83	
5	stretchers	mahogany	$^{13}/_{16}$	21	2	51	$6^{13}/_{16}$	173	

DTBE = dovetail both ends

Hidden lapped dovetails. The stretchers connect to the hub and the leg with $1/2$"-thick lapped dovetails. They are $3/4$" wide at the hub end and 1" wide at the leg.

Never to be seen. These joints won't show in the finished table, but they must be strong. The sockets in the legs were wasted with a small router; the sockets in the hub with wasted with a Forstner bit. I then pared them all to size with a chisel.

beneath the plug, but it seemed to me that these joints needed more than a mechanical fastener.

I don't really know how the original is held together at the intersection of the leg and shelf. Loose tenons seem the obvious solution to us today, but at the time a dowel or two flanking the screw would have been more likely. I decided to use Festool Dominos for loose tenons, along with a screw to pull the assembly together. It's hard to clamp a pentagon.

At the top of the legs, stretchers seemed necessary, but it was a puzzle deciding how to connect them to the legs. There isn't any structure visible in the photo I was working from, so my solution is a best guess. I used a lapped dovetail at each end of the 2"-wide stretchers, and in the center made a five-sided hub piece that holds them all together.

Together Twice to Make it Nice

All the parts for this table came from a single plank of mahogany about 14" wide and 12' long. I made all the joints and dry-assembled the entire table before doing any of the decorative work.

The hub is the piece I worried most about. It is like a keystone that affects the location of the other joints. Any variations in this piece and the legs would twist and throw off the joints at the shelf. Because it was too small to safely cut on the table saw or miter saw, I cut it on the band saw. I then made a small shooting board, as shown in the lower right photo on page 45, and trimmed the hub to size with a low-angle block plane.

I made a full-size printout of my drawing and used that to check the parts and assemblies as I made them. I cut a rabbet at each end of the stretchers with a tenoning jig on the table saw, leaving $1/2$" thickness for the dovetails. I hand cut the dovetails and used them to lay out the sockets in the hub and the top of each leg. Numbering each

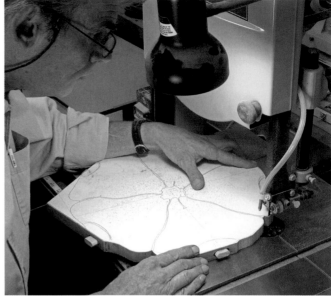

LEFT: Straight fitting. All the joints were made and all parts dry-assembled before doing any of the shaping to the legs and shelf.

ABOVE: Rapid layout. Gluing a full-size paper pattern to the shelf blank eliminates transferring the pattern. The paper will stay in place through the cutting process.

stretcher and its hub location helped keep the parts in order.

Because the hub was so small, I couldn't use a router to remove the waste for the sockets, so I used a Forstner bit at the drill press to establish the flat bottom of the sockets and cleaned up the sides with a chisel. For the sockets in the legs, at the other end of the stretchers, I used a ¼" spiral up-cut bit in a small router with a fence to cut a smooth bottom and back for each socket. Again, I cleaned up the corners with a chisel.

Then I dry-fit the hub to the stretchers, and test-fit the assembled hub and stretchers to the legs. After a bit of tweaking to the joints, I glued the stretchers to the hub, but left the stretcher-to-leg joints loose.

I cut the shelf to size, and made sure that it fit the perimeter of the legs and assembled top hub. I centered a Domino

in each edge of the shelf at the maximum depth and at the center of each leg at the minimum depth, with the top of the shelf 7⅛" above the bottom of the leg. I glued the Dominos into the shelf only, drilled a counterbored hole and drove a No. 8 × 1½" screw through each leg and into the tenons in the shelf.

After squaring up the shelf and legs, I was ready to cut the parts to final shape. When I was satisfied that everything was tight and square, I took it apart to cut the profiles.

The Shape of Things

I used spray adhesive to glue full-size paper patterns to the blanks for the shelf and top. I also glued a full-size pattern to a piece of ½" Baltic birch plywood to make a template for the legs. The top and shelf were cut to shape at the band saw. Where the shelf meets the legs, I left a flat area in the curve for the joint. I ended the curves about ½" away from the intersections with the legs so I could

trim right to the meeting point after the legs were shaped and smoothed.

The plywood pattern I made for the legs has the pattern on only one side. After cutting the pattern just outside the lines on the band saw, I smoothed the plywood edges back to the lines with a rasp.

I marked one side of each leg, then flipped the pattern over to mirror the outline on the vertical centerline. This saved some time in making the pattern, and it ensured that the legs would be symmetrical.

After cutting the outside shape of the legs at the band saw, I drilled holes near the ends of the cutouts, and I used a jigsaw with a narrow blade to rough-cut the shapes. I clamped the pattern to the legs, then trimmed the outside edges and the cutouts with a ¼"-diameter flush-cutting bit in a small router.

A Little Carving

Before removing the paper pattern from the top and shelf, I traced the lines of the carving with the sharp point of my knife. After darkening these thin lines with a pencil, I used a 60° V-tool to establish the depth and sides of the lines. I followed that with a ⅛"-wide No. 11 gouge. The profile of the lines is mainly the profile of the U-shaped tool, so the only real challenge in carving was getting smooth, consistent lines.

The lines that define the lobes were rounded slightly at the top with a skew chisel. The central portion of the carving is slightly domed. This is the only portion of the top surface that isn't flat. After carving, I smoothed the flat surfaces of the top with a plane, following up with a scraper and 240-grit Abranet (a new abrasive on a flexible mesh-like base that's not paper. Abranet cuts fast, leaves a smooth surface and doesn't load up).

Living on the Edge

The band-saw marks on the edges of the top and shelf were removed with a rasp. The edges were further refined with a modeler's rasp. One of the good things about using a hand-stitched rasp is that the surface left by the tool is a series of tiny grooves. A cabinet scraper quickly removes the high spots between the grooves, leaving a smooth surface.

The corners were broken with a few strokes of the fine-cut modeler's rasp, followed by sanding with a small piece of Abranet, folded to make a slight radius. When the top and shelf were complete, it was time to move on to the edges of the legs.

Another advantage to using the rasp is the ability to use the half-round side to shape inside curves as seen in the upper right photo on page 50. Many of the curves on this piece closely matched the curve of the rasps, so I believe that the original maker likely used the same technique and tools.

I used the same procedure and sequence of tools to smooth the edges of the legs and the cutouts at the top of each leg. The router bit left a decent surface, but there were a few chatter marks on long surfaces, and some burning in the tight inside corners. I wanted these edges to be as nice as the flat surfaces so I planned on it taking awhile.

Actually it took quite awhile. Smoothing the edges of the legs took about half the time I spent on this

Taking a stab at marking. Cutting through the pattern with the point of a knife establishes the layout lines for the carving.

Shape from the tool. After starting the carving with a V-tool, a deep, narrow gouge cleans up the cuts and defines the profile of the lines.

entire project. What slowed this step down were the tight corners at the buds on the legs, plus the cutout areas. In these places, the grain direction of the mahogany changes from long grain to end grain and then back again in the span of a few inches.

No one area was difficult to smooth, but the number of curves increased the overall length of the perimeter, and each area required a different approach. I found a stool to sit on, and settled in to get it right. When I was satisfied with the rasping and scraping, I went over the entire table with Abranet to obtain a consistent, smooth surface.

Together at Last

I made one final dry assembly, screwed the legs to the shelf, then tapped the top stretchers into the tops of the legs. I marked the intersections of the shelf and legs, and carefully carved the shelf edges down to these points.

The final assembly was quick and painless. With screws holding the legs to the shelf, and the dovetails at the top of the legs, I didn't need any clamps. After applying glue to the end grain of the mortises in the legs, I applied glue to the tenon ends in the shelf, put the legs in place and drove the screws.

After making sure the legs were square to the shelf, I applied glue to the sockets at the top of the legs, then pushed and tapped the stretchers into place.

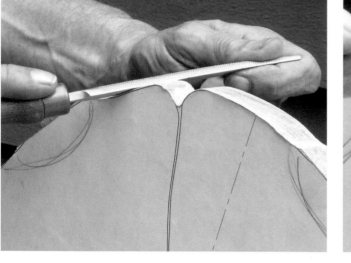

PHOTOS ABOVE: Rasp to the rescue. The flat side of this rasp removes the band-saw marks on most of the edge. The round side gets into places the flat side can't reach. Many of the finished tight curves are defined by the shape of the tool.

LEFT: A close scrape. The hand-stitched rasp will leave shallow, narrow grooves. A cabinet scraper follows the rasp to remove the high spots between the grooves and leaves a fine surface.

Finally, the screw holes were filled with mahogany plugs. After the glue in the plug holes was dry, I pared the plugs flush with the face of the leg using a ¾" chisel. I then went over the face of each leg with my scraper and Abranet.

At the center of each stretcher, I drilled a ³⁄₁₆"-diameter hole, and with the tabletop upside down on my bench, I lined up the assembled table base with the top. Each of the legs is centered in a lobe of the top, and the grain and pattern of the top is aligned with the shelf. In each of the five holes I drove a No.8 × 1¼" washer-head screw. The holes are larger than the shanks of the screws, allowing the top to expand and contract.

I've seen original versions of this table in both mahogany and oak. Mahogany is a beautiful wood, and I wanted a finish that would show it off without filling the grain or looking polished. I used dark walnut Watco Danish oil for the first two coats and natural Watco Danish oil for the final three.

I applied the oil liberally, let it soak in for about 15 minutes, then reapplied more oil. I wet-sanded the table with a Scotch-Brite pad on the first coat, let it sit for another 10 minutes, then wiped the surface dry. I waited a day between coats, then saturated the surface, allowed the oil to sit for 15 minutes, then wiped the surfaces dry.

Gustav Stickley's talent as a designer is often downplayed by those who aren't familiar with his entire career. The straight lines and masculine proportions of his Craftsman furniture can lead a person to believe that his entire body of work contains no curves or delicate shapes.

The Poppy Table was one of three similar tea tables produced in 1900. All three are exquisitely proportioned, sensitive designs based on floral forms. The style can be seen as a bridge between Art Nouveau and American Arts & Crafts. These early gems show that Gustav Stickley's tremendous talent for design was not dependent on the direction it was focused.

Final cut. After shaping the legs and the shelf, the intersection is blended with a No. 1 straight carving chisel. Leaving these small areas oversized until almost the end of the project resulted in crisp detail in a highly visible place.

It isn't cheating. The original table had face-grain plugs in the faces of the legs. It is reasonable to assume that there are screws beneath the plugs. A Domino loose tenon reinforces these joints.

First coat. Dark walnut Danish oil helps to accentuate the grain of the mahogany. Two color coats were followed by three coats of natural Danish oil.

Last tap. The assembled hub and stretchers fit into the dovetail sockets at the top of the legs. When everything is lined up, they are tapped home, completing the assembly without using clamps.

The Lost Stickley Table

BY ROBERT W. LANG

Most original Gustav Stickley furniture can be easily identified by model number. This was, after all, factory-made furniture and pieces were designed to be made in multiples. When you come across an antique, you can look it up in an old catalog to identify it. However, the only known example of this small table appeared at a Sotheby's auction in late 2004.

This uncataloged piece was likely a prototype, never put into factory production. What makes it unique is the front and back splay of the legs. It's this slight angle that gives this table more character than straight-legged versions that were mass produced. It's also the likely reason this piece never got beyond the prototype stage.

This table features many of the Stickley design elements that appear in other pieces. There isn't much material in it, but there is a good deal of labor-intensive, head-scratching joinery involved. This probably made it too expensive to be marketed at a reasonable price, but that does make it a great project on which to practice and develop joinery skills.

The anonymous cabinetmaker who built this prototype lived when it was a great time to be a woodworker. Hand-tool skills had not yet been forgotten, and machinery was in use to make life in the shop easier.

As I planned how I would make this piece, I realized it made sense to do some of the work with machine methods, while on other parts it would be quicker and easier to make some joints by hand.

First Things First

Before cutting any lumber, I made a full-size section drawing on a piece of plywood. This helped me plan the sequence of building, and the sizes of the joints. It also established a reference to the exact size and shape of the parts.

While I was building this table, I referred to this drawing rather than relying on calculations, numbers and measuring. My CAD program tells me that the angle of the legs is 3.56° and that the length of the bottom edge of the rail between the legs is $15^{17}/_{32}$". Neither of those pieces of information is needed, and trying to build to the numbers instead of referring to the full-size drawing only slows things down and invites mistakes.

I made the legs by laminating two $^{13}/_{16}$"-thick pieces together, then cover-

Using a full-size section drawing is essential; it lets me set angles and shows the exact sizes of parts without any of the risks of measuring.

THE LOST STICKLEY TABLE • INCHES (MILLIMETERS)

QUANTITY	PART	STOCK	THICKNESS	(mm)	WIDTH	(mm)	LENGTH	(mm)	COMMENTS
1	top	QSWO	$^{13}/_{16}$	21	$15^3/_8$	391	21	533	
2	top aprons	QSWO	$^{13}/_{16}$	21	$4^1/_4$	108	$17^7/_8$	454	$1^1/_4$" ATBE
2	lower rails	QSWO	$^7/_8$	22	$5^1/_4$	133	$13^5/_8$	346	$1^1/_4$" TBE
1	lower stretcher	QSWO	$^3/_4$	19	5	127	16	406	$1^{13}/_{16}$" BSTBE
4	legs	QSWO	$1^5/_8$	41	$1^7/_8$	48	$22^1/_4$	565	Angle both ends
1	back apron	QSWO	$^{13}/_{16}$	21	$4^1/_4$	108	$13^5/_8$	346	$1^1/_4$" TBE
1	rail below drawer	QSWO	$^{13}/_{16}$	21	$^{13}/_{16}$	21	$12^5/_8$	321	$^3/_4$" TBE
1	drawer front	QSWO	$^{13}/_{16}$	21	$3^1/_2$	89	$11^1/_8$	283	Bevel both edges to fit
2	tenon keys	QSWO	$^1/_2$	13	$^5/_8$	16	2	51	taper to fit through tenons
2	drawer sides	maple	$^5/_8$	16	$3^1/_4$	83	$15^7/_8$	403	
1	drawer back	maple	$^5/_8$	16	$3^1/_4$	83	$11^1/_8$	283	
1	drawer bottom	maple	$^1/_4$	6	$10^1/_2$	267	$15^1/_4$	387	
2	web frame stiles	poplar	$^3/_4$	19	2	51	$17^1/_4$	438	notch around legs
2	web frame rails	poplar	$^3/_4$	19	2	51	$9^3/_4$	248	$^3/_4$" TBE
2	drawer runners	maple	$^{11}/_{16}$	17	$^9/_{16}$	14	$15^3/_4$	400	fit between legs & beside drawer
2	drawer stop	maple	$^{11}/_{16}$	17	$^9/_{16}$	14	6	152	fit behind drawer

QSWO=quarter sawn white oak; TBD=tenon both ends; BSTBE=beveled shoulder tenon both ends; ATBE= angled tenon both ends

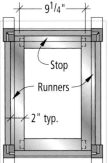

Web frame plan

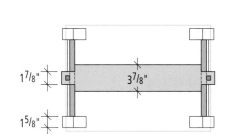

Lower rails, stretcher &
tenon key plan

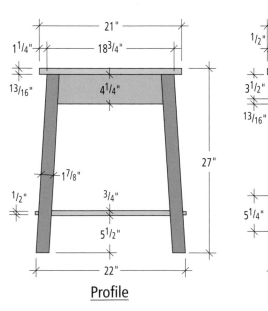

Profile

Elevation

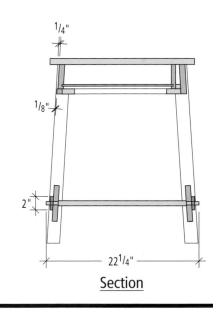

Section

ing the edge seams with ⅛"-thick veneer that I resawed from the same boards I used for the other parts of the legs. This is the method originally used by Gustav Stickley to show quartersawn figure on all four edges of a leg. To keep the thin pieces flat, I glued and clamped all of the legs together at one time.

After trimming the edges of the veneer flush with my smoothing plane, I cut the angles at the top and bottom of each leg. I then returned to the full-size layout to locate the mortises. The mortises in each leg are in different locations, so I marked each leg's position in the table on its top. As I made other pieces, I marked which leg they joined to with a red lumber crayon.

The mortises on the back of the front legs, and the front of the back legs are parallel to the top and bottom of the legs. I put an angled block of scrap on the bed of the hollow-chisel mortiser to make these mortises.

The Best Made Plans

I planned on making the remaining mortises in the legs with the mortiser, but on the second mortise, the machine broke down. Faced with a deadline, I switched to plan B and made these mortises with my plunge router.

The through mortises that pierce the lower front and back rails are at an angle to the face, and I'd planned to use an

Thin veneers tend to buckle when clamped. Gluing them in a stack applies even pressure to keep them flat.

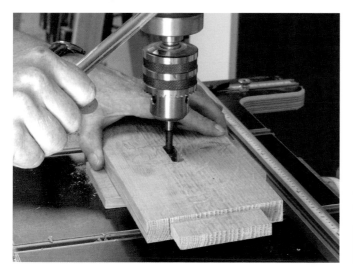

The angled mortises on the lower rails were roughed out with a Forstner bit on the drill press. A tapered block under the workpiece makes the holes at the correct angle.

An angled block of scrap wood tilts the leg to cut an angled mortise parallel to the top of the leg.

angled block on the bed of the mortiser to make them. Instead, I used a similar setup on the drill press. I removed most of the waste with a Forstner bit, then cleaned up the openings with chisels and rasps.

I made the straight and standard tenons on the ends of the lower rails on the table saw. I used a miter gauge to cut the tenon shoulders, and a jig that rides on the fence to cut the cheeks.

I considered making the angled cuts on the remaining tenons on the table saw, but realized each angled setup would need to be done twice: One to the right and one to the left. I decided to make a guide block that could be reversed for my handsaw, as seen in the photos at bottom left and right.

This was a quick and accurate method, and I was able to make all four saw cuts for each joint in sequence. This helped to keep the parts in order, and prevented making any miscuts by machine.

I dry-fitted the front and back legs with the top rails, and checked this assembly against my full-size layout. The angles matched, so I knew I could determine the length and angle of the lower stretcher directly from the full-size drawing. The critical length on this part is the distance between the shoulders of the through tenons. The angled parts of these tenons are short, but they need to be exact. I didn't want to risk a miscut on the table saw, so I used another angled block to guide my handsaw.

The Key to a Good Fit

I did use the table saw tenoning jig to cut the wide cheeks of the through tenons on the lower stretcher, and the band saw to cut the edge cheeks. I made all of these cuts a hair big. Through tenons always demand some hand fitting. I used chisels, rasps and a shoulder plane to fit the tenons, checking the fit frequently as I came close to the finished size.

With the through tenons fit, there were only two mortises remaining: Those for the keys that hold the lower stretcher to the lower rails. These look difficult, but are actually the easiest joints to make in the piece. With the tenon fit in its mortise, I made a pencil mark at the intersection.

Taking the pieces back apart, I made another line slightly behind the first one. This puts the mortise just behind the intersection, and ensures that the key pulls the two lower rails tightly together. Luckily a repair part for the mortiser arrived, and I could cut these mortises with one stroke of the ½" chisel. I used

After squaring the corners of the mortise with a chisel, I use a rasp to finish smoothing the inside of the angled joint.

The quick and easy way to make the angled cuts for the through tenons is with a handsaw, guided by an angled block of wood.

These angled shoulder cuts would be tricky to make with power tools.

After fitting the through tenon, the location of the second mortise is laid out, keeping the back of the hole just behind the face of the rail.

The mortise is cut with one plunge of the hollow-chisel mortiser. A piece of scrap below the cut supports the tenon, keeping the wood from breaking on the back side.

a piece of scrap under the tenon to support it while the cut was made.

In most pieces with a keyed tenon, the mortise is angled slightly to allow the key to wedge in place. Because the rails are tilted back and the stretcher is horizontal, the angle of the rail allows the key to wedge in a straight mortise. To make the keys, I cut a few long pieces of scrap to slightly more than the ½" width of the mortise by ⅝". I cut pieces about 6" long, and cut the taper on the band

saw. I used my block plane to remove the saw marks, and bring the keys down to a snug fit.

This method let me get a good fit without worrying about the length of the keys. When I was happy with the fit, I marked ¾" above and below the protruding tenon to get the finished length of the keys.

The last parts to be made were the narrow rail below the drawer and the web frame. The rail is thin so that it

can be turned 90° to show quartersawn figure on its face. It is also beveled to be parallel with the front faces of the legs. The web frame is made from poplar, and is mortise and tenoned together. When I had all the joints fit, I made a dry assembly of the table. Then I took the pieces back apart so I could plane, scrape and sand all of them before gluing the entire table together.

I glued in stages, making subassemblies of front and back legs, and the top aprons. I cut some angled blocks and attached them to the top of the legs with masking tape so that the clamps would pull straight on the angled legs.

After letting the glue dry on these, I put one of the leg assemblies flat on my bench. I put glue in the mortises, and put in the upper-back rail, the small rail below the drawer, and the lower rails, with the stretcher in place between them. I then brushed glue on the tenons, and placed the second leg assembly on top. Turning the table upright on my bench, I clamped the joints and began to worry about the drawer.

Half-blind dovetailed drawers don't bother me, but I'd never made one with the face tilted back at an angle. I decided to lay out the tails with the same angles they would have if the drawer front were vertical. This makes the top and bottom angles of the tails different in relation to the slanted drawer front which made the layout tricky, but it looked right when the joints were completed.

After cutting the tails by hand, I laid out the pins on the ends of the drawer front, and removed most of the waste with an upcut spiral bit in my trim router. This speeds things up, and gives a perfectly flat surface where the back of the tail rests on the bottom of the pin. I then used a chisel to pare down to the layout lines.

The pull was made from a cutoff piece from one of the legs. I trimmed it down to 1¼" × 1¼" by about 3" long. The pull finishes at 1⅛" but the extra length gave me something to hold on to while cutting it to shape. I laid out the shape of the pull on two adjacent faces, and cut it out on the band saw. I didn't

As the tenon key is fit, the length above and below the through tenon changes. I leave the key long and mark the length once I have a good fit.

After cutting the key to length, I round the edges above and below the completed joint.

worry about the exact size of the radius below the pyramid shaped top; that would come from the shape of my rasp.

After cutting one face, I taped the scraps back on the block with clear packing tape and cut the adjacent side. With the rough cutting complete, I clamped the extra length in my vise, and finished shaping the pull with a rasp. The finished pull is held to the drawer front with a No. 8 × 1¼" screw from inside the drawer.

I wanted an authentic looking finish, but didn't want to go to the trouble of fuming it with ammonia. I used W.D. Lockwood Dark Fumed Oak aniline dye diluted with alcohol. I brushed on the dye, and wiped it with a rag. I then brushed on two coats of amber shellac. After letting the shellac dry, I attached the top with figure-eight fasteners. I took off the gloss of the shellac with a Scotch-Brite pad and applied a coat of paste wax.

The assembled web frame is notched around the legs. After fitting the drawer runners between the legs, they are screwed in place, and the drawer stop is also attached with screws to the frame.

I laid out the tails with the same angles from horizontal that I would have if the drawer front were vertical. The knob is cut with the band saw and shaped with a rasp.

After routing most of the waste, I use a chisel to pare the pins down the rest of the way. The router quickly establishes a consistent depth.

Drawer pull

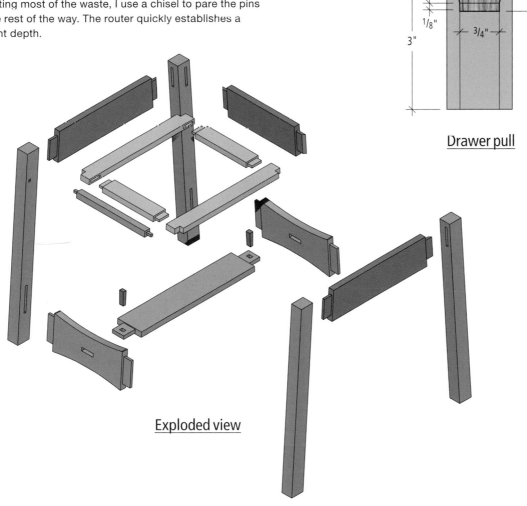

Exploded view

Ribbon Table

BY JOHN HUTCHINSON

If architect and furniture designer Alvar Aalto (Finland, 1898-1976) is considered to be one of the founding fathers of modern design, then Eileen Gray (Ireland, 1878-1976), who shared his profession and time on Earth, must be a founding mother. For my ribbon table, I borrowed design elements from his sensuous bentwood stacking stool and her machined glass-top side table. I guess that makes me a modern grandson.

The stability and strength of Baltic birch plywood made it my material of choice. Aalto could bend it two ways but I wanted to up the ante by twisting it in the third dimension. Segmented, radiused corners, combined with a variation on finger joinery connecting the straight vertical pieces, proved to be a successful way of pulling off the illusion. The top and bottom are made from two pieces, biscuit-joined together.

Careful Layout

I can tell you that the outside radius of the arcs is 4", and that the length of the straight finger extensions is 1½", but I can't give you the exact width. That's something you'll have to measure because the width of the bends must be equal to the thickness of the nominal ¾" stock you purchase. I used my dial caliper to come up with the $^{47}/_{64}$" dimension shown in the illustrations. So what's the big deal about a $^{1}/_{64}$" variation from true ¾"? A lot when you're trying to bring so many surfaces into alignment from so many directions.

I printed nested corner patterns on standard copier paper after generating

This obligatory "Man Drills Holes In Board" shot is here to remind you that accurate drilling, with a backup scrap to prevent tear-out, is key to a number of forming and glue-up steps. A $^{17}/_{64}$" brad-point bit clears the way for the ¼" registration dowels.

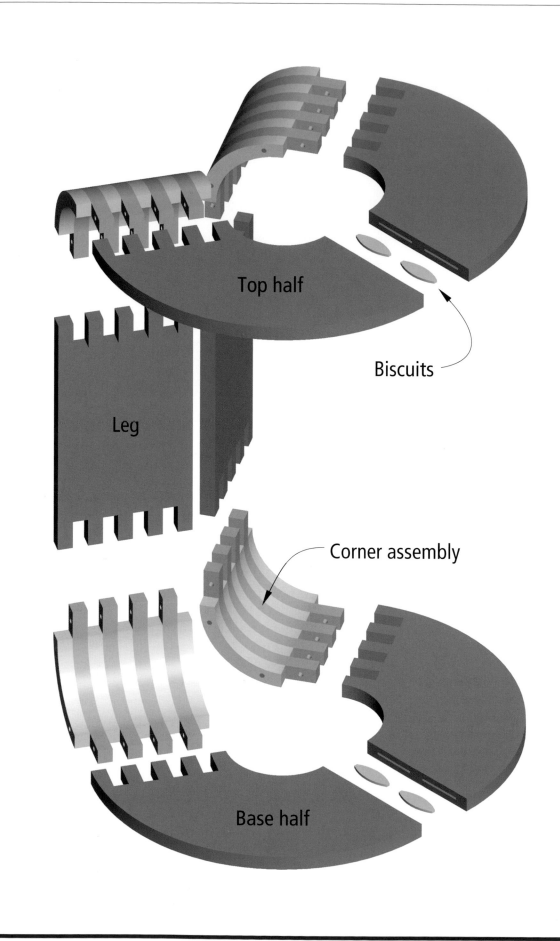

Top half

Biscuits

Leg

Corner assembly

Base half

Nesting the patterns for the corner segments produces a minimum amount of waste. Make the cuts just outside the lines. You'll be a band saw master by the time you get to your 36th smiley.

Here's the whole story on the pattern-routing jig — one perfected pattern mounted to the bottom of the plastic guard, four protruding registration dowels, three spacers/stabilizers (with UHMW Slick Tape glides) arrayed around the pattern, and a couple handles.

them through the CAD software on my computer. The same accuracy, however, is achievable by using a square, a dime-store compass and a ruler.

A Whole Bunch of Holes

With a $^{17}/_{64}$" brad-point bit secured in your drill press, drill the four registration holes in each of the radial corner segments. Four holes may seem excessive until the segments fall prey to the flush-trimming bit. It's amazing how a little cylinder of metal, with two innocent-looking cutting edges, can exert enough force to bend ¾" plywood as if it were overcooked spaghetti. I tried to get by with only the two inner holes and ended up with chatter marks at the unsecured extensions of the arcs.

Rack of Ribs

You know that I'm a band saw guy if you've seen any of my previous projects. There's something about becoming "one

With a rough-cut corner segment resting on the router table, and registered to the perfected pattern just below the plastic guard, feed the segment into the cutting edges of the flush-trimming bit.

with the blade" and tracking a cut $\frac{1}{32}$"
outside of a line that gives me repeated
doses of obsessive/compulsive satisfaction. So much for my problem. Your
task will be to rough-cut 36 arcs out of
a rectangle. After nesting your patterns
on the stock to minimize the waste, start
rough-cutting slowly and carefully, stay-
ing just outside the lines. You'll have the
rhythm in no time.

A Passion for Sanding?

Pattern routing the corner segments
isn't really necessary if your idea of the
perfect day in the shop is one devoted to
sanding. If that doesn't float your boat,
read on. The router-table jig that I made
for handling these small parts consists of
a rectangle of $\frac{3}{8}$" polycarbonate plastic,
two purchased jig handles, one finely
tuned pattern, four $\frac{1}{4}$" registration dowels, and spacers consisting of two layers
of the plywood stock. The spacers need
to be arrayed around the pattern in a
manner that prevents the jig from tip-
ping as you run it over the router table.
Remember to always feed the parts
against the rotation of the bit, never with
it. When the dust has cleared, you'll have
a perfectly matched stack of bends.

But before you can glue up your corners, 20 of the pieces need to be shorter
than the others to form the fingers. You
can trim them to size on the band saw,
or you can set up a jig and use your table
saw (see lower photo, page 66).

Corner Glue-up

My ingredients for this operation were:
$\frac{1}{4}$" registration dowels, a flux brush,
cup of water, polyurethane glue, paper
towels. And if you don't already own
gloves, get some. I went macho-glove-
less for the first corner glue-up and
ended up with Incredible Hulk hands.
Nothing but time releases polyurethane
glue from your skin. Before applying any
glue, I placed the segments on a damp-
ened paper towel, let them sit for a few
minutes, and then flipped them. Baltic
birch plywood is pretty inert stuff and
the moisture absorbed from the paper
towel helps to activate the glue. Brush a
liberal amount of glue on both sides of

Alternately stack
short and long cor-
ner segments over
7" lengths of $\frac{1}{4}$"-
registration dow-
els for a perfectly
aligned glue-up.
Trim the dowels
flush to the outside
surfaces after the
glue has dried.

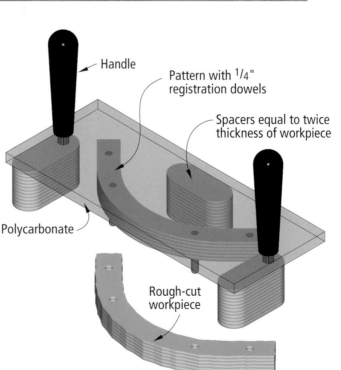

Handle

Pattern with $\frac{1}{4}$"
registration dowels

Spacers equal to twice
thickness of workpiece

Polycarbonate

Rough-cut
workpiece

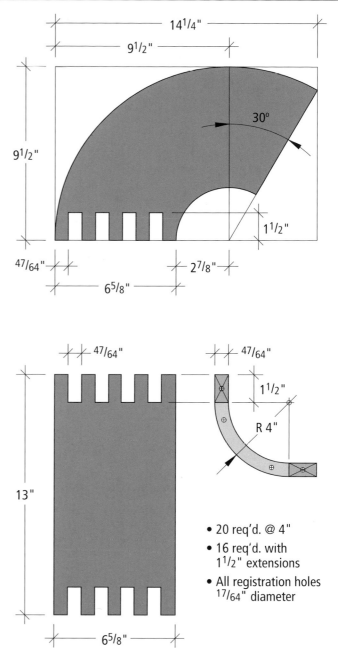

My dado sled is nothing more than a scrap of plywood fastened to a couple wood runners. The fence is mounted square to the table and perpendicular to the blade. Here, I'm removing the finger-joint waste from a tabletop half.

- 20 req'd. @ 4"
- 16 req'd. with 1 1/2" extensions
- All registration holes 17/64" diameter

the five short and four long bends. Next stack them alternately on the dowels. When the sandwich is complete, apply a few clamps. Almost instantly, you'll have a big foamy mess of glue squeeze-out. Don't be tempted to tidy things up by wiping the foam with one of your paper towels. Doing so will lead to the sanding that you avoided by pattern routing. Be patient, let it dry, and then cleanly slice it away with a scraper.

Dado Sledding
I made a simple table saw sled for the dado cuts in the "legs" and table halves.

Although it seems counter intuitive, I don't recommend using a dado stack to make the notches. Because the thickness of plywood varies slightly within a single sheet, I found it best to trace the fingers of the bends on the straight sections and then nibble away the waste with a ripping blade. Start the cuts at the middle of the waste area and work outward, sneaking up to the pencil lines. This method of cutting saves you from fussing with shims and is more forgiving and far less aggressive than a dado stack.

Getting It All Together
I glued up the base in two vertical halves and then glued the halves together, aligning the top and bottom surfaces with biscuits. The only thing you really need to watch is the right-angle attachment of the bends to the flats. I accomplished this by first clamping a flat to my workbench and then pulling the fingers together with a pair of long bar clamps. I intentionally pushed the joint beyond 90° then pulled it back to square with a couple hand clamps. The rubber pads on the long clamps allowed this kind of micro-adjustment.

Finish Line

I knew from day one that I wanted this to be a painted piece. Aalto was a fan of primary colors so I followed his lead with a cheerful cherry red. Your careful measuring and pattern routing in the early stages of the race will pay huge dividends when you near the finish line. A little wood filler, a little sanding, and you're good to go. I usually don't gush over a finishing product, but Krylon's motto of "no drips, no runs, no errors" is no idle boast. It's vital that the paint stays where it's placed when applying the finish in three dimensions simultaneously.

Topping it Off

You can use any 19"-diameter disc of material for the top (solid wood, stone, metal) but it really deserves a circle of glass to display the undulations of the base. I ordered my ⅜"-thick top, with pre-drilled mounting holes, from a local glass fabricator. I separated the top from the base with black rubber bottle stoppers. When I can visualize a connection detail, but don't know how to accomplish it, I always head for those mysterious, arcane parts drawers at the hardware store. I'd almost settled for doorstop bumper replacements (have you checked yours lately?) when I stumbled on two drawers of cork and rubber bottle stoppers in every conceivable size. Eureka! To pick up on the machine aesthetic of Gray's side table, I through-bolted the glass to the base with stainless steel machine screws, finish washers and cap nuts.

Can't Help but Wonder

Some day, someone's going to take a shot at the ribbon table in solid wood. My gut instinct tells me that this is impossible due to expansion/contraction considerations, but I haven't taken the time to evaluate the force vectors. It might work or it might explode. Do I have a volunteer?

Trace the outline of the fingers of a glued-up corner to the legs, as well as the top and bottom halves, after clamping them in alignment on your workbench. The holes in the fingers are merely "leftovers" from the pattern-routing process.

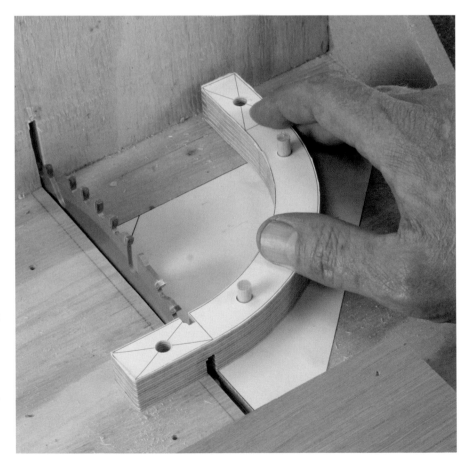

After starting to remove the straight extensions on 20 of the 36 corner segments on the band saw, I realized that by mounting a few more registration pins on the back of my dado sled I was able to make quick work of another repetitive task. I love it when I can get double duty out of a jig.

The secret to successfully joining corner pieces to flat pieces is keeping everything flush and square. Keep it flush with the little guys. Pull it together and up to square with the big guy.

Inspiration

The Aalto Stacking Stool and Eileen Gray Table are available from Design Within Reach, online at www.dwr.com.

IMAGES COURTESY OF DESIGN WITHIN REACH

Variation

If you like the form but need a larger table, make two bases then top them with a long sheet of glass or other flat material.

One afternoon, start to finish, is all it takes — even for a new woodworker.

PROJECT
10

Tornado Table

BY STEVE SHANESY &
JOHN HUTCHINSON

If mid-20th-century modern furniture design were as popular as the Arts & Crafts style is today, then thousands of these tables would be turning up for sale at craft shows any day now. Why? Anybody can build this table. And the more tables you build at once, the less time each one will take.

In spite of its simplicity and minimal materials, the table is very sturdy, owing to the geometry of the dowel placement. Isamu Noguchi (1904 - 1988), a sculptor and designer recently honored with the issue of U.S. Postal Service commemorative stamps, designed the table in the 1950s using a cast-iron base and chrome-plated steel rods. Wooden dowels, even ⁵⁄₁₆"-diameter ones as used in our model, provide ample strength.

Many different materials can be used to make the table. In addition to the wood or steel dowel options, the base can be solid wood or plywood. The top can be solid wood, plywood covered with plastic laminate or even glass with a ring of plywood to capture the top of the dowels and support the glass. Marble, granite or slate are still other possibilities.

The Secret to its Simplicity

When you've settled on the materials, the first order of business (and the genius that makes the table so easy to build) is making one simple jig. This is what will guide your drill bit when boring the holes for the dowels.

You'll need something to use as a guide for the drill bit, which we'll call the

The drilling jig is made from four pieces of wood, with the center piece cut at the proper angle before gluing the blocks in place. The metal drill bit bushing is then glued in place using epoxy.

drill bit bushing. Aluminum or copper tubing can be used for ¼" or ⅜" dowels, but for ⁵⁄₁₆" dowels, which we used for this project, you should buy a 1" long × ⁵⁄₁₆" threaded rod connector and drill out the threads. Just make sure the inside dimension of whatever you choose to guide your drill matches your dowels' diameter.

To build the jig, first rip and crosscut a 2"-wide × 6½"-long board. The thickness of the board should be the same as the outside dimension of the drill bit bushing. On this board, cut a 56° angle across its width at one end (use a miter saw or a miter gauge with a 34° setting).

Next, cut two 2"-wide × 6½"-long pieces of scrap wood (the thickness

isn't critical). These will be glued to the angled piece to create a space to capture the drill bit bushing. Glue the drill bit bushing to the angled section of the jig using epoxy.

After the glue has cured, cut a notch in the bottom of this assembly and attach the long, transverse "wing" board. This board provides you with a place to attach the clamps that will hold the jig in place while you drill your holes for the dowels. Secure the wing to the jig using four countersunk drywall screws.

Cutting Circles

With the jig built, you can cut the top and base to shape. You can use a band saw

69

TORNADO TABLE • INCHES (MILLIMETERS)

QUANTITY	PART	STOCK	THICKNESS	(mm)	WIDTH	(mm)	LENGTH	(mm)	COMMENTS
1	top	maple hdwd	1/2	13	22 d	559			
1	base	maple hdwd	1	25	14 d	356			
5	dowels	maple	5/16 d	8			23 7/16	595	
5	dowels	maple	5/16 d	8			23 5/8	600	

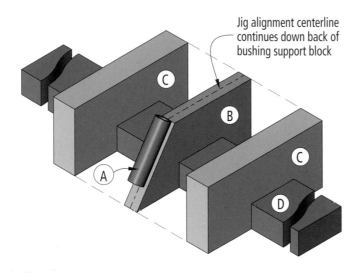

Jig alignment centerline
continues down back of
bushing support block

(A) Metal tube drill bit bushing (inside diameter = dowel diameter)

(B) 2"x 6 1/2" bushing support cut at 56° (thickness = bushing outside diameter)

(C) 3/4"x 2"x 6 1/2" blocks

(D) 3/4" x 1 1/2" x 24" clamping "wing"

or jigsaw for this, but a perfectly round shape is best achieved by using a router with a circle-cutting jig. Although you can purchase this jig, a simple shop-made version will handle this project easily.

Mount a piece of 1/4"-thick plywood that's about 24" long to the base of your router. Drill a hole so a straight bit can pass through the jig. For the three radius sizes required for this project (the top, and the outside and inside circles of the base) drill a small hole for a finish nail that will be the pivot point of the jig.

Where you drill these pivot holes depends in part on whether you are cutting the outside edge of the top or base or the inside edge of the hole in the base. To cut the outside edge of the top and base, you don't want to include the

diameter of the straight bit in your measurement; for the inside hole, you do.

Next, prepare the two square blanks for the top and base from 1/2"-thick material of your choice. Each blank should be at least 1/8" bigger than the finished size. On the underside of each plywood blank (the side that won't show) find the center by drawing two lines from corner to corner of each square. The center is where those lines intersect. Mark that spot with an awl for the finish nail that is the pivot point of your circle-cutting jig.

Insert the finish nail in the appropriate hole in the jig and hammer it in the center of the blank. When cutting the circles in the base, you can drive the nail clear through because — if your design

calls for it — the center piece is later cut away and discarded. Cut the outside circle first. (The inside circle is cut after you drill your holes for the dowels.) Do the same thing for the top, except this time don't drive the nail all the way through.

When cutting all the circles, you should make the cut in three passes, so set the depth of your router bit's cut accordingly. Be sure to clamp each blank to your bench top. You'll likely want to protect your work surface from the last router bit pass by putting some scrap below the work.

Also, keep in mind that when you later cut the inside circle of the base, the outer ring should be clamped down so it isn't damaged by the router bit at the moment it's cut free of the outer ring.

Cut the top and the outside base circles. As mentioned earlier, before cutting the inside base circle, you'll need to drill the dowel holes first because you'll need to use the waste material of the inside circle to align the jig.

Drilling Holes

Prepare to drill the holes for the dowels using the jig you made and the hole-drilling pattern. Copy the pattern at 100%. Then make five copies, trim to the pattern border and match them up so that corresponding, overlapping lines are in place, as shown on page 74. Tape the five pages together, then tape them to the top side of the base.

Study the pattern and sort out the various circles. The very outside circle is the outside diameter of the top. The next circle in is the outside diameter of the base. It contains the five pairs of small circles that are the drilling locations for

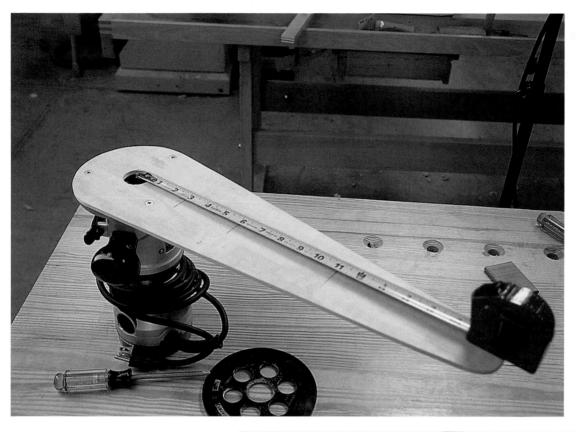

A finish nail serves as the pivot point for the circle-cutting jig. For outside cuts, measure from the inside edge of the router bit; use the outside edge of the bit for measuring inside cuts. Mark the radius distance on the jig, then drill a small hole for the nail.

the holes in the base where the dowels will be glued. *Note: Each drilling location has a straight line (green in the drawing) that connects it to the location in the top for gluing the other end of the dowel.*

Before clamping the jig in place and drilling your holes, mark the centerline of the guide bushing on the back of the jig.

Transfer the drilling locations from the paper template to the work. Use an awl or other pointed implement to softly mark each hole's center. Then follow the straight "dowel" line mentioned earlier about 8" back and softly mark another point. Designate pairs of dimples that go together. When all these are made for the base, remove the template, keeping it intact, then connect the paired dimples with a pencil line. (Or, you can make two copies of the pattern, attach one to the top and one to the base, and drill right through each pattern.)

To clamp the jig to the work, you'll need to elevate it. Use short lengths of 2×4s. Position the jig as shown on page 72.

Use the drill bit bushing as a sighting device so you can see the center of your marked hole. Align the pencil mark on the back bottom edge of the jig with the

Underside of top

Make cut counterclockwise

Blank clamped to scrap plywood or bench

Mark the center of the circle with an awl. Then use the point of the nail in the jig to drop in the hole. Give the nail a couple of taps with a hammer to secure it. Cut the circle by moving the router counterclockwise. Make the cut in several passes, lowering the bit about ⅛" after each pass.

Tape the five-piece pattern together and lightly secure it to the underside of the top. Use an awl to mark the hole's drilling center for the dowels. Make two more marks, one to represent the hole center for the base and another along the line indicating the dowel path. Mark the center about 8" back from the dowel center for the top.

Connect the dots made by the awl with a pencil line. The pencil line will represent the dowel's path from the top hole to the base hole. You'll use this line to set up the drilling jig in proper alignment.

straight line for that hole location. Verify the position by sliding your brad-point drill bit through the bushing. If the point hits the dimple, it's perfect.

Clamp the jig to the work and drill a ¼"-deep hole. Because you're drilling at an angle, one side of the hole will be longer than ¼". To establish a consistent hole depth, mark on your drill bit where you should stop drilling when the mark reaches the top of the bushing. Repeat the process for each hole center on the base and the top. Once you drill all the holes in the base, place the template on the underside of the top piece and follow the same steps to drill the mating holes. To make assembly easier, re-drill the holes in the top using a bit that's 1/64" larger than 5/16". It's not necessary to use the jig — just chase the existing holes with the larger bit.

Now you can rout out the inner circle of the base.

With the drilling jig clamped in place, drill a ¼"-deep hole for the dowel. You should mark your drill bit with a pen or piece of tape to tell you how deep to drill. Obviously, you don't want to drill through your top.

Before assembly, you may want to apply edge veneer tape to the exposed plywood edges. Use pressure-sensitive adhesive-backed veneer tape because of the size of the inside circle of the base.

Assembling the Storm

It's time to cut your dowels to length — five at 23⅝" and five at 23⁷⁄₁₆" to create a 20"-high table when assembled. Designate the lengths by color-coding the ends.

Next, dry-fit the base, dowels and top. First insert the dowels in the base. Each pair will make a V-shape. Insert the slightly longer dowels first in the left hole of each pair. Next, place the shorter dowels in the right hole making sure these dowels overlap outside all of the previously placed dowels. Study the 3-D illustration on page 75 to get a clearer picture of how it all works.

When you're satisfied with the assembly, take the table apart. Sand it and get ready to finish the base, dowels and underside of the top. If you want, finish the good side of the top, too. Just be careful not to damage it during final assembly.

Before applying any finish, plug the dowel holes and tape off the ends of the dowels. This will ensure that you're gluing wood to wood, not finished wood to finished wood. To finish the dowels, consider screwing cup hooks in one end so you can apply the finish and then hang them to dry.

For final assembly, place the top upside down and glue all the dowels in the top first. Then apply glue to the holes in the base and carefully slip the dowels in their respective holes. Be sure all the dowels are seated home. Measure the distance between the base and top to make sure they're parallel. This will ensure a table with a top that's parallel to the floor. While the glue is drying, place a weight on top of the base.

The Tornado Table described here is basic and representative of the original Noguchi table. You can see from the gallery that the variations of tornado tables are limited only by your imagination and materials.

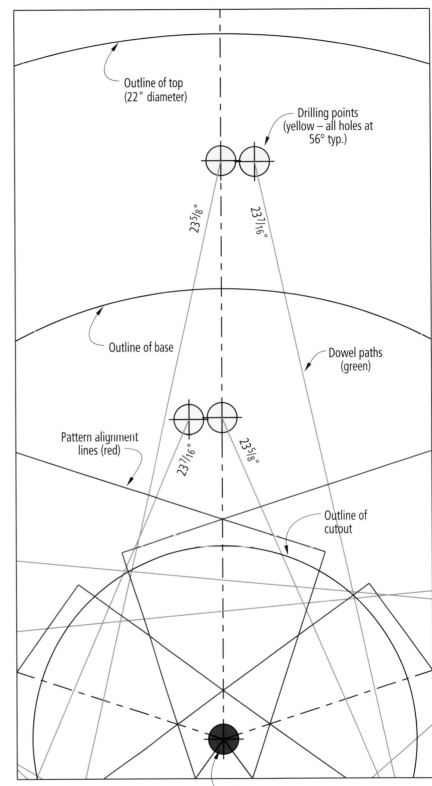

Full-size pattern

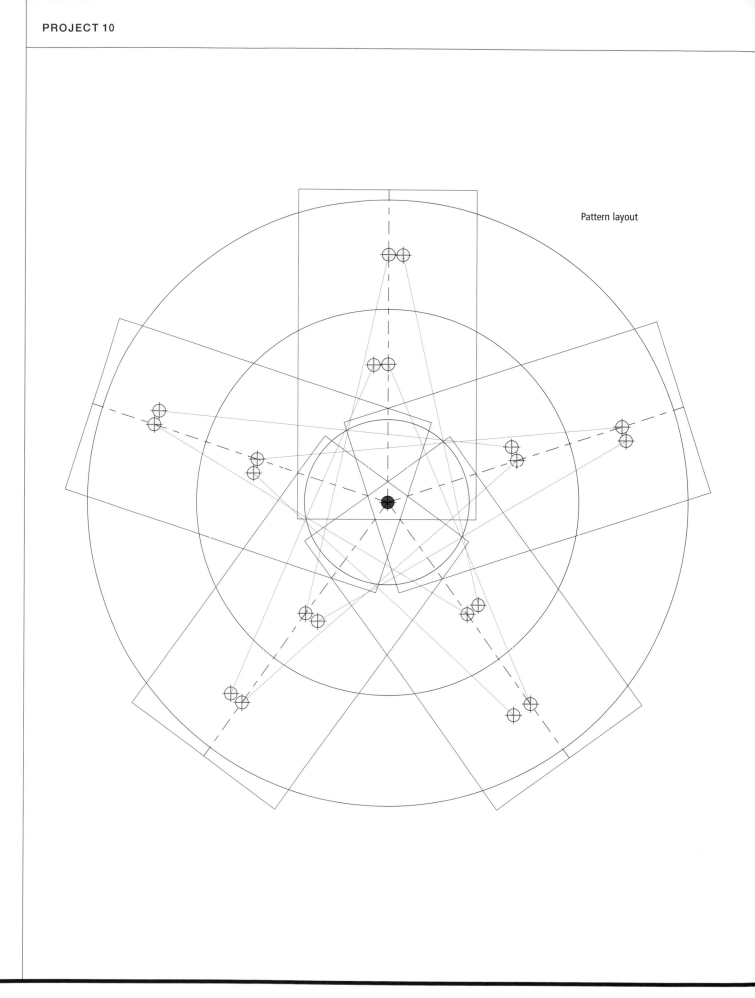

Pattern layout

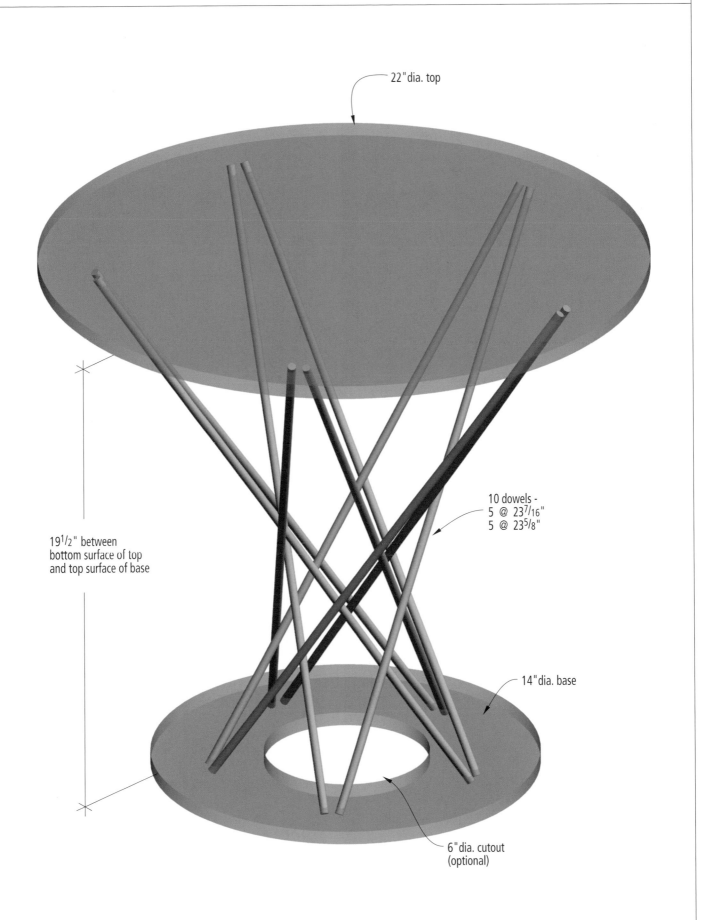

22" dia. top

10 dowels -
5 @ 23$^{7}/_{16}$"
5 @ 23$^{5}/_{8}$"

19$^{1}/_{2}$" between
bottom surface of top
and top surface of base

14" dia. base

6" dia. cutout
(optional)

The Hyperboloid: A Shape For Atomic-Age Furniture

As a child of the 1950s, I used to classify myself as a Baby Boomer. After researching Isamu Noguchi's Tornado Table, I've decided to switch titles to "Offspring of the Atomic Age." (The fact that my father worked for the Atomic Energy Commission doesn't hurt, either.)

If commercial nuclear power has a birthday, it would be Dec. 8, 1953. That was the day President Eisenhower gave his "Atoms for Peace" speech. As a result, the first wholly commercial power plant was ordered in 1955 and built in 1959 by Commonwealth Edison in Morris, Ill. Coincidentally, Noguchi presented his design for the rocking stool (yes, the table started as a rocker) to furniture manufacturer Knoll Associates in 1955. When inverted and with a few dowels added, the Tornado Table takes on the shape of a nuclear power facility's cooling tower. How much more "atomic" can you get? Despite its current negative conno-

tations, the shape of the cooling tower was the icon for a bright new tomorrow in the mid-1950s.

As a pure geometric form, the shape of the Tornado Table (and the illustration below) is what is known as a one-sheeted hyperboloid. For more information on all the cool math, check out http://mathworld.wolfram.com/Hyperboloid.html. Apparently, hyperboloids came in one- and two-sheet varieties.

But what about three sheets? Yet another Internet search gave me the answer. The phrase "three sheets to the wind" dates to 1821. The "sheet" is a reference to a rope on a sailboat. To have a sheet loose in the wind is bad seamanship; to have three loose means you are not capable of controlling the boat i.e., wasted. And you thought you'd only be learning about woodworking.
— JH

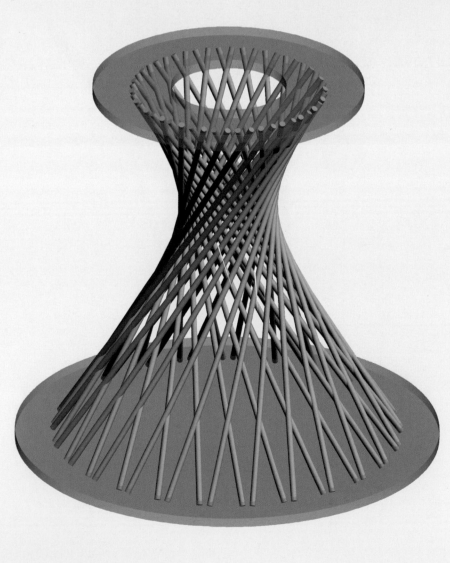

Popular Woodworking Staff Tables

Steve Shanesy

MATERIALS: walnut top, white oak base, steel supports

THE IDEA BEHIND IT: I wanted to get closer to the look and materials of the original Noguchi design. The base is turned, giving it a slight domed shape. The steel stock is bend at the base and secured with clinch nail. The walnut top is a single board and features a pencil edge often seen on Knolf furniture pieces of the era.

Linda Watts

MATERIALS: white oak

THE IDEA BEHIND IT: I delight in sitting on my front porch on a warm afternoon, so my goal was practical. I wanted a side table that could withstand the weather and hold a good book, a glass of iced tea and a planter of flower. I cut a hole in the top to inset the lipped planter for stability and finish the table with a light coat of boiled linseed oil.

Chris Schwartz

MATERIALS: cherry base and dowels, sugar pine top

THE IDEA BEHIND IT: I was going for a high-tech, high-texture look, so all the surfaces are finished with hand tools. The rippled surface of the top was created with a scrub plane, The chamfers on the base and underside of the top were made with a drawknife, block place and scrapers. The circle in the base was shaped with a small gouge.

David Thiel

MATERIALS: poplar top and base, hardwood dowels

THE IDEA BEHIND IT: Black lacquer has always held a magical appeal for me. With such a simple table, a gloss black finish seemed an obvious was to dress it up. I left the dowels natural as a counter-balance to the stark reality of the top and base. The edge of the top was radiused above and a heavy chamfer applied below to slim the appearance.

Michael Rabkin

MATERIALS: poplar top and base, hardwood dowels

THE IDEA BEHIND IT: Baseball has always been a big part of my life. I changed the circular base to a home plate and painted the entire table white. The my friend Amy (a great artist) painted the red stitching on the top so it looks like a baseball.

Kara Gebhart

MATERIALS: maple plywood top and bases, hardwood dowels

THE IDEA BEHIND IT: I wanted a top with a more fluid shape, but there was the stability issue. John suggested creating a two-base tornado "storm". The amoeba-shaped top is two 22"-diameter circles connected with curves. The overall height is 17" and I chose ¼" dowels. The drilling angles remained the same. I finished it with spray lacquer.

This historical reproduction is easier than it looks, thanks to a tricky rabbet.

PROJECT
11

Limbert Tabourette

BY CHRISTOPHER SCHWARTZ

The curves, cutouts and captured shelf of this small table make it look like a daunting project for the beginning woodworker. But thanks to some sharp design work from our project illustrator, this tabourette actually is duck soup.

Or, should I say, "rabbet" soup.

At the core of this table is an unusual rabbet joint that joins the four legs of the table. The rabbets nest inside one another and, when assembled, look like a pinwheel when viewed from above. As a bonus, this joint allows you to make all four legs from one simple template.

But how do you clamp such a curvy form with this unusual joint? If you own a nail gun, then you already have the answer.

This noteworthy joint might be the only thing that separates my reproduction from a museum original. Using historical photographs, we went to great pains to ensure this tabourette looks exactly like the table that appeared in Charles P. Limbert Co.'s 1905 furniture catalog. If you are unfamiliar with Limbert furniture, you should know that this Grand Rapids, Mich., company produced Arts & Crafts furniture with a European flair. Instead of straight lines and massive proportions, Limbert preferred curves. The furniture remains popular to this day. The No. 238 sold for $7 in 1905; a recent example fetched $1,600 at auction. Constructing this rep-lica, as you'll see, is easier than affording an original.

Start With the Legs

You can build this project with just two 8'-long 1×8s, making it affordable and easy to build — even if you don't have a jointer or a planer in your shop. Limbert's company built this table in quartersawn white oak, though we've also built it in walnut and cherry for a more contemporary look.

The first order of business is, as always, to get your stock flat and true. Cut all your pieces to length and true one long edge of each board. Set aside the four boards for the legs and glue the remaining boards edge-to-edge to create the panels you will need for the top and shelf.

You're going to make the legs using a plywood template, a router and a pattern-cutting bit. But before you start cutting curves, you should first cut the ³⁄₈" × ³⁄₈" rabbet on your four legs that will join the four pieces together.

This rabbet is the most critical part of the project. It needs to be precise to ensure the legs nest together seamlessly, so check your work carefully as you go. An inexpensive dial caliper will make the work easier.

I like to cut my rabbets on the table saw using a dado stack that's buried in an accessory fence. This allows me to cut my rabbets in one pass and has given me consistent results — especially when I add a featherboard to the setup.

With your rabbets cut, fit the four pieces together to check your work. Tweak your saw's settings until everything fits. You'll be able to tune up your joints by hand later if you know how to use a shoulder plane.

One Template, Four Legs

With the rabbets cut, it's time to make the plywood template that will shape the legs. Use the scaled diagrams we've provided. To make the template, you can use ¼" plywood if you like, though thicker plywood, such as ½" or ¾", will make your routing easier, as you'll see later on.

Using your band saw or jigsaw, cut slightly wide of the line. Leave a small nib of waste at the foot and the top of the leg that will allow you to screw this template directly to your lumber.

Clean up the curves on your template using sandpaper or files. Make the curves as smooth as possible. To ensure your curves are fair, I recommend you shape a piece of scrap with your template before you move on to the real thing. A trial run will point out rough spots or bumps that need more attention with the file.

To rout the shape of the legs, first lay the pattern on your work and line up the long, straight edge of the pattern with the rabbeted edge of the piece. Trace this shape onto your wood.

Remove the pattern and trim your leg close to this line using a jigsaw or band

LIMBERT TABOURETTE • INCHES (MILLIMETERS)

QUANTITY	PART	STOCK	THICKNESS	(mm)	WIDTH	(mm)	LENGTH	(mm)	COMMENTS
4	legs	white oak	3/4	19	8	203	26	660	oversized for pattern routing
1	top	white oak	3/4	19	16	406	16	406	
1	shelf	white oak	3/4	19	10½	267	10½	267	

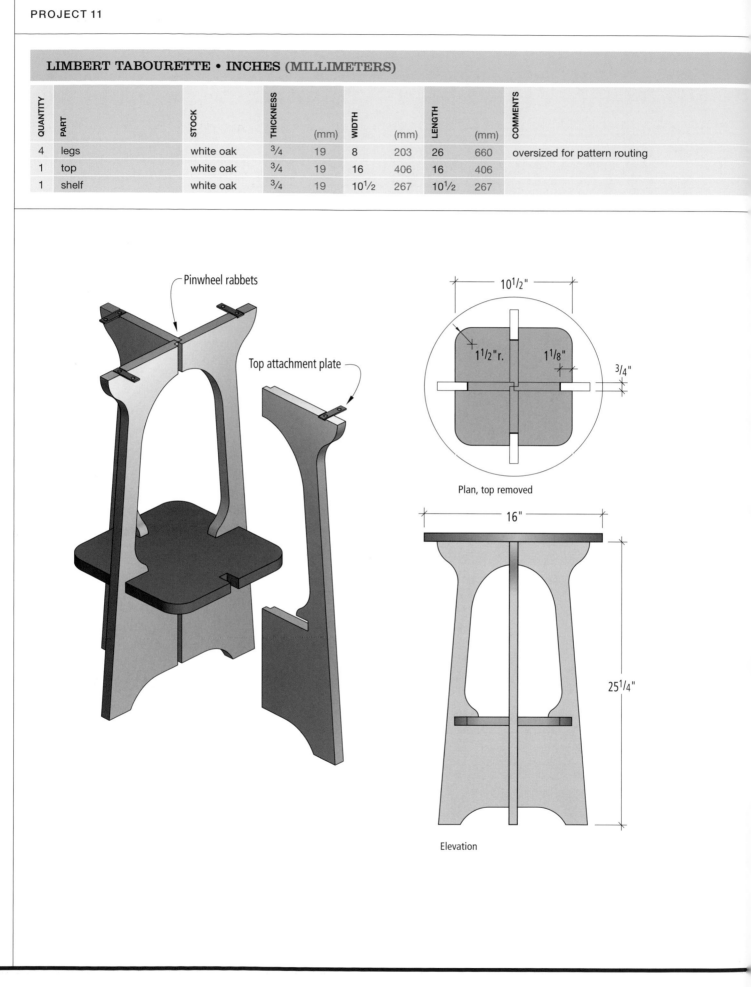

Pinwheel rabbets

Top attachment plate

10½"

1½"r.   1⅛"   ¾"

Plan, top removed

16"

25¼"

Elevation

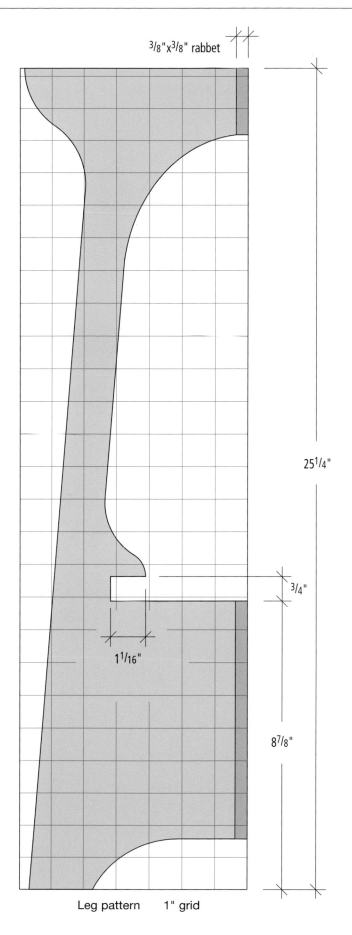

3/8"x3/8" rabbet

25¹/4"

3/4"

1¹/16"

8⁷/8"

Leg pattern   1" grid

saw — get within ¹/₁₆" to make it easier on your router and pattern-cutting bit. Save your fall-off pieces because they can help you clamp the legs together later in the game.

There are a couple of ways to rout the legs. You can do the operation on a router table, if your table is big enough. Or you can clamp the work to your bench and use a hand-held router.

The real trick is the router bit itself. There are two kinds of pattern-cutting bits: One has the bearing at the end of the bit; the other has the bearing above the cutting flutes. I generally prefer bits with the bearing on the end, especially when working with a hand-held router. That's because you can work with the pattern clamped to your workbench (if your pattern is thick enough). If this is the route you choose, clamp the pattern to your bench using a vise and bench dogs — make sure your bench dogs don't interfere with the bearing on the end of the bit. Affix the work to the pattern with screws or double-sided tape and rout it to shape.

With the shape routed, you'll immediately see that the notch that holds the shelf will need some additional work. The round router bit won't cut that area square, so square out this section with a jig saw, band saw or even a handsaw and chisels

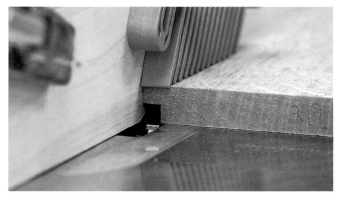

Cut the rabbets using a table saw with a dado stack or a router table with a straight or a dado cutting bit.

With the patterns taped together, attach it to a piece of plywood using a spray adhesive. This 3M product is available in the glue section of most home-center stores.

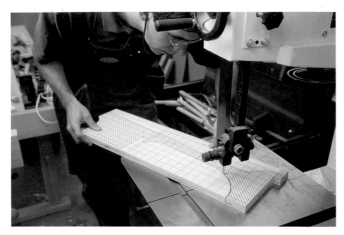

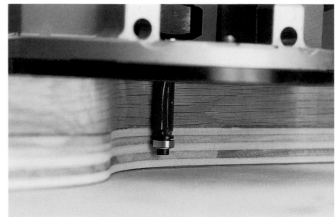

When trimming your pattern to rough size, cut as close to the line as you dare. The closer you are now, the less you'll labor your router later. But if you go over the line, you'll be in trouble.

Move the router around the piece in a counterclockwise pattern. As the grain changes direction in the piece, you might want to climb-cut a bit in places (cutting clockwise) for a cleaner cut. Just keep a firm grip on the router when you do this.

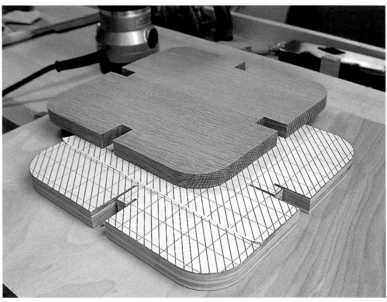

I nailed my pattern to a piece of scrap plywood and clamped that to my bench. This made routing the leg a simple operation that could be done in one pass.

A template for the shelf can simplify things if you're making several tables. I cut the notches on each edge of the pattern with a table saw and cleaned out the interior waste with a chisel. Double-sided tape held the shelf on the pattern during routing.

— whatever works for you. This also is the time to remove the small pieces of waste that you used to screw the work to your template.

Shape the other three legs in the same manner. Remove all the machining marks with sandpaper or hand tools (a spokeshave and smoothing plane would be appropriate).

The Other Curves

After shaping the legs, the top and shelf are pretty simple. The lower shelf requires notches on the four sides and round corners, as shown below. You can make a template for this operation, too. Cut the notches with the same tools you used to clean up the notches in the legs.

You can round the top in a variety of ways depending on what sort of tools you have. A router circle-routing jig is ideal. You also could cut it close using a band saw or jigsaw and sand it round on a disc sander.

This is the best time to finish the table's parts. Begin by sanding all the surfaces. Start with 100 grit, then move up to 180 or 220. I'm a hard-core hand-tool enthusiast, so I skip the sandpaper and use a smoothing plane and a card scraper to prepare my wood for finishing. Either way is fine. Once your wood is perfect, tape off all your glue joints with blue painter's tape.

I use a tried-and-true finishing process we've developed in our shop that emulates the deep reds and browns of a fumed ammonia finish without the downsides of that dangerous chemical.

We explained the entire process in detail in our June 2002 issue (*Arts & Crafts Finish*, available for sale at our website).

Essentially, you dye the project with a reddish half-strength water-base aniline dye. After that's dry, wipe on a coat of warm brown glaze. Then add a topcoat finish — we spray lacquer. The finish takes some time, but it's worth the effort.

Assembly

Putting the base together is easier than it looks; the trick is to do it in stages. First study the pinwheel rabbet in the diagram. Then take two of the legs and join them at a 90° angle as shown in the illustration. Here's how: Put glue in the rabbet, put the lower shelf in place and nail the two pieces together. You read that right, nail it. I've used a 23-gauge pinner and an 18-gauge nailer for this operation. Both fasteners work, but the smaller pins are less likely to split the wood. Place the fasteners so that when you assemble the entire table the nail holes will be covered by the other rabbets.

Now add a third leg to your first assembly in the same way. What you have left is what you see in the construction drawing: A three-legged table with a groove running down the assembly. And you have a fourth leg with its mating rabbet. Attaching this leg is a bit of a trick. I recommend either band clamps or making clamping cauls.

If you want to make clamping cauls (as shown below) you can use the fall-off pieces from band-sawing the legs to shape. These work, but they won't mate perfectly. The better way is to make another copy of the leg pattern and use that to saw and sand a set of cauls. To make the cauls easier to clamp to your project, tape the cauls to your clamps' heads. This allows you to assemble the project by yourself.

Using your cauls, clamp the fourth leg in place until the glue is dry, then attach the top. I used brass mending plates that have two screw holes bored in them. These simple bits of hardware allow the top to move with the seasons. To install them on the table's base, use a chisel to make a notch that's just a little bigger than the mending plate. The plate needs to pivot a bit when the top expands and contracts.

The notches shown in the photo are 3/32" deep by 5/8" wide and are 1 1/8" in from the outside edge of each leg. Screw each plate to the base. Once you install all four, screw the base to the top.

Now that you're done, be sure to save your templates and clamping cauls — because you're ready to go into production.

Nail one leg to the other so that the nail holes will not show when the piece is together. It's easy to do, but it's also easy to make a mistake. Use the diagram as a guide and an extra set of hands helps immensely.

I made clamping cauls using the patterns for the legs. Sand the edges of the cauls to avoid marring your finished edges. I also taped the cauls to my clamps, which made them easy to get in position without help.

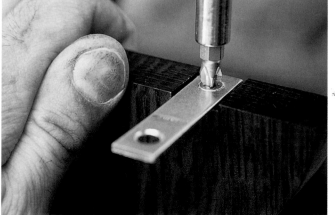

The shallow notch at the top of each leg holds the mending plates (found at my local home-center store). Make the notch a bit wider than the plate to allow it to pivot. This allows the top to expand and contract with the seasons.

Simple joinery makes a table in the classic style of the
Greene brothers a rewarding and easy project.

PROJECT
12

Greene & Greene Side Table

BY STEVE SHANESY

If you don't mind a little cheating, you can make this table quite simply. You see, the "pegged" mortise-and-tenon joints aren't really pegged at all. They are simple dowel joints, and the "pegs" arc merely inlaid and applied pieces of ebony. But even if you feel the slightest twinge of guilt about taking such short cuts — please don't. The brothers Greene and Greene, renowned architects and designers of the late Arts & Crafts period didn't hesitate a moment to use screws in their classic furniture. A little liberty on this project follows right along in the tradition.

I built this table from cherry. The legs require 2"-thick material and the top requires 1½"-thick stock. The aprons and stretchers finish out at ⅞" thick. If you use thinner material, you could reduce both the top and legs by ½", and the aprons and stretchers could go to ¾" stock. That will keep the proportions just about right.

Prepare all your stock to the final sizes as given in the cutting list. Next prepare the template for routing the so-called *cloud lift* patterns on the aprons and stretchers. These are Greene and Greene design signatures and were borrowed from the Japanese.

Cloud Lift Template
The two-sided template is made from ¼" Baltic birch plywood with the two

When routing the cloud lifts, the top-mounted bearing on the straight router bit follows and duplicates the pattern shape onto the table apron. Before routing, most of the waste material is removed with a band saw. Note the aprons ends are aligned with pencil marks on the template and the part is held to the template with brad nails.

Here I'm rounding over the edges with a ¼"-radius router bit. Almost every edge on the project gets this treatment. The exception is where parts join together, such as the apron, stretcher ends and apron top edge.

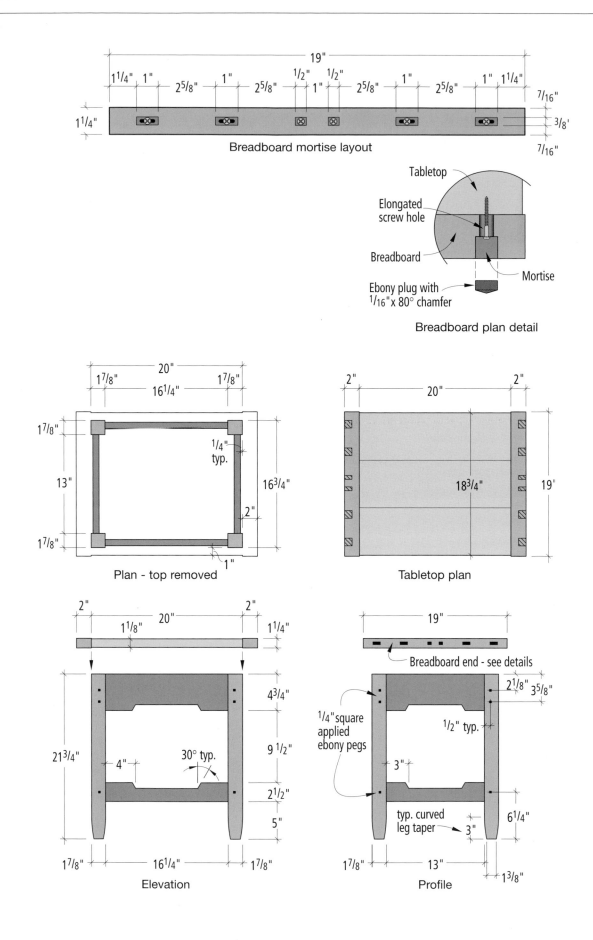

Breadboard mortise layout

Tabletop

Elongated screw hole

Breadboard

Mortise

Ebony plug with 1/16" x 80° chamfer

Breadboard plan detail

Plan - top removed

Tabletop plan

Elevation

30° typ.

1/4" square applied ebony pegs

typ. curved leg taper

Breadboard end - see details

1/2" typ.

Profile

GREENE AND GREENE SIDE TABLE • INCHES (MILLIMETERS)

QUANTITY	PART	STOCK	THICKNESS	(mm)	WIDTH	(mm)	LENGTH	(mm)	COMMENTS
4	legs	cherry	$1^7/_8$	48	$1^7/_8$	48	$21^3/_4$	552	
2	aprons	cherry	$^7/_8$	22	$4^3/_4$	121	$16^1/_4$	413	
2	aprons	cherry	$^7/_8$	22	$4^3/_4$	121	13	330	
2	stretchers	cherry	$^7/_8$	22	$2^1/_2$	64	$16^1/_4$	413	
2	stretchers	cherry	$^7/_8$	22	$2^1/_2$	64	13	330	
1	top	cherry	$^1/_2$	13	$18^3/_4$	476	20	508	
2	breadboards	cherry	$1^1/_4$	32	2	51	19	483	

patterns (one is slightly longer than the other) cut on the long edges of the same piece. Plan on using the template along with a straight router bit with a bearing of the same dimension as the bit diameter. Draw the design on the plywood following the dimensions in the diagram. The "lift" is ¾". Before band sawing to the line, drill ½" holes in the inside corners of the pattern. Drilling these holes is much easier than band sawing such a tight radius. After carefully band sawing to the line, sand the band-sawn edges so that they are smooth and straight. Next, on the template, mark each pattern edge with a line that represents the ends of the two different lengths of aprons and stretchers used in the project.

Before using the templates to rout the design, first band saw away most of the waste on the parts. Using the template, draw a pencil line of the design on each apron or stretcher, then band saw to about 1/16" from the line. The router will clean up the rest.

To prepare for routing, set up a router table with a router and the ½" straight bit as mentioned earlier. No fence is required for this type of pattern cutting. To begin routing, align the part so that the ends match up with the lines previously drawn and so that the leading edge of the pattern aligns with the edge of the part. Attach the part to the template using two small brad nails. You can putty the nail holes later, but even so, select the "b" side of the part that will go to the inside of the table base as the side to nail to. Run each part this way. If you use cherry, do your

best not to hesitate in the corners of the cut to minimize burning.

Shape the Legs

Next, turn to the legs. First shape the bottom to the gradual tapering curve as seen in the diagram. Start the detail 3" up from the bottom. The slight curved taper removes only ¼" per side at the end of the leg. Now make a template of the pattern so you can draw a pencil line for each side of the leg. Then band saw and sand to the line.

With the parts of the table base shaped, go back to the router table and insert a ¼" roundover bit in the router. Run the profile on all the long edges of the legs, stretchers and aprons, except for the top edge of the apron, which remains square.

Right-Sizing Dowels

If your dowels are too snug, there's an easy fix called a dowel skinner. In this project, I found my ⅜" dowels were too tight for my ⅜" hole. The solution was to drill a hole in ⅛" or thicker mild steel that was 1/64" smaller than the dowel. Then just drive your dowels through the hole with a hammer and you'll get a perfect fit.

Dowel Joints for Base

To assemble the legs, aprons and stretchers, drill the holes for the ⅜" dowels and sand the parts to 150 grit. Use two, 2"-long dowels for each joint and position them so that when assembled, the apron sets back ¼" from the outside face of the leg.

When all the dowel holes are drilled, dry-fit the assembly before actually gluing it together. When I assembled my base, I glued and clamped it in two stages. First assemble one set of legs, aprons and stretchers. Then complete the assembly after the first assembly is dry. Take care not to apply too much glue because squeeze-out in the joint is difficult to clean up and can lead to finishing problems later.

Make the Top

Now turn your attention to the tabletop. The breadboard ends with ebony plugs are another Greene and Greene signature detail. I made the breadboard ends ⅛" thicker than the top, leaving them 1⁄16" proud of the thickness of the rest of the top. They also are slightly longer. This additional length anticipates eventual expansion of the top.

Prepare your top's main boards and glue them up. When dry, square up the top and cut it to its final size. The breadboards are attached easily with a 2½"-long screw in each of the plugged holes. Be sure and make elongated screw slots in the breadboard to anticipate wood movement in the top. To make the square grooves in the breadboard ends, use a mortising machine or chain drill the holes and then square them up with a chisel. The depth of the hole is 1". The size of the small holes is ⅜" wide by ½" long. The longer holes are 1" long.

Before attaching the breadboards to the top, go back to the router table and round over the long edges of the top and the outside edges of the breadboards. The edges of the top and breadboards that join together remain square. As with the table base, pre-sand the top before assembling the top and breadboard ends. When done, clamp the ends to the top so they remain in perfect position while screwing the ends in place.

Simple joinery makes this project easy. A pair of dowels join each apron and stretcher end to the leg. This vintage Stanley No. 59 doweling jig makes this process especially easy due to its adjustability (see the story facing page), particularly when drilling the holes in the legs to provide the ¼" setback of the aprons.

Ebony Plugs and Pegs

The ebony plugs used on the table all stand about ⅛" proud of the surface. The top of each plug is shaped so that it looks faceted, or slightly beveled on the top. The ebony plugs for the breadboards are first made as a ⅜" × ½"-long stick. Carefully make two 10° cuts on one of the long ⅜"-dimension edges to create two of the facets. Next cut them to length, but a little long. Fit each one as they are installed. I fit mine by sanding. Also sand the other two facets on the top surface. When ready to install, add a slight amount of glue and carefully tap them into place. The process is a bit

No mortising machine? You can still speed along the process of cutting the plug holes in the breadboard ends. After marking out the locations, drill out most of the waste, then square up the ends and side walls with a chisel.

tedious, but it takes just about an hour to complete.

The smaller pegs for the mortise-and-tenon joints are ¼" square. To make these, cut an ebony stick ¼" square and about 12" long. Facet the top to make a shallow pyramid shape by sanding, then hand-saw off the shaped end about ⅛" long. Repeat the process until you have at least 24 "plugs." To apply the "plugs" use cyanoacrylate (what most people call Super Glue). Carefully mark the location of each plug, add a tiny drop of glue and set it in place. The glue cures quickly and no clamping is required.

Finish sand the top and base with 220 grit sandpaper. This last sanding must be done by hand due to the plugs project-ing off the surface. I finished the project using two coats of a clear satin finish spray lacquer that comes in an aerosol can. A wiping varnish or polyurethane also would be appropriate. Whichever finish you use, sand lightly between coats for the smoothest results.

You're almost done. Attach the top to the base using whatever method you prefer. I used 1"-square wooden cleats and screws. Again, be sure your method of attachment accommodates wood movement in the top.

Old Stanley Doweling Jig The Best

There was a time when I used a lot of dowels in furniture building. Back then, the jig I used was the self-center-ing kind. A few years ago a woodworker friend showed me a vintage Stanley doweling jig he picked up at a flea market. Its design is quite similar to the current Stanley offering, but the quality of the materials are far superior to today's models.

The great feature of this design is the variability of spacing the dowel hole locations and the ease of align-ing the hole center to your predetermined location. Since purchasing my own vintage Stanley, my self-centering jig hasn't come out of the drawer. Chances are you can buy your own vintage Stanley No. 59 or No. 60 at auction on eBay (ebay.com) for about $25. Just make sure the one you bid on is complete. The bushings for guiding your drill are interchangeable depending on which size hole

you want. A complete jig would include bushings for ¼", ⁵/₁₆", ⅜", ⁹/₁₆" and ½" drill bits.

If you do buy one of these tools without bushings (or if you need odd-size bushings), Stanley still sells them as replacement parts. Call 800-262-2161 during business hours and select the option "replacement parts."

Not ready to build the Morris chair? Try your hand at this side table to hone your skills.

PROJECT
13

Stickley Side Table

BY DAVID THIEL

Patterned after the model No. 562 taboret shown in the L.&J.G. Stickley catalog of 1914, the original of this table now sells for $1,600 at auction.

As with all white oak Arts & Crafts pieces, wood figure is important to make a simple design stand out. Choose the best figure for the top and the panel pieces. If the stretchers and legs are also well-figured, so much the better.

After cutting the legs to size, mark the best faces for showing off the grain. Then cut ³⁄₈" × 2⁵⁄₈" × 1"-deep mortises in the legs for the stretchers, and ³⁄₈" × 1¹⁄₈" × 1"-deep mortises for the aprons. These mortises are centered on the width of the legs and located as shown in the diagram. I used a benchtop mortiser for this step, but you could also use a plunge router with an up-spiral bit to cut them.

Now change the bit (either mortiser or router bit) to a ¼" bit and mark and cut the ¼" × 5³⁄₈" × ½"-deep mortises for the panels in the aprons and stretchers.

With the mortises complete, head for the table saw and get ready to cut tenons. I use a rip blade to form my tenons. I cut the cheeks first, then define the shoulders, so there isn't a chance of the shoulders being accidentally notched by the saw blade during the cheek cut. By cutting the shoulder last, any "notching" will happen against the tenon cheek.

When making the shoulder cut on the table saw, it's easiest to use the rip fence to define the 1"-tenon length. If you use the fence to the right of the blade, and the miter gauge to the left of the blade you will trap the fall-off piece between the blade and fence, causing it to shoot back from the blade. Instead, set the fence for 13" to the right of the blade and use the miter gauge to the right of the blade as well. This way you can cut both tenoned ends with a single setup, and the waste will fall harmlessly to the left of the blade.

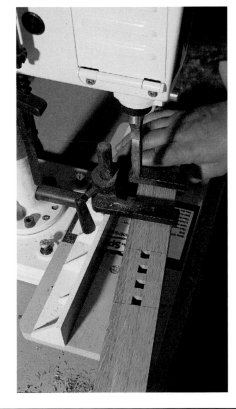

If you're paying careful attention, you will realize 1" tenons are going to bump into one another in the mortises. After cutting the tenon shoulders, reset the fence and the blade angle to cut 45° miters on the ends of the tenons.

Don't leave the saw yet. You still need to form the ¼" × 5¼" × ½" tenons on both ends of the panels. You might have noticed that all of the tenons are ⅛" less wide than the mortise dimensions. This is no mistake. When the side panels are positioned between the stretchers and

LEFT: The best method for mortising is to first bore the areas at either end of the mortise, then space the next few mortises the width of the mortising chisel. In this case, the spacing works almost perfectly. The goal is to allow the chisel bit to have enough wood to drill straight without wandering from side-to-side. On some mortises the spacing between the first holes will be less than the width of the chisel.

ABOVE: Complete the mortise by drilling away the waste between the first mortises. This allows the mortise chisel to cut most efficiently without pulling to the left or right and bending the chisel.

STICKLEY SIDE TABLE • INCHES (MILLIMETERS)

QUANTITY	PART	STOCK	THICKNESS	(mm)	WIDTH	(mm)	LENGTH	(mm)	COMMENTS
4	legs	white oak	2	51	2	51	$21^{1}/_{8}$	537	
4	stretchers	white oak	$^{7}/_{8}$	22	3	76	14	356	1" TBE
4	aprons	white oak	$^{7}/_{8}$	22	$1^{1}/_{2}$	38	14	356	1" TBE
4	panels	white oak	$^{1}/_{2}$	13	6	152	$8^{1}/_{2}$	216	$^{1}/_{2}$" TBE
1	top	white oak	$^{7}/_{8}$	22	20	508	20	508	
16	pegs	oak	$^{1}/_{4}$ D	6			$1^{1}/_{2}$	38	

TBE = Tenon, both ends

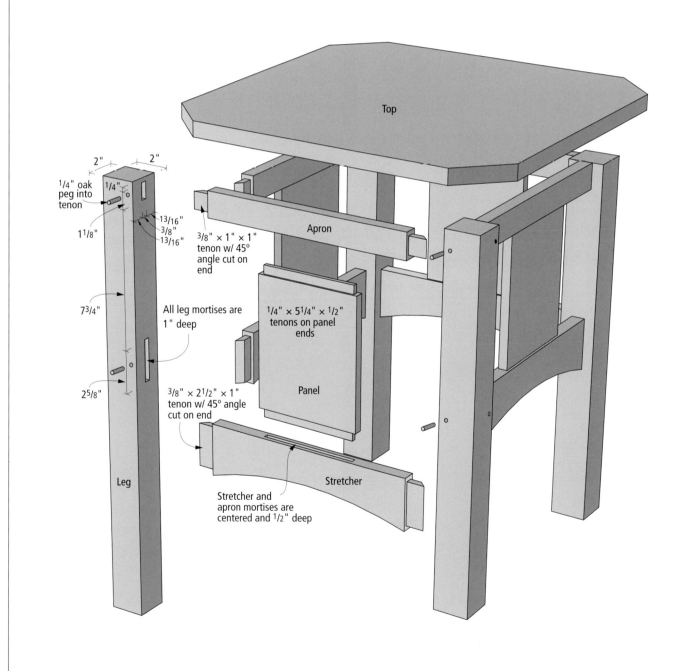

Top

2"   2"

$^{1}/_{4}$" oak peg into tenon

$^{1}/_{4}$"

$^{13}/_{16}$"
$^{3}/_{8}$"
$^{13}/_{16}$"

$1^{1}/_{8}$"

$^{3}/_{8}$" × 1" × 1" tenon w/ 45° angle cut on end

Apron

$7^{3}/_{4}$"

All leg mortises are 1" deep

$^{1}/_{4}$" × $5^{1}/_{4}$" × $^{1}/_{2}$" tenons on panel ends

$2^{5}/_{8}$"

$^{3}/_{8}$" × $2^{1}/_{2}$" × 1" tenon w/ 45° angle cut on end

Panel

Leg

Stretcher

Stretcher and apron mortises are centered and $^{1}/_{2}$" deep aprons, the shoulders of the panel tenons will fit snugly against the stretchers and rails. If the mortises in the legs were the exact width of the tenons, and off by even a little bit, they would force a gap between the panels and the two rails. The 1/8" extra space on the tenons is to allow for wood movement.

Next, mark the 1"-high curve on the bottom edge of each stretcher and cut the shape on the band saw. The easiest way to mark this curve is with a flexible 1/8" wood strip bent to the 1" mark and then traced with a pencil.

One last step before assembly. The top is held in place by tabletop fasteners. These are screwed into the underside of the top, and fit into 1/8"-wide grooves in the aprons. These fasteners allow the top to adjust to wood movement without affecting the base. Run these grooves on all four aprons on the table saw. This will let you decide which way the top will fit later.

You're ready to sand, then glue up the base. A dry fit is definitely a good idea to make sure everything fits and to make sure you know how to hold everything in place once the glue goes on.

With the base glued and clamped, cut the pieces for the top, and glue them together. To reduce the amount of sanding necessary, a few biscuits added to the joint will help align the pieces and keep them from slipping during glue-up.

When the base is ready, mark each of the peg locations on the mortise-and-tenon joints, and drill a 1 1/4" × 1/4" hole at each location. Then peg the holes with 1/4" oak dowels. Cut the excess dowel length flush to the table leg and finish sand.

Unclamp the top and sand it flat. Then mark 2 1/2" in from each corner and run a line at a 45° angle to clip the corners of the top on the band saw to an octagon shape. Then finish sand the top.

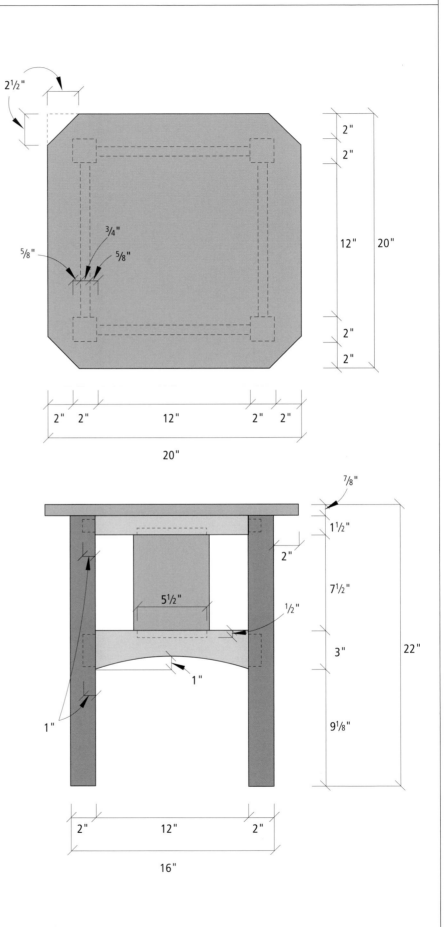

Build a traditional table with help from a tool usually reserved for carpenters: the power planer.

PROJECT
14

Porringer Side Table

BY JIM STUARD

As I get a little older, I get more sedentary. My wife says I'm just looking for more places to set a drink down. In that spirit, I decided to draw on my experience making period furniture to come up with an end table for the living room with a curly maple porringer top. This table comes from a design that is roughly 250 years old, which places it squarely in the country interpretation of the Queen Anne style.

According to Leigh Keno, a noted New York antiques dealer and a regular on PBS's popular Antiques Roadshow, the term porringer is merely a convenient way for antique dealers to classify this type of table and probably has nothing to do with the way the table was used originally. Using the English word porridge (oatmeal) as the root word, the term is likely no more than 150 years old. Porringer is used today to describe a small soup or cereal bowl with a handle. Antique dealers most likely tried to use the name to pass off the round oversized corners — which were no more than a decorative element — as the accessories of a small breakfast table. That said, porringers in good condition will fetch thousands of dollars due to their rarity.

Making Aprons

This table was made with mortise-and-tenon construction. Start by cutting the apron parts according to the cutting list. Next, cut the $\frac{1}{4}$" × 4"-wide × $\frac{7}{8}$"-long tenons on the ends of the aprons and the scrollwork as shown in the illustration.

Then drill the pocket holes for attaching the base to the top. Do this on a drill press with a $1\frac{1}{4}$" Forstner bit. Use a shop-built jig using the diagrams later in the story to hold the aprons in place while drilling.

Leg Blanks

Although the legs look complicated, they are not. The secret is using an offset turning technique. First cut the blanks $\frac{1}{8}$" longer than in the cutting list. This gives you some room to work with when turning the pad on the end of the foot.

Use a straightedge to make an "X" from corner to corner on both ends of the blank. This will aid in finding the center as well as marking the offset. Now, on the bottom of the legs, determine which corner will face out; then, on the bottom of each leg, measure $\frac{1}{2}$" from the center to the corner opposite the outside corner. This is the offset for the leg. Remember, the farther away from the center you go, the thinner the ankle (the area just above the pad) will be. Going any farther than $\frac{1}{2}$" is dangerously close to having a leg pop off your lathe.

Mark a line completely around the blank 6" down from the top of the blank. This area will remain square. To save time roughing the blank, lay out a $1\frac{1}{2}$"-diameter circle on the foot end of the blank. Set your jointer to 45°. Using the circle as a guide, lower the infeed table to the point where you can take the corner off, leaving about $\frac{1}{32}$" outside the circle. Go slowly as you joint up to the line where the turning starts. Now mount the blank in the lathe between the center points with the top towards the lathe's drive center. Cut a small kerf at the line where the turning stops. Don't cut too deeply or you won't be able to remove the kerf as you turn. With a roughing gouge and a skew chisel, turn a cylindrical blank from the saw kerf to the foot. Then use a skew chisel to round the corners of the pummel (the square part of the leg) where it meets the turned portion. Repeat this procedure on all four legs. Now you're ready to do the offset turning.

Turning the Offset

Before resetting the legs, measure up from the bottom $\frac{1}{8}$" and from that mark another $\frac{5}{8}$". Turn the lathe on and follow the marks around with a pencil. Take a parting tool and set it on its side. Cut a small incision at the $\frac{5}{8}$" mark. This creates a shadow line from which to begin the offset turning. Set the lathe for its lowest speed and reset the tailstock so the leg is mounted in the lathe using the offset mark. This might look like an awkward setup, but as you remove material the leg will turn with more stability. Finish the straight part of the leg with a skew chisel and the ankle with a roughing gouge. Finally, turn the pad foot as

PORRINGER SIDE TABLE • INCHES (MILLIMETERS)

QUANTITY	PART	STOCK	THICKNESS	(mm)	WIDTH	(mm)	LENGTH	(mm)	COMMENTS
1	top	maple	³/₄	19	20	508	30	762	
4	legs	maple	1¹/₂	38	1¹/₂	38	21¹/₄	540	
2	long aprons	maple	³/₄	19	5	127	18³/₄	476	
2	short aprons	maple	³/₄	19	5	127	10³/₄	273	

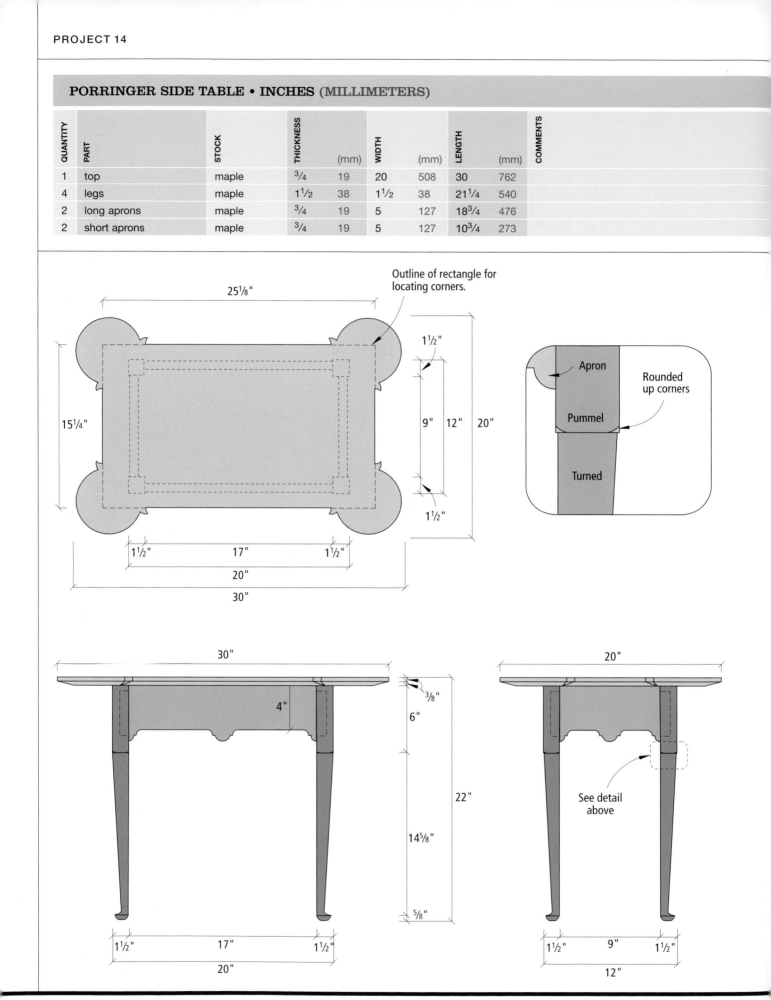

Outline of rectangle for locating corners.

Apron

Rounded up corners

Pummel

Turned

See detail above

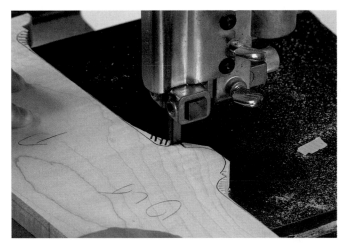

Lay out the scrollwork on the bottom of the aprons using the dimensions in the illustrations or make a pattern. If using a pattern, glue it to ¼" plywood, cut it out, trace the pattern on your aprons and cut them out on a band saw. Make relief cuts on the inside radii so you can remove the material easier.

Make sure that the bottom of the pocket is at least ⅞" from the top edge of the apron to prevent the screws from poking through.

CUTTING CORNERS: First mount a blank between centers with the top towards the drive center. Then use a saw to cut a small kerf on each corner at the line 6" from the top. Don't cut too far or you won't be able to remove the kerf. With a roughing gouge and skew chisel, turn a cylindrical blank from the saw kerf to the foot. At this point use a skew chisel to cut a small rounding up on the square corners of the top (see diagram). Repeat on all the legs and you're ready to do the offset turning.

shown in the photo. Now it's time to sand the legs. Start with 120-grit sandpaper and finish with 150 grit.

Now cut the ⅜" × ⅞" × 4" mortises in the legs, 5⁄16" in from the edge and ½" down from the top. Be careful when marking the locations of your mortises to make sure the turned feet face out. You'll notice that the mortises meet slightly at their bottoms. Plane away a little of the tenon where they meet. Now glue the base together. Start by gluing

the legs and the short aprons together; then glue them to the long aprons.

After the glue is dry, finish sand the entire base, then lay out the holes for the cherry pegs. Any dark hardwood will do for the pegs, but cherry sands smooth and the end grain stains a dark color. Drill a ¼" hole 1" deep. Follow suit with 3⁄16" and ⅛" bits, creating a tapered hole. After shaping 16 square pegs (tapered on four sides to a point), tap one in until you feel and hear it seat. The sound of

the hammer hitting the peg makes a distinctly different sound when it seats. No glue is required for this as you are running a peg completely through the leg. It won't be coming out anytime soon. Cut the pegs, leaving 1⁄32" showing and sand until it is a rounded-over bump. Drill ¼" holes into the pockets from the top of the base for attaching the top.

Make and Attach the Top

The top is the easier part, but it can make or break the whole project. Wood selection is key. One hundred years ago, you could get extremely wide, highly-figured curly maple at a low price. Amazingly, most old porringers were one- or two-board tops. That's clear-figured wood 10"- to 20" wide! Regrettably, those days are gone, and you will have to make do with the painfully high-priced, narrow lumber you get today.

I had to try the Amish sawmills in eastern Pennsylvania to find a retail source for decent curly maple. I managed to find decent 4/4 lumber that's about 7" wide and a nice piece of 8/4 for the legs (I wasn't sure how thick the legs would be when I started so you could probably get away with 6/4 for leg stock).

For the top, lay out a 15¼" × 25⅛" rectangle in the center of the top. Make a pattern for the top using ¼" plywood as you did for the aprons. When you lay the

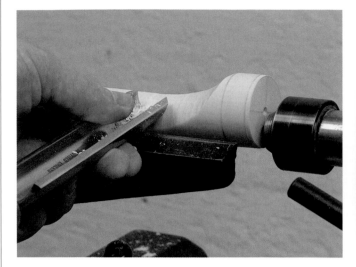

When you turn the lathe on, the leg's spinning creates a ghost image of what the finished leg will look like. Remove that "ghost" material with a roughing gouge. Stop at the second line that you drew earlier. Lay the gouge on its left side at the second line and slowly rotate the gouge clockwise as you go to the left. Go very slowly until you get the hang of how the wood reacts to the gouge.

The last thing to do on the legs is turning the pad on the foot. You do this last, as removing the foot material also removes the offset center. Reset the bottom of the leg into the original center, and, using a parting tool, turn away this "extra" length until it's about $3/8$" diameter. This gives you some extra distance from the live center. Then, using a small spindle gouge, turn the pad of the foot till it meets the $3/8$" diameter. Sand the pad the same as the leg and you're done turning.

inside corner of the pattern over the outside corner of the drawn rectangle, the outside of the radius should just touch the edge of the top. Trace the pattern on all four corners and cut out the top using a jigsaw.

When you are done cutting the shape of the top, chamfer the edges. Chamfering the edges lightens the overall look of the table, and the chisel work underneath has a very sculptural feel. Before chamfering, scribe a line that is half the thickness of the top on the entire outside edge of the top. Next, use an adjustable square to mark a line around the underside of the top, 1½" from the edge.

I chamfered the edges with a power planer. It's a tool used mostly by carpenters to remove material from doors when fitting and installing them. And in that role, this tool is unequalled. Finish-sand the top to 150 grit.

The last assembly chore is to screw the top to the base. Begin by laying the top upside down on a blanket. Center the base on the top and screw it down with No. 10 × 1½" wood screws.

To finish the table, I hand scraped the top with a Stanley No. 80 cabinet scrap-

When you've done all you can with a power plane, use chisels and planes to remove material down to the marked line.

er. With the lack of abrasive sandpaper 250 years ago, this is how the old tables were made ready to finish. Scraping with a properly prepared scraper blade will show up as rows of slight depressions (1/32" deep) with ridges about 2½" apart.

I stained the wood with aniline dye, applied one coat of boiled linseed oil and finished the table with four coats of dark shellac. This imparts a nice honey brown color to the curly maple and is easy to repair. Now where did I put that drink?

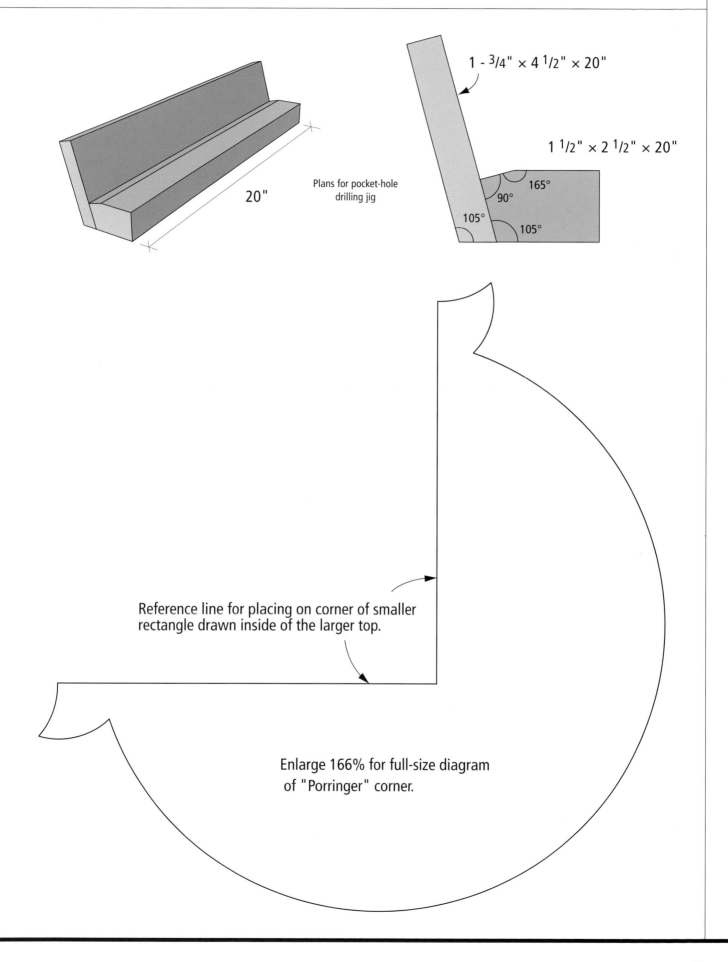

$1 - {}^3/4" \times 4 {}^1/2" \times 20"$

$1 {}^1/2" \times 2 {}^1/2" \times 20"$

20"

Plans for pocket-hole
drilling jig

165°

90°

105°

105°

Reference line for placing on corner of smaller
rectangle drawn inside of the larger top.

Enlarge 166% for full-size diagram
of "Porringer" corner.

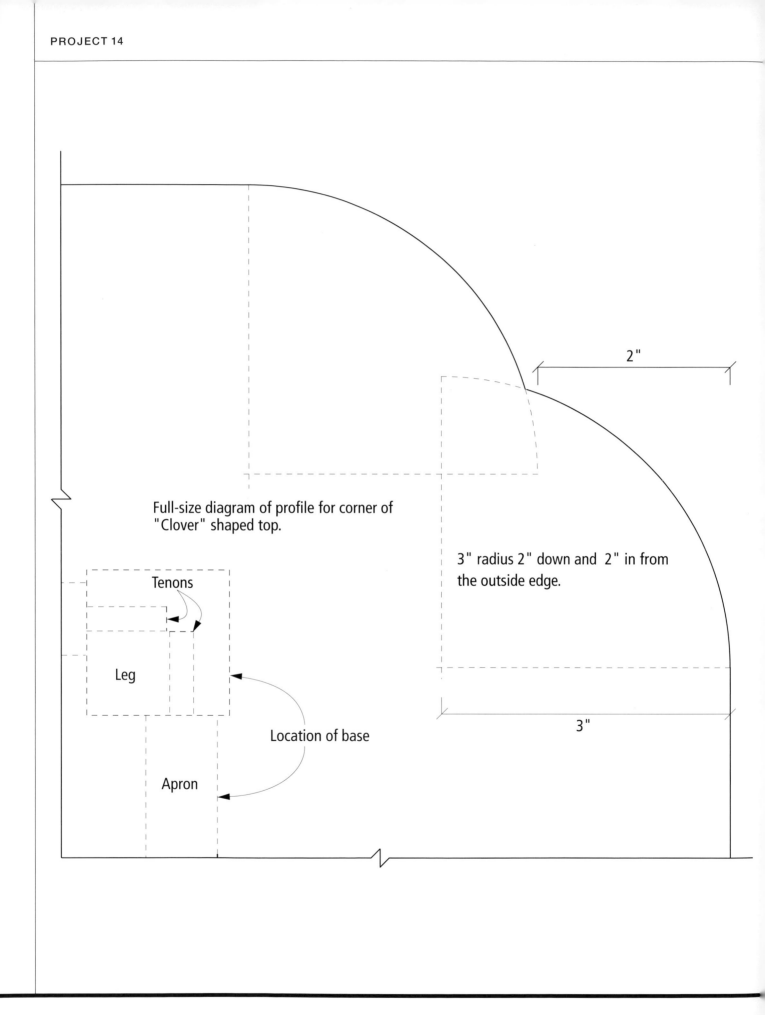

2"

Full-size diagram of profile for corner of "Clover" shaped top.

3" radius 2" down and 2" in from the outside edge.

Tenons

Leg

Location of base

Apron

3"

Enlarge 166% for full size.

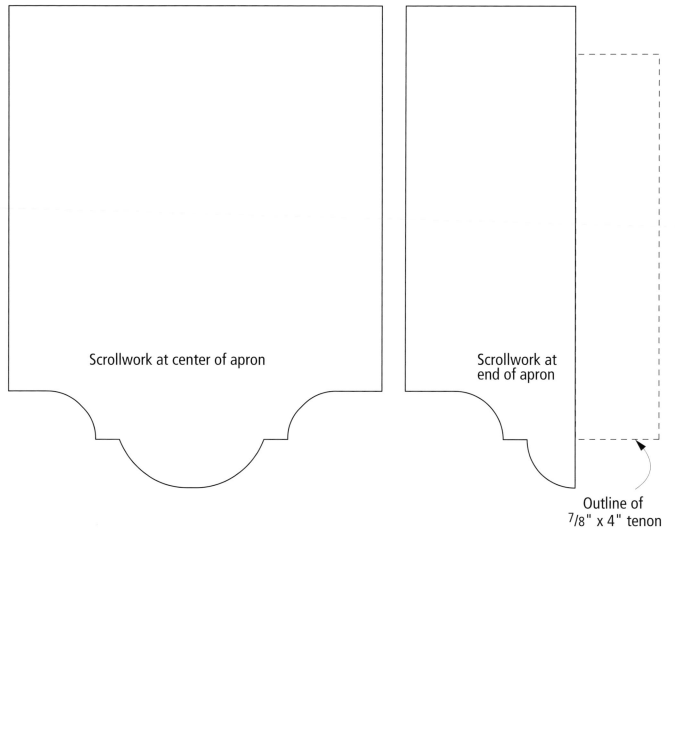

Scrollwork at center of apron

Scrollwork at
end of apron

Outline of
$7/8$" x 4" tenon

A simple-to-build and handsome coffee table that has ample storage for extra magazines and newspapers.

Coffee Table

BY GLEN HUEY

A coffee table is generally the focus of the living room. Sure the couch is the big comfortable sitting place, but the coffee table is the heart of the area. Where else do you prop up your feet? Where are the important magazines stored, to be pulled out when needed? The answer is your coffee table.

This particular table caught my eye because of the overall design. It is not too Country or Arts & Crafts and it will fit into either design quite well. It will also look proper within a contemporary setting.

The construction of this piece is uncomplicated. The top and shelf units are made of four individual pieces of lumber, which will help limit the total amount of wood movement versus using one solid glued panel. The legs are comprised of two pieces each and are attached to the top and shelf with screws. Add in the pieces that put the finishing touches on the sides and ends and this coffee table is ready for a finish.

And the finish could not be any easier to complete if it were painted, which would also be a nice look if you chose not to use the red oak as shown — but first things first.

Making the Top and Shelf

Construction begins with the top and shelf pieces. Each of the two identical assemblies is made of four pieces of stock cut to the required length. Take the time to knock the sharp edges off of the pieces. This can be done with 100-grit sandpaper or if you would like a more pronounced rounding of the corners, use a hand plane to make the cuts on all the edges of each piece.

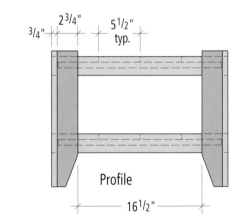

Plan

Elevation

Profile

COFFEE TABLE • INCHES (MILLIMETERS)

QUANTITY	PART	STOCK	THICKNESS	(mm)	WIDTH	(mm)	LENGTH	(mm)	COMMENTS
8	top and shelf boards	oak	$3/4$	19	$5^{1}/2$	140	$40^{1}/2$	1029	
6	battens	oak	$3/4$	19	$2^{1}/2$	64	$21^{3}/4$	552	
8	leg sides	oak	$3/4$	19	$3^{1}/2$	89	$18^{3}/4$	476	
4	end rails	oak	$3/4$	19	$2^{1}/2$	64	$16^{1}/2$	419	
4	side rails	oak	$3/4$	19	$2^{1}/2$	64	35	889	
40	No. 8 × 1¼ wood screws								
16	No. 6 × 1¼ pocket screws								

Knocking the corners off of all the edges will provide a shadow line as the pieces are place side by side. Don't try to find the joint — celebrate it!

Lay four pieces together as shown, aligning the ends, and add clamps to hold them in place. Attach the battens and the top and shelf are complete.

Patience is required when cutting the leg stock. Get close to the line and finish the edge with a plane.

A set-up as shown will allow you to create the beveled feet whether you have a sliding compound miter saw or simply use a miter jig with a hand saw.

Position four of the top/shelf pieces on a flat surface, such as your bench top, with the best face down toward the bench and align the ends. Add clamps to help pull the pieces tightly together as well as to keep things from shifting as you attach the battens.

The battens are pieces of 1×4 that are cut a ¾" less in length than the overall width of the assembled panel. Position three battens so they are about 2" from both ends and one is centered. To attach the battens use one screw (No. 8 × 1¼") directly in the center of each of the 1×6 pieces. Use a tapered drill with a countersink before installing each screw.

Having the screw located in the center of each piece will help to keep the wood stable with seasonal adjustments. The pieces will be allowed to move but the total movement is, in essence, cut in half because the pieces will only move from the center outward. If the pieces were screwed at both edges, the screws would restrict the movement and a crack or split might occur. Repeat these steps for the second assembly and set them aside for the time being.

A Leg Up

Cut the leg material to size and set four of the pieces to the side. The remaining four pieces need to have ¾" taken from one edge. Mark the cut line and use a jigsaw to make the cut as close to the line as possible without crossing. Use a hand plane to straighten and square the cut edge to the line.

I made the angled foot cuts at the miter saw, though they also could be made with the jigsaw and cleaned up with a hand plane. In using the miter saw we can't set any angle past 45° (+ -). We need to make a steeper cut, so we need to base the cut off of the 90° setting. Position the saw to cut a 15°, place a temporary stop in place (bottom right photo facing page) and set the cut to

A strong glue joint and the correct orientation of the legs is important.

Stack the pieces of the table in any way you can to ready them for clamps. I found a neat way to use soda cans.

Mark the top or bottom edge of your shelf. You will need to get those cans out and precisely locate the shelf back in position.

Everything may be in position, but if your table is not square to the flat surface, you will find it extremely difficult to add the finishing pieces to the table.

leave 2⅛" of stock at the bottom edge of the leg. Make the cut on the four full-width pieces, then set the stop so the cut is made at 1⅝" on the pieces that were ripped with the jigsaw.

After the legs are assembled, the idea is to have identical views while looking at either face. You'll notice that the difference in the layout of the two cuts is exactly ¾", which is the amount ripped off with the saw.

Add glue to the ¾" edge of the narrow blanks and clamp the leg assembly together. Make sure as you tighten the clamps that the pieces don't slip. *A little trick I've learned over the years is to add*

a little playground sand to the glue before adding clamps. The sand keeps the pieces from sliding, but indents into the wood, so the joint will still pull tight. Repeat the steps for each pair of leg blanks and set the legs aside to dry.

Time to Assemble

Position the top with the face down and raise the unit off of the bench with a couple of ¾" scraps. Next you need to find a way to position the shelf so your hands can be free to position the legs and add clamps. You can get a friend to help or think outside the box and find a special support system. The shelf should

hit the legs 3½" above the terminating point of the angled cut. I found that two stacked soda cans worked great.

Set the cans at each corner and position the shelf, face down, on top of the can supports. Next, position the legs at each corner and add a clamp to each side. Once the clamps are in place, mark the location of the top edge of the shelf as it hits the legs. This is so you can correctly position the shelf after removing the cans.

Loosen the clamps slightly and slide the shelf upward. Remove the cans and tighten the clamps while repositioning the top at the marked lines. Do the same

Joining the legs to the top and shelf is easy with screws. Please don't use drywall screws, they will break, leaving you with much bigger problems.

The remaining pieces need a tight fit. Butt one end to the legs and mark the cut end to achieve that fit.

A pocket screw connection will hold the rails in place while you add the nails to complete the construction.

With a piece of the scrap wood and a plug cutter, you can make plugs that exactly match your project.

for the opposite end and you are ready to attach the legs to the top and shelf.

Before joining the two, make sure that the entire table, as it is to this point, is square to the bench. Tapping the unit with a rubber mallet or a hammer and a block of wood can make slight adjustments. Again, use the tapered pilot-drill and drive a No. 8 × 1¼" screw through each leg and into both the top and the shelf. Each leg will have a total of eight screws installed.

Before the clamps are removed, cut and fit the remaining pieces that complete the sides and ends. A snug fit is

required. Use a pocket hole jig to drill a hole at the lower edge of each of the rails. Follow the manufacturer's instructions to create the pockets. After the pieces are fit and readied for the screws, attach the pieces to the leg assemblies with the recommended screws.

Drive nails into the side rails, three per side, and through the end rails into each piece that makes up the top and shelf. Two nails per piece — ½" from each edge. Use a drill bit or begin the hole with the nail itself in the drill. The nails will allow for seasonal movement and help keep the wood flat because as the

lumber moves, the nails will bend to and fro. Screws hold things fast and wouldn't allow for this natural happening.

The construction is complete once you have filled the screw holes. The countersink part of the pre-drill leaves room for a ⅜" plug. These plugs can be purchased from the supply store, or cut from scrap material with a matching ⅜" plug cutter. Add glue in the hole and on the plugs and tap them in place with a hammer. Trim any additional material with a small saw or a plane and allow them to dry before finish sanding.

Knock down all sharp edge and corners before starting the staining process.

With these four finishing products you will complete your finish in a short time.

Wipe on, let sit, and wipe away. Repeat that twice, once with the stain and once with the oil and you are ready to add your top coat of shellac.

Preparing for a Finish

Before we look into that easy finish I mentioned, we need to get the table ready for finish. This involves sanding the flat surfaces with 120- and 150-grit sandpaper as well as rounding the ends of all the tops of the legs and the sharp corners. Use a file or rasp to ease the edges of the leg tops and carefully sand the areas smooth.

Once everything is sanded and ready, the staining is next. The staining process begins with a coat of Olympic Special Walnut wood stain. Use a clean rag to apply the stain. Rub on a heavy coating, allowing the stain to sit and penetrate the wood pores for about 15 minutes. Then wipe away any excess stain. This has to sit for at least 24 hours before moving on.

Once the stain is dry we move to the second coat of finish. This is a coat of dark walnut Watco Danish Oil. Apply this in the same way as the stain. Put on a generous coat, allow the oil to seep for 15 minutes and wipe away any excess. Please take caution with these oily rags as they can become fire hazards if not properly treated. *(Hang the rags on the edge of a garbage can and let them dry. Then they can be safely tossed into the garbage can.)*

After the oil has dried for more than 24 hours we can apply the next coating — shellac. Rag a coat of shellac over the entire table. Try to not lap your application. Putting additional shellac over an area that already has a coat may produce lap marks, which will show in the final product. Keep a wet edge as you apply the top coat.

When the shellac is completely dry, a few hours later, lightly sand with a piece of No.0000 steel wool or a piece of 400-grit sandpaper. This will knock down any nibs left from the shellac. The final coat before using your table is a layer of paste wax. Rub it on, allow it to set and dry, then polish the surface to a warm sheen.

If you are like me, you will find a number of uses for a finish this easy. Move the table into your living room and add books — or maybe just your feet.

A graceful slipper-footed design enhanced with additional period details.

PROJECT
16

Slipper-Foot Tea Table

BY GLEN HUEY

In Colonial America, prior to Paul Revere's famous midnight ride, colonists adopted many of the lifestyles of English citizens. One such behavior was afternoon tea. Of course, you couldn't be of a wealthy class and partake in tea without having the necessary serving implements – including a tea table.

Tea tables came into vogue in the early 1700s and were built in many designs such as tray-topped, round-topped and porringer-topped tables with either carved cabriole legs or turned cabriole legs. A tray-topped design with carved legs was by far the most high-end table one could possess.

After the tea party in Boston, the idea of afternoon tea all but disappeared in the American colonies, but the furniture design survives to this day.

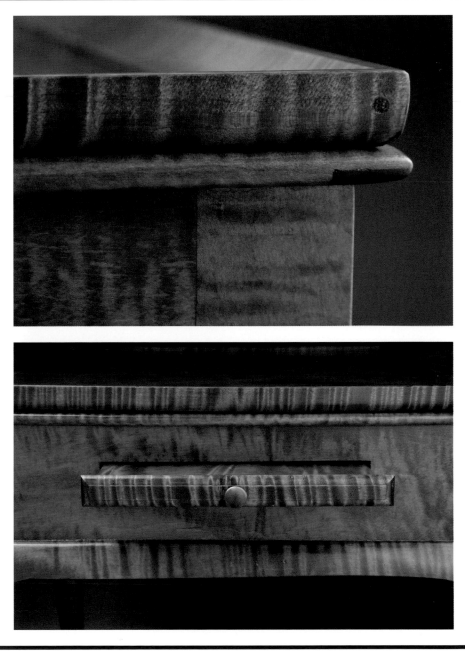

SLIPPER-FOOT TEA TABLE • INCHES (MILLIMETERS)

QUANTITY	PART	STOCK	THICKNESS	(mm)	WIDTH	(mm)	LENGTH	(mm)	COMMENTS
4	legs	tiger maple	3/4	19	2 1/2	64	26 1/2	673	
2	end aprons	tiger maple	3/4	19	5 3/4	330	18 1/2	47	1" tenon both ends
2	side aprons	tiger maple	3/4	19	5 3/4	330	26 7/8	683	1" tenon both ends
1	top	tiger maple	3/4	19	18 3/4	476	26 15/16	684	
8	wooden clips	tiger maple	3/4	19	7/8	22	2 1/2	64	
KNEE RETURN BRACKET									
2	end brackets	tiger maple	3/4	19	2 1/8	54	16 1/2	419	
2	side brackets	tiger maple	3/4	19	2 1/8	54	24 7/8	632	
2	side aprons	tiger maple	3/4	19	5 3/4	33	26 7/8	683	1" tenon both ends
CANDLE SLIDE PARTS									
2	support	tiger maple	3/4	19	1 3/4	44	26 3/4	679	
2	candle slides	tiger maple	9/16	14	8 1/4	210	8	203	
2	candle-slide fronts	tiger maple	3/4	19	7/8	22	8 1/2	216	
TRAY MOULDING PARTS									
2	long beads	tiger maple	3/8	10	7/8	22	29 1/8	740	
2	short beads	tiger maple	3/8	10	7/8	22	20 3/4	527	
1	long cove	tiger maple	3/4	19	2 1/2	64	32	813	
1	short cove	tiger maple	3/4	19	2 1/2	64	23	584	

SUPPLIES

Horton Brasses Inc.
2 - brass desk interior knobs, 1/2" #H-42

Cabrioles Without a Lathe

Queen Anne-style furniture makers focus on curves and achieving a light, graceful look. Cabriole legs are all about curves, and to give a lighter look to the design, slipper feet were the choice for many tea tables.

Forget the lathe. A slipper foot is shaped by hand. To begin work on the legs, copy the pattern from the drawing. Next, transfer the shape to a piece of hardboard or thin plywood. Each leg requires you to trace the pattern onto two adjacent sides of each leg blank. Transferring from paper would be tedious. Mill the leg stock to size and trace the pattern to the stock.

At the band saw you'll need to cut to the lines. Freehand cutting is the only option, but there are a few tips to make the task easier. Starting with one face, begin cutting on a straight section of the leg. Cut halfway, then carefully back the blade out of the cut. Cut the balance of

that profile entering from the opposite direction, but stop prior to reaching the previous cut. That creates a bridge that holds the waste material in place so the leg pattern remains on the second face. If the blade shows signs of being pinched as you back out of that cut, squeeze

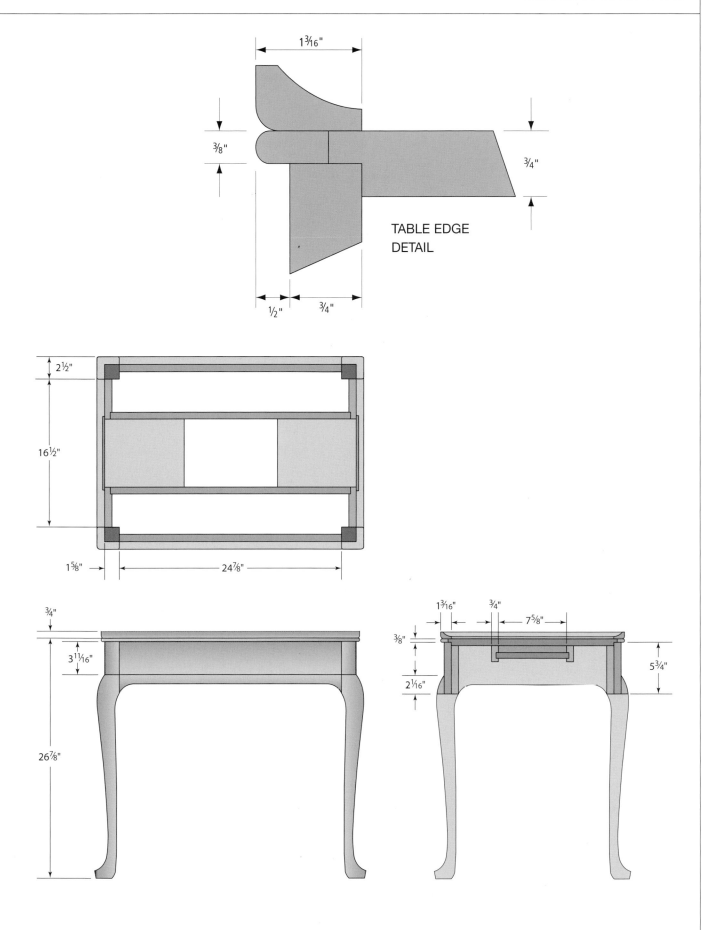

TABLE EDGE
DETAIL

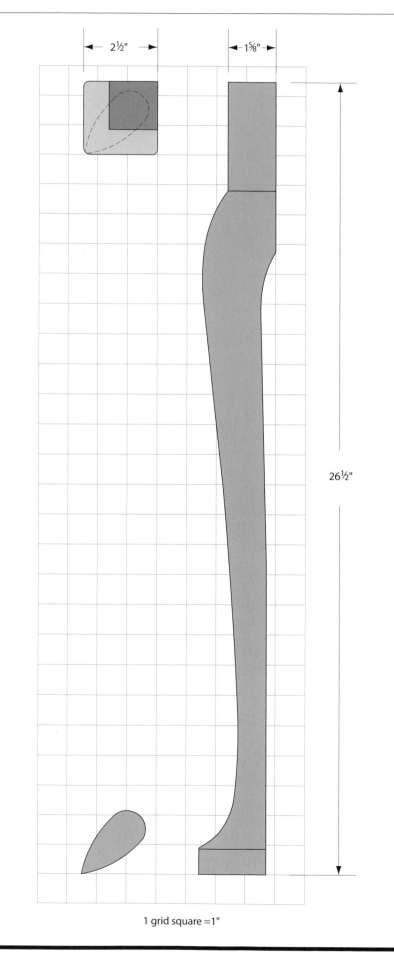

2½"   1⅝"

26½"

1 grid square =1"

the leg at the straight cut to allow ample room for extraction.

Complete the band saw work on the remaining lines for the first face of the leg. On the second face there's no need for a bridge, so saw away until the parts fall free.

Then it's back to the first face to break down the bridge. When the cuts are all completed, you have a square-shaped leg that is in need of shaping.

From Round to Square

Shaping the legs looks more intimidating than it is. Start at the ankle and make that area completely round. To guide me, I use a pattern that's made with a 1" drill bit. Drill a hole in a plywood or hardboard scrap then split the hole down the center. The resulting half-circle is used as a template for rounding the ankle, as shown at left.

Next, shape each leg from round at the ankle to square at the knee. Work one leg at a time shaping each edge from bottom to top. The transition is gradual. Use your hands to feel the shape. A Shinto rasp is my tool of choice for shaping legs. I like the aggressiveness of the tool when roughing out the profile.

Smooth the leg with the second side of the Shinto or other rasp but save the finish sanding until the foot area and above the knee is shaped.

All sized and ready to work. If you begin the leg layout work with the stock milled to size, it doesn't matter whether you match the knees or the heels when tracing your patterns.

Simple is better. A simple shop-made jig is the perfect tool for defining the shape of the ankle of a cabriole leg. This slim tea-table ankle is 1".

Shaping a Slipper

Shaping the leg is a rather quick task. But, the work on the individual feet is where the majority of shaping time is spent. Begin shaping the foot by drawing an "X" on each foot's bottom. Next, make a pattern of the foot from the drawings just as you did for the leg. Center the pattern on the foot bottom with the point matching the front corner of the leg. (See bottom photo.) Trace the pattern onto each foot.

Use a combination square to draw 45°-angle lines across the foot, parallel to the pattern. Extend those lines up the sides of each foot then saw away the waste material. The lines on the sides guide your sawing to keep from wasting needed material. It's easy to cut too close to the ankles.

Shape the foot to the pattern making sure you keep the sides of the foot perpendicular to the foot's bottom. Pay particular attention to the rear of the foot. The heel has to roll down and blend in with the foot's shape.

Finish shaping the foot by drawing a matching profile ⅛" inside the foot bottom. Each side of the foot is then beveled slightly to that profile. The heel continues to roll to the inside line.

Shaping the top of the foot is the next task. Using hand tools for this is real work. The simplest method I've found is to use a spindle sander. Install a 3" drum with a coarse-grit sleeve on the sander, then slowly sculpt the top of the foot. The idea is to level the foot's top and make a gradual transition to the ankle. Check your progress often. As you get near the ankle, begin to slowly rotate the leg and form the beginnings of the roundness that transitions to the full-round ankle.

Once the shaping of the leg and foot is completed, move to the band saw to remove the waste material from the top block. There is a certain order in which to make this cut. The first cut is with the knee positioned facing the saw's table. To make the second cut simply rotate the leg 90° so one face of the knee is facing up. Following this procedure allows the leg to be fully supported as you cut.

A foot pattern to match. Transfer the foot pattern to hardboard to make repeated layout easy. If you start shaping with a matching pattern, the end results should match as well.

Work to your plan. The majority of the waste in shaping the slipper foot is removed with a saw. It's important to plan the layout lines and cut to those lines. Deviations could alter the foot shape.

Shape with power. Hand tools can achieve a flat foot top, but power sanding at a spindle sander is quick, accurate and repeatable. Goodbye hard-to-work end grain.

Shape the knee, as well as the area above the knee, then sand the entire leg with 150-grit sanding discs. At this time stand the legs side by side and look for any variations in shape. This is the time to fine-tune the legs so they match. But, don't get carried away with this task. Remember — the legs stand 17" apart at minimum. Slight variations will be imperceptible in the finished table.

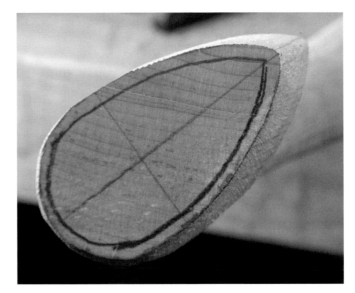

Tapered sides. The edges of the feet taper ⅛" while the heel continues to roll to the floor. Draw the inner profile freehand.

Profile and Fit the Aprons

Aprons join the legs with mortise-and-tenon joints. Positioning the legs to cut a mortise in the correct location is a bit tricky. Place a support under the top block of the leg to keep the knee off the surface. As you can see in the lower left photo facing page, I cut the ¼" × 4¾" × 1" mortises with the back of the leg block against the fence of a dedicated mortise machine.

Aprons are cut to size according to the cut list and tenons are formed on both ends of each apron to fit the mortises. Before assembly takes place, slot openings for the candle slides have to be cut into the end aprons. Locate the slot, then use a plunge router with a ⅝" straight bit to create the opening. A straight fence attached to the router makes this quick work. Chisel the corners square, then begin work on the inside face of the apron.

On the inside of each end apron there are two ¾" × 21⅛" × ¼"-deep dados that capture the candle-slide supports. The supports are held down from the top edge of the aprons ⅜" to accommodate the recessed top and are press-fit into the candle-slide openings. A straight fence and ¾" pattern bit work great to make the dadoes. Again, square the corners with your chisel.

Sand the aprons through 150 grit, then fit one apron to a mating leg. Hold the apron flush with the top edge of the leg, then draw a pattern on the lower apron edge so the rounded profile of the knee bracket area continues onto the apron as in the top left photo following

page. (A 5" sanding disc makes a perfect pattern. See top left photo page 116.)

Blend the radius of the pattern up 1¹⁄₁₆" on the apron. Repeat the pattern on both ends of each apron then make the cuts at the band saw. Smooth the edges with light sanding at a spindle sander.

Now it's time to assemble the base of the table. It's best to assemble the base in two steps. First, glue the side aprons to the legs. After the glue is set, assemble the end aprons to the legs. Add glue to both the mortises and tenons, then slip the joints together, making sure to keep the top edges flush. Allow the glue to dry, then sand the entire workpiece to 180 grit. You'll have to touch up the sanding later

A right way to cut. There is a specific cut order to remove the waste from the two faces of the leg block. Choose wisely and the work is quick.

A top with movement. Wooden clips hold the floating top to the table base and allow for seasonal movement. This relieves any cross-grain construction concerns.

Leg support. To cut the mortises into the legs, you need to add support under the top block so the knee is off the table. Add a small wedge below the knee to stabilize the piece.

Plough out the groove. A plunge router and straight bit make quick work of cutting the candle-slide opening. Of course, an attached fence is a must-have.

Right with the pattern. Routing the dado for the candle-slide supports is a snap. Use a pattern bit with a straight fence that you set right on the layout line.

during the project, but this is the best time to do the majority of the work.

Next, you'll need to create small slots for the wooden clips used to secure the top. A couple options for cutting the slots are a router or router table with a ¼" slot-cutting router bit (the tea table is light and compact enough to hoist onto your router table), or use a biscuit joiner and complete the slot in two overlapping cuts.

Position the slots from ½" to ¾" down from the top edge of the aprons. With the slots located in this position, the tongue of each wooden clip is set toward the middle. (See top-right photo.) If you slide any further down the apron, you'll likely cut into the candle-slide opening in the end aprons.

At-hand solution. It takes time to set up a compass or trammel to lay out the curve necessary for the transition from knee to apron. Shop items such as this sanding disc do the job — and are usually right at hand.

Dressing up the apron. The knee-return brackets add visual interest to the overall design. Once the proper thickness is achieved, transfer the profile and begin to shape the returns.

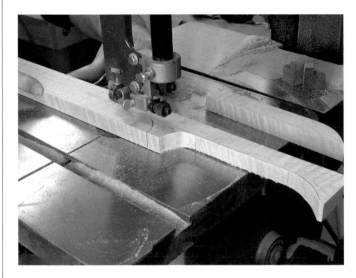

Keeping balance. To keep the stock level throughout the cut, leave tabs on the knee-return brackets. Create a tab as you reach the end of the band saw table. The tabs are later removed with the stock positioned face up.

Waste not, want not. Bevel the table saw blade to remove as much waste as possible from the knee returns without cutting into the profile portion.

Shaped Knee-return Brackets

Another feature that adds interest to the design of this tea table is the shaped knee-return brackets. On most carved cabriole-legged furniture, the knee returns extend to or slightly over the aprons or other rails. However, on some tea tables the brackets extend from leg to leg, adding shape and shadow lines.

Begin with blanks that fit snug between the knees of the legs. Draw pencil lines along the leg curvature to transfer the shape to the returns. Also,

transfer the design from the bottom edge of the aprons onto the returns.

Angle the table saw blade then position the fence to remove as much waste as possible.

The flat surface on the face of the returns is enough to hold the pieces flat at the band saw to cut the apron-matching design. But, if you make a continuous cut, the flat area is removed and the piece becomes unsteady. It's best to make the cut in sections to leave short portions of flat area intact. This allows you

to maintain control throughout the cut.

Use a spindle sander or drum sander at the drill press to smooth to the lines. Again, the flat areas help maintain control. Once the edges are smooth flip the piece and, using a pencil or marking knife, connect the straight portions to provide a line to remove the balance of the waste material. Return to the band saw to remove the final waste material then sand those areas; the return brackets are now ready for final shaping to the leg profile.

Final shaping is done with a small hand plane. Work the profile to match the leg area, then finish smoothing with rasps and by sanding. Finish sand the returns to 180 grit.

The brackets are glued to the lower edge of the aprons — no fasteners are needed. To keep the glue from squeezing out above the bracket where it would be difficult to remove, make a shallow table saw cut just below the top edge of the bracket on the back face. That cut acts as a reservoir for excess glue. Add a thin bead of glue to the bracket below the cut then position the brackets to the apron. Add a few spring clamps until the glue is set.

Adding the Candle Slides

While the glue sets, cut and fit the candle-slide supports. Fit the pieces to the base then mark the exact location of the slide opening. Cut a $5/8" \times 1/4" \times 10"$ groove at each opening.

A straight bit and a router table are your best bet for this task. Align the layout marks with the router bit, set the fence and create the groove. Setting a stop for the length of cut allows easy removal of the support after the groove is cut. The supports are held in place with a small amount of glue where the bottom of the slide fits the dado in the end aprons.

Next, make the candle slides so they fit the opening. Mill the material, making sure to orient the grain across the opening. Then create the front piece for each slide with all edges profiled with a $1/4"$ roundover router bit.

Mill this profile on wide stock, then slice the fronts at the table saw. This eliminates working with small pieces. Run the four edges to create a $1/16"$ shadow line on the profile (as you would when profiling drawer fronts), then rip the fronts off. A zero-clearance insert keeps the moulded piece from dropping into the saw.

Finish sand the candle-slide parts to 180 grit and prepare to attach the fronts to the slides. Align the fronts with a $1/4"$ above the slide and equal distance to each side. Again, a small amount of glue does the job. Add a thin bead of glue, position the fronts to the slides then use tape to hold the connection until the glue has dried. Use small brass screws as stops to keep the slides from being pulled from the base. Those stops are applied after finishing is complete.

Turn for alignment. With the opening for the candle slides transferred to the support, locating the cutting position of the matching router bit is all that's needed to create the groove. Turn the carbide cutter perpendicular to the fence to set up the cut.

Shave to shape. The best way to shape the knee-return brackets is with a small hand plane. Watch the grain direction and the results should be near finish-ready.

Saving the digits. Profile the edges of the candle-slide fronts on a larger piece of stock, then rip the individual pieces to size. At no time do my fingers get close to the blade.

No brads allowed. To keep from marring the fronts of the slides, use tape and a small bead of glue. The tape acts as a clamp until the glue sets.

Thicker is better. With the bead-frame stock at 3/8", it has plenty of rigidity to shape at a router table. There's no need to rip profiled moulding from wider boards.

Easy does it. Cut the half-lap joinery on the bead frame using the table saw and a miter gauge. Pushing the stock back and forth across the blade creates a smooth level surface.

Beginning the Tray Mouldings

In order to properly size the top, you'll need to build the first layer of tray moulding, which is the beaded frame. The overhang of the completed frame is ½" all around. Prepare the four pieces of stock then rout the edge profile with a ⅜" bead-forming router bit.

The beaded frame is joined at the corners with half-lapped joinery. Make the necessary cuts at the table saw and keep in mind the orientation of the pro-filed edge. It's easy to remove the incorrect portion of the joint.

I found it best to create the bead, then round the corners at the joints after assembly, versus joining the frame and moulding it afterward. This allows you more control working with the thin stock.

Assemble the frame with glue. Small F-style clamps apply pressure to hold the corners tight. You need to check the assembly for square as you walk through the glue-up. Once the glue is dry, make sure the overhang is correct, then use a thin bead of glue and 23-gauge pins to attach the frame to the table base.

Free-floating Table Top

Because this table has mouldings in a cross-grain relationship to the top, I elected to attach the tray mouldings to the top edge of the base and allow the top to float. With the bead frame in place, fit and install the top.

Mill the top to size and thickness, then fit the top inside the bead frame. Because wood moves across the grain, you'll need to take into consideration what season of the year you're building the piece. Allow ⅛" if you're in low-humidity times to almost no gap if you're building with humidity on the high side. As for the length of the top, wood doesn't move much with the grain, so I fit that area snugly.

The top is rabbeted along all sides to fit flush with the bead frame. I use a two-step rabbeting method at the table saw, but there are many ways to cut rabbets. Select the method that works best for you.

Whatever method you choose, there is one additional step necessary before the top is attached to the base. You need to remove material at the corners of the top that correspond with the leg posts. Use a straightedge and flush-cut router bit to remove the waste.

With the milling of the top complete, sand the piece to 180 grit, add a drop of glue to the exact center of the end aprons, then position the top to the base. The glue adds extra hold to the top, forcing any movement outward to the sides and divides overall wood movement in half. Each half acts independently.

Add the wooden clips to the base and installation of the top is complete. The clips are made at the table saw, counterbored for screws, then installed with No. 8 × 1¼" wood screws. The clips allow the top to move, but keep it tight to the base.

Framing the tabletop. The bead frame is the first layer of moulding. It's joined at the corners with half-lap joinery and captures the recessed top.

Trim to fit. Any straightedge and a pattern router bit, in this case a ⅝"-diameter bit, produces a clean cut at the top corners to allow for the recessed top to fit in position.

Make cove moulding. This is the setup used to create cove mouldings. With the fence above the blade, you're responsible for holding the stock tight to the fence. A featherboard helps with that task.

Creating the Tray's Cove Moulding

The tray's cove mouldings begin as two pieces of flat stock milled to ¾" thick. Next you'll need to produce a cove cut centered on the stock that results in the correct end measurements for the cove once the stock is ripped into two matching pieces.

At the table saw, with the blade height adjusted to ½", position an auxiliary fence for the cut. Twisting the fence manipulates the cut, so it's necessary to find the exact setup position. I take two pieces of stock and draw my cove profile on opposing ends. Position the drawn profile toward the blade and maneuver the auxiliary fence until the infeed and outfeed of the blade align with the layout marks. Once found, lock the position of the fence.

The lower photo at right shows the setup at the table saw. I like my auxiliary fence on the outfeed side of the blade, and I've secured the stock in position with a magnetic fence to keep the moulding from moving.

Lower the blade, then make successive cuts — each time raising the blade incrementally to produce a cove profile matching the desired design. Take the last pass very slowly in order to remove as many mill marks as possible, which will reduce the amount of sanding.

Finish sand the tray cove mouldings to 180 grit, then use a table saw to split the stock in half, forming two identical strips per piece. Each piece is routed with a ⅜" roundover bit on the bottom edge to reflect the edge treatment of the profile of the bead frame below. Finish sand any rough areas before fitting the moulding to the table.

Those mouldings are attached to the table with brads located so the top is free to move. The brads extend through the cove moulding and the bead frame into the aprons. Fit each piece of moulding in place, then temporarily attach it to the table with one 23-gauge pin at each end. When the task is complete, the mouldings and pins are easily removed.

Clean up any pencil lines. Add a thin bead of glue to the cove, position the mouldings to the table and attach them with brads — the square holes left from the brad gun mimic antique, square-head nails.

To secure the coved corners, peg each miter with a short length of ⅛" dowel.

Race to the Finish

For the finish I elected to stain the piece with water-base aniline dye stain (a 50-50 mixture of golden amber maple and brown walnut), add a single coat of boiled linseed oil to highlight the stripes, then topcoat with a few layers of shellac.

Normally I would rub out the shellac to achieve a dull sheen. To save time and effort, I elected to spray a single coat of dull-rubbed-effect lacquer to achieve that sheen. If you don't spray your finish, try wiping on a coat of satin polyurethane or wiping varnish.

Add the brass knobs and brass screw stops to the candle slides and you're ready to sit down for an enjoyable afternoon of tea — or coffee — if you haven't been able to get over that entire taxation-without-representation mess.

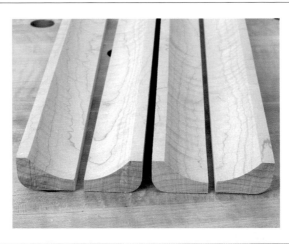

Ready to miter. The tray cove moulding is created as a single cove moulding then split exactly down the center to provide twice the length.

Prep work saves patience. Half the battle in fitting the tray cove is determining where the cut lines are located. Lay out 45° lines that bisect the corners, then cut to those lines.

Two Tub Tables

BY STEVE SHANESY

I suspect most woodworkers would rather spend an entire day hand sanding than get involved with a project that requires cutting compound miters. And I think they have good reason. Not only are compound miters hard to get right (although I hope to change that for you with this article) but just about every book or magazine article has a different way of doing them. To complicate matters further, some sources even give you conflicting settings for the blade tilt and miter gauge.

Over the course of the last three years I have evolved a system that has two basic rules to follow to make cutting these pesky joints nearly bulletproof. First, make a mock-up — a miniature one — once you have made your blade and miter gauge settings. Chances are it won't be perfect the first time so you tweak your adjustments until the mock-up is right. Second, don't change the settings in order to cut the other side of the part once the first side is cut. Turn

the piece over and move it to the other side of the blade instead. Why? Because it's next to impossible to find the perfect setting on the opposite side of the table saw's miter gauge. The same is true for the track arm of a radial arm saw or the miter setting of a compound miter saw.

Armed with these rules, your compound miters have a 90 percent chance of success. The last 10 percent comes from making sure your stock is flat, you hold it firmly when cutting and, of course, you find the "right" angle settings. I say "right" for two reasons. One, you may go to a source that isn't correct. Second, the miter degree markings on most woodworking tools are inaccurate or too crude for the "on the money" setting a tight-fitting compound joint requires.

A Tale of Two Tubs

In this article I'll show you how to make these two occasional tables. One uses black walnut and has sides that square up at the top in what I call a "crown." The second, which is easier to build, is made from birch plywood and runs the angle all the way until it meets the lid, which on both tables is removable for storing things. Further, the second table is butt-jointed at the sides, not mitered like the walnut version. To keep everything straight, I'll describe the steps in constructing the walnut tub table first.

Start by gluing up five panels, four of which are slightly more than 22" wide and 17" long. Make the panel for the top oversized so you can cut it to size after the base is assembled. As you prepare your stock and glue up the panels, make

sure your panels stay flat, or the angle you cut later for the miter joint will not be true. You'll note that the grain on the walnut table runs up and down and is continuous from the angled sides to the crown at top. The length of the side panels you glue up will accommodate the crown.

Once glued, sand your panels just shy of your final grit. Next, take the panels to the table saw and cut them square but still oversized. Now crosscut the lower portion of each side from the "crown" piece that will be glued back later. Make this cut at 14¼". This length will allow you to make angle cuts cross grain at the bottom edge and the miter edge where the top piece joins the side and not lose any height.

Next cut the crown pieces to length (and I do mean length because it is the dimension that goes with the grain) to 2¼". Now set the table saw's blade to 15° and cut this angle on the lower edge of the sides' bottom on all four pieces. You should remove only enough material to make the angle and no more. Now change the blade angle to 7½"° and cut the complementary angles for the joint where the side and crown join.

Cut the Compound Miters

Set the crown pieces aside for now. Prepare a piece of stock that's at least 42" long to screw on to your table saw's slot miter gauge. Put at least 30" to the right side. Run your table saw blade over to 43¼°. Set your miter gauge to 75½° on the left scale of the miter gauge. Now you are ready to make a small model to check your angle settings. I suggest

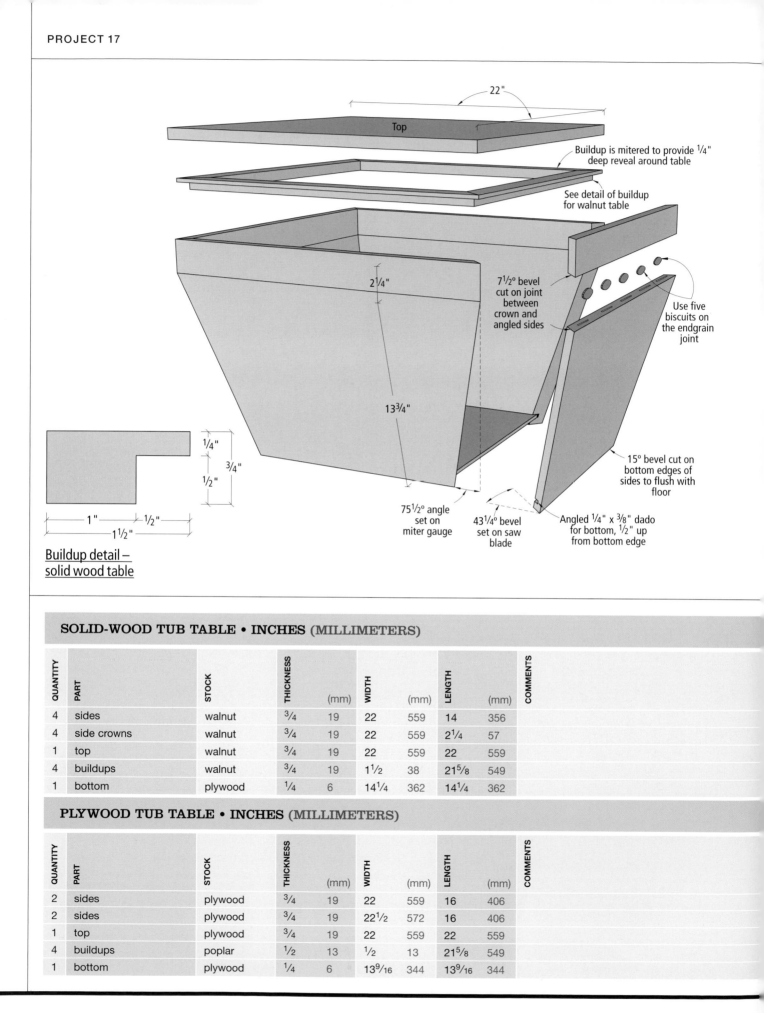

22"

Top

Buildup is mitered to provide ¼"
deep reveal around table

See detail of buildup
for walnut table

2¼"

7½° bevel
cut on joint
between
crown and
angled sides

Use five
biscuits on
the endgrain
joint

13¾"

¼"

¾"

½"

15° bevel cut on
bottom edges of
sides to flush with
floor

1"   ½"

1½"

75½° angle
set on
miter gauge

43¼° bevel
set on saw
blade

Angled ¼" x ⅜" dado
for bottom, ½" up
from bottom edge

Buildup detail –
solid wood table

SOLID-WOOD TUB TABLE • INCHES (MILLIMETERS)

QUANTITY	PART	STOCK	THICKNESS	(mm)	WIDTH	(mm)	LENGTH	(mm)	COMMENTS
4	sides	walnut	¾	19	22	559	14	356	
4	side crowns	walnut	¾	19	22	559	2¼	57	
1	top	walnut	¾	19	22	559	22	559	
4	buildups	walnut	¾	19	1½	38	21⅝	549	
1	bottom	plywood	¼	6	14¼	362	14¼	362	

PLYWOOD TUB TABLE • INCHES (MILLIMETERS)

QUANTITY	PART	STOCK	THICKNESS	(mm)	WIDTH	(mm)	LENGTH	(mm)	COMMENTS
2	sides	plywood	¾	19	22	559	16	406	
2	sides	plywood	¾	19	22½	572	16	406	
1	top	plywood	¾	19	22	559	22	559	
4	buildups	poplar	½	13	½	13	21⅝	549	
1	bottom	plywood	¼	6	13⁹⁄₁₆	344	13⁹⁄₁₆	344	

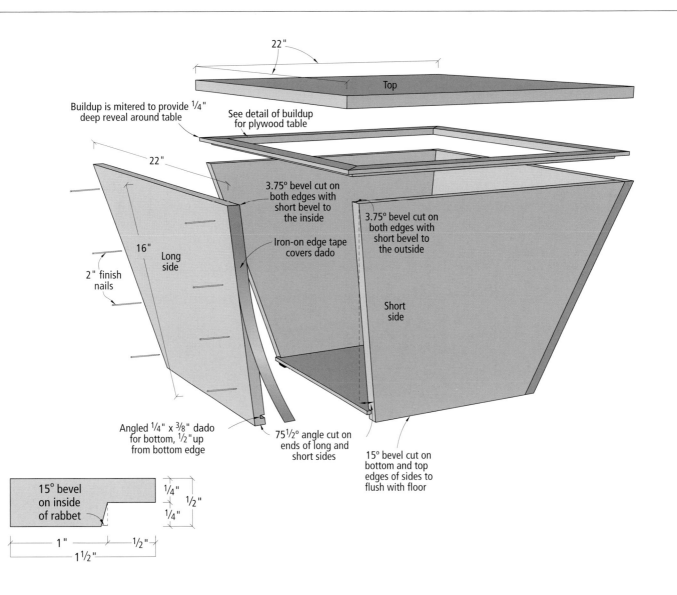

22"

Top

Buildup is mitered to provide ¼"
deep reveal around table

See detail of buildup
for plywood table

22"

3.75° bevel cut on
both edges with
short bevel to
the inside

3.75° bevel cut on
both edges with
short bevel to
the outside

16"

Long
side

Iron-on edge tape
covers dado

2" finish
nails

Short
side

Angled ¼" x ⅜" dado
for bottom, ½" up
from bottom edge

75½° angle cut on
ends of long and
short sides

15° bevel cut on
bottom and top
edges of sides to
flush with floor

15° bevel
on inside
of rabbet

¼"
½"
¼"

1"
½"
1½"

using a piece of scrap plywood about 6"
wide and about 30" long.

Make your first cut by trimming one
end of the sample board. Now clamp a
stop block about 6" to the right of the
saw kerf in the fence. Next take the sample board and turn it over, then place the
just-trimmed end against the stop block
and make a second cut. Again, turn the
sample board over, place it against the
stop block and make another cut. Repeat
two more times and your four sample
sides will be cut.

Place all four sides together and
check for gaps in the mitered corners. If
there's a gap in the inside of the miter,
slightly reduce the angle of blade tilt. If
open on the outside, increase the blade
tilt angle. For a slight opening, ¼° to

½° should be all the correction needed.
Continue adjusting and checking until
there are no openings in the joints or
rocking motion when holding them in
your hands and applying pressure.

Cut Your Good Panels

Because you have already cut the bevels
on the top and bottom edges of the
sloping side panels, you have desig-
nated which sides face out. As a result,
while cutting the compound miters,
you'll need to keep track of which side
faces where.

After the first cut, clamp a stop block
to the right end of the miter gauge fence
that will give you the 22" finished width
at the top after making the second miter
cut. I made a 15° bevel cut on the stop

block I used, which prevented it from
slipping during the cut. Now study the
photos on the previous page for the correct cutting and turning sequence for
the sides.

Before moving any saw settings, use
masking tape to dry assemble the four
sides to make sure everything checks
out. Before gluing the sloping sides
together, cut biscuit slots in the joint
where the sloping side and its mating
crown piece go together. I used five
biscuits evenly spaced on each joint.
Remember, this is virtually an end-grain
butt joint so you must rely on the biscuits to make a sound joint. Be sure and
angle the fence of your biscuit joiner to
7½° for proper alignment. Cut the dado
for the bottom using your table saw.

Make the first cut with the outside face down, the bottom edge against the fence and the panel to the left of the blade.

To make the second cut, turn the panel so the outside face is up and the top edge is against the miter gauge fence. Cut the other three panels the same way.

Glue the Compound Miters

The best way to glue up this awkward assembly is to tape the joints with masking tape. First lay out the parts face up and apply two layers of tape strips along the length of the joint. Make sure the sharp edges are touching and that the top and bottom edges are aligned. With the last joint still open, carefully turn the entire taped-up assembly over and spread wood glue in the joints. Now tip the pieces up and slide the bottom in place before taping the last joint. When it's taped up, check for any open joints that could be caused by being out of square or by not taping the joint edges close enough.

While this dries, begin cutting the crown pieces to finished size. Each piece needs a 45° miter joint. Be sure to match the grain with the sloping portion of the side. To glue the crown to the base, cut a piece of plywood that's 22" square, the same size as the top area. This piece gives you the clamping surface you need to draw the crown to the sloping sides. Stack a few pieces of wood under the base so you can get clamp ends under it.

Complete the Top

In addition to cutting the top to finished size, you must also add four strips to the underside to create the small "reveal" or "quirk" detail between the top and base. These strips also serve to keep the top in position because they nest inside the sides.

Study the drawings of these strips on the previous page. Because the reveal

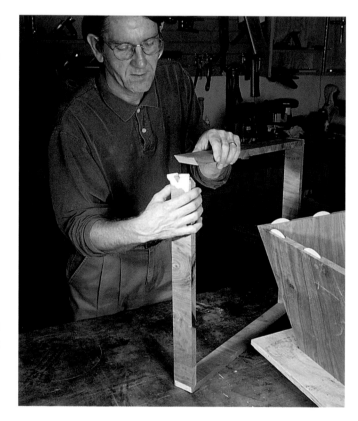

Carefully cut and fit each of the four pieces for the "crown." Dry-assemble them in place before gluing, but wait until the glue on the sloping sides has completely cured.

is ¼" square, cut your wood strips so you create a rabbet that leaves ¼" thickness and sets back ½". Make two strips this way. Make the other two strips you need with a ⅝" setback and use these on the sides of the top that run with the grain direction. This additional space will allow the top to expand in humid conditions without pushing out the sides and ruining the miter joints. The top remains loose for easy removal.

To prepare the pieces for finishing, sand up to 150 grit. Be careful sanding at the transition point of the sloping side to

the crown. You want to maintain a crisp joint line. The walnut had both great figure and color. So I only applied two coats of clear finish and let the beauty of the wood shine through.

For me, the two rules of making sound compound miter joints worked perfectly again. Yes, I had to fine tune my setup after I made my mock-up, but I didn't change any settings once I had it right. The results were dead on and my frustration from not "getting it right" was virtually non-existent. Follow these simple rules and you'll get the same results.

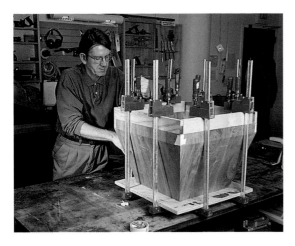

Use a small amount of polyurethane glue on the joints and tape the corners as shown in the photo before applying glue. After all the surfaces are glued, set the crown in place and clamp it down. Check to make sure the corner joints are nicely closed. If they need help, clamp across them as needed.

Miter the ends of the strips and screw them to the top as shown. Use elongated slots for the screw clearance holes where top expansion is expected.

After attaching the lid strips to the lid, trim any overhang on the miters with a chisel.

Building the Plywood Tub

The plywood tub table is constructed much like the solid walnut version with a few exceptions. If you plan to build this simpler version, familiarize yourself with construction of the walnut version as well.

The main differences are the absence of the crown and the joinery for the sloping sides. Instead of a compound miter, the sides are butt-jointed together. The two sides that overlay the adjoining sides are $1\frac{1}{2}$" wider so the overall width of all the sides remains equal when assembled.

To cut the angles on the sides, prepare the miter gauge fence as described earlier. Only this time, set the gauge degree setting to $75\frac{1}{2}°$, and tilt the blade to $3\frac{3}{4}°$. Make the cuts as described previously.

There's one more modification to this unit. In making the pieces that create the reveal and are attached to the underside of the top, Cut the rabbet using a 15° angle as shown in the diagram.

To color the birch plywood, I used a brown walnut stain before clear coating. Make sure you give the stain at least eight hours to dry.

Cutting the dado for the bottom applies to both tables. Change the angle setting of the saw to 15° in order to cut a dado to hold the $\frac{1}{4}$"-thick bottom in place. Set the fence so that the bottom will start $\frac{1}{2}$" up from the bottom. The blade height should be $\frac{3}{8}$". Make two passes using a regular thickness blade to allow the bottom to slip into place. While you have the blade set, cut your bottom with a 15° bevel on all four edges.

Before gluing and nailing the sides together, use iron-on veneer tape on the edges of the sides that will be exposed. Make sure your parts are aligned exactly flush before hammering the nails home. After assembly, use more veneer tape on the top edges of the sides and on the edges of the top.

An anachronism in its time, this table now fits perfectly in our homes.

PROJECT
18

Prairie-style Coffee Table

BY DAVID THIEL

Frank Lloyd Wright would probably be dismayed to see a coffee table built in his Prairie furniture style. In fact, he and his fellow early 20th-century designers all would have been disturbed by the concept of a coffee table. Eating or drinking in the living room? Unheard of! That type of informality in furniture is a product of the latter half of the 20th century.

But, there is a fine old Russian proverb that says necessity is the mother of invention. And so I offer you the Prairie-style coffee table. At least it'll keep my kids from leaving plates, glasses and remote controls on the floor.

This project is an adaptation of a number of Wright's pieces, utilizing applied moulding to a generally simple design. The shelf is placed high on the legs and extends beyond the base to match the wide and low look of Wright's Prairie-style buildings and furniture.

The construction is simple, with the most complicated joint being a mortise-and-tenon attachment on the legs, which I've simplified even further for you.

Ground-up Construction

I started building the table at the base with the four legs. For a larger table I would have used a mitered or lock-

PHOTO BY AL PARRISH; SPECIAL THANKS TO UNIVERSITY OF CINCINNATI ALUMNI ASSOCIATION

The lower stretchers tie into mortises cut in each of the four legs. I made the mortises ½" wide so I wouldn't have to cut tenon cheeks on the stretchers. Unfortunately I only had a ⅜"-wide mortising chisel, so I overlapped the mortise cuts to achieve a ½"-wide mortise.

mitered leg to make sure the dramatic grain commonly found in quartersawn white oak was visible on all four sides of the legs. But for a table this small, the work really didn't justify the benefit, so I started with 2" × 2" white oak turning blanks, choosing the straightest grain possible.

With the legs cut to length, the first step is to mark the mortise locations and then make the mortise holes. Traditionally it makes sense to make the

mortises and then fit the tenon to the mortise. Because I'm short-circuiting the tenon process by using part of the stretcher as the tenon, I needed to make the mortise match the tenon this time.

The next step is assembling the stretchers. This is where the fun starts. The two stretchers are of an I-beam design, with a top and bottom that are horizontal, and a middle piece that is oriented vertically. The top and bottom stretcher pieces are 9½" long, which is

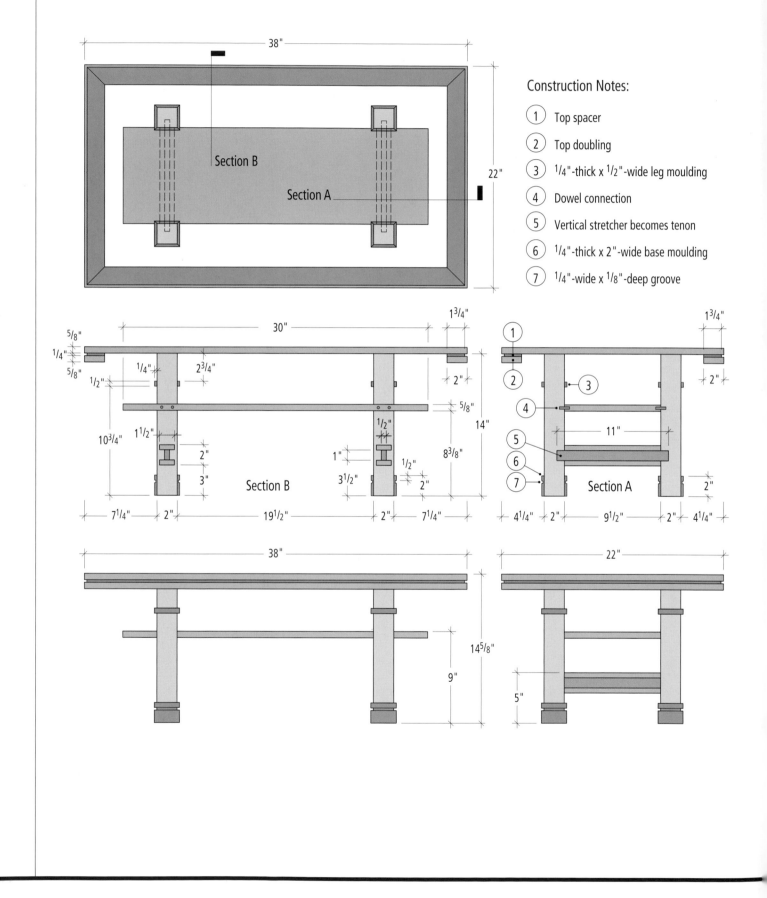

Construction Notes:

1. Top spacer
2. Top doubling
3. 1/4"-thick x 1/2"-wide leg moulding
4. Dowel connection
5. Vertical stretcher becomes tenon
6. 1/4"-thick x 2"-wide base moulding
7. 1/4"-wide x 1/8"-deep groove

Section B

Section A

PRAIRIE-STYLE COFFEE TABLE • INCHES (MILLIMETERS)

QUANTITY	PART	STOCK	THICKNESS	(mm)	WIDTH	(mm)	LENGTH	(mm)	COMMENTS
1	top	white oak	5/8	16	22	559	38	965	
2	top spacers	white oak	1/4	6	1 3/4	45	21 1/2	546	MBE
2	top spacers	white oak	1/4	6	1 3/4	45	37 1/2	953	MBE
2	top buildup	white oak	5/8	16	2	51	38	965	MBE
2	top buildup	white oak	5/8	16	2	51	22	559	MBE
1	shelf	white oak	5/8	16	9 1/2	241	30	762	
4	legs	white oak	2	51	2	51	14	356	
4	stretchers	white oak	1/2	13	1 1/2	38	9 1/2	241	
4	stretchers	white oak	1/2	13	1	25	11	279	3/4 TBE
32	leg mouldings	white oak	1/4	6	1/2	13	2 1/2	64	MBE
32	leg mouldings	white oak	1/4	6	2	51	2 1/2	64	MBE

*MBE=miters both ends; TBE=tenons both ends

the actual size of the space between the legs. The middle stretcher is 11" long. When the three pieces are assembled, the middle piece extends ¾" on either side, creating the tenons.

It's important that the stretchers fit tightly against the legs, so I assembled the stretchers while they were in place in the legs. Before you do that, though, sand all the pieces, because it's next to impossible to sand inside the channel once the stretcher is assembled. By squaring the stretchers to the legs while assembling, everything fits tightly without a lot of extra fitting.

The other part of the support structure on the table is the shelf. Traditionally this would be positioned much lower, but the Wright design dictates a higher shelf. Useless you say? Posh! It's the perfect height for hiding the remotes and the TV Guide. Maybe they won't all end up stuck in the couch cushions if they have a proper home.

The shelf is attached to the legs using dowels. I used only one dowel per leg on this version. Because it's such a small table and the top is attached to the legs as well, one dowel is adequate for a small-scale table.

However, if you look at the drawing, we've shown two dowels at each location. One thing that's nice about this design is if you cared to scale this up to dining

With the mortises cut, it was time to assemble the three-piece stretchers. To ensure a square fit, I first squared the center stretcher piece while it was fit into the mortise. Remember, no glue at this point!

With the center stretcher square, it's simple to pin the upper and lower stretchers in place, maintaining the square relationship and forming the tenons on the stretchers simultaneously.

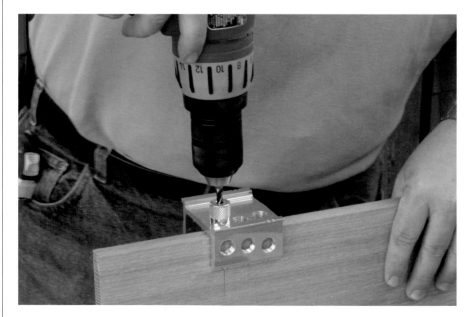

The shelf is dowelled into the legs to make assembly simple. A dowelling jig makes this even easier. Locate the dowel holes on the legs 4¾" down from the top of the legs and centered. The locations on the shelves are 4¼" in from the ends and centered on the thickness of the shelf.

table size, all the proportions would still work and it would be an attractive larger table. In that case, two dowels per leg would be recommended.

At this point, leave the stretchers and shelf separate from the legs. We still have some detailing to do on the legs before assembling the base.

Mitering Small Mouldings

There are two moulding details on the leg — a lower "foot" and a small upper strip. The upper piece is ¼" × ½" material mitered around the perimeter of the leg. The lower moulding is ¼" × 2" material that has a ⅛" × ¼"-wide groove cut into the length, ½" down from the top. I cut the groove in two passes on the table saw on a long strip before mitering the pieces to length.

The first time I ever saw one of Wright's Prairie designs, I looked at the mouldings and thought, "Wow, that's simple! All you do is miter the pieces and nail them on!" Well, that is the process, but it's not as simple as it seems. While fitting a single miter isn't too awkward, getting four miters to align perfectly around a leg is darn tricky. In fact, this step turned out to be the most difficult part of the project.

I started out assuming that I could simply use my miter saw and a stop block to cut the pieces. But working with such small pieces is actually a little scary. Your fingers are too close to the blade. A table saw could work as well, if you have a sled that works with the blade either tilted or beveled to 45°. But, again, the small pieces and the concern of tear-out make it a task not for the faint of heart.

Instead, I relied on a slower method, but one that proved more reliable. After rough-cutting the moulding pieces to length (using a clamping jig on the miter saw). I hand-fitted each piece using a small disk sander with the table set to a 45° angle.

Tiny Nails

After fitting the pieces to the legs, it's a good time to sand all the pieces before attaching the mouldings. It's just easier to get in the corners this way. Then it is as simple as adding a little glue and nailing them in place. Actually, I pinned the pieces in place using a 23-gauge pneumatic pinner. I love this tool. The pins are so small that the hole looks like a freckle on the wood. The holes are easily filled, or you can be a little lazy and let the stain cover up the hole.

One tip when using a pinner (or nailer) like this: Rather than drive all the pins straight into the piece, angle the pins toward one another. While it's unlikely the pins will fail, this will add extra strength to help keep the moulding from ever pulling loose.

Start with the lower moulding, setting the leg upright on your work surface as you attach the pieces. This helps to make sure you have a flat bottom to the leg and helps align the pieces at the miters.

The next step is the upper mouldings. You'll need to add some location lines to the legs to orient these mouldings. Measure down 2¾" from the top of the leg to the top of the mouldings.

Base Assembly

At this point you're ready to assemble the base. Work with two of the legs flat on your work platform, with the mortises facing up. Add glue to the one set of dowels and tenons and attach the shelf and two stretchers to the legs. Then add glue to the remaining dowels and mortises, and attach the other two legs.

At this point, stand the base up and allow the legs to sit flat on the work platform. Then clamp across the legs to hold everything together while the glue dries. Use a square to double check the angle of the legs to the shelf while clamping the base. Set this aside to dry and turn to the top.

Doubling the Top

Part of the look of the top is achieved by recessing a piece of ¼"-thick material between two thicker pieces, leaving a ¼" × ¼" channel that creates a delicate shadow line on the top's edge.

One of the other benefits of this process is making the top look more substantial without adding too much weight.

After running the ⅛"-deep × ¼" groove in the lower mouldings using the table saw, they were ready to miter and hand-fit on a sanding disk. This is the tricky part, so take your time. Then glue and pin the pieces in place.

The same mitering technique is used to fit and attach the upper mouldings on the legs. Remember that part of the leg is hidden behind the top's built-up edge, so locate the moulding 2¾" down from the top of the legs.

The spacers required to create the ¼" × ¼" shadow line are mitered and held ¼" in from the edges, then pinned in place (no glue). The pieces don't need to be 1¾" wide. My scrap was narrow, but no one will know.

The buildup pieces work the same as the spacers, but they're held flush to the top piece.
A square works well to orient the pieces before pinning through the spacers into the top.

I used figure-eight fasteners (available from Rockler) to attach the top. These allow the top to move seasonally without affecting the base.

top piece for a good look. I used a square against the table to align the doubling, then used 1⅛" pins to nail through the doubling and the spacer into the top.

Attaching the Top

I attached the top to the legs using figure-eight-shaped fasteners that are recessed into the tops of the legs — not just recessed, but also given a little extra space so the fasteners can swivel on the screws in the legs. This solves the wood-movement problem at this joint, allowing the top to expand with changes in humidity without affecting the base.

Drill a hole matching the diameter of the fastener, just to the depth of the thickness of the fastener. Then widen the hole to allow that fastener to swivel.

After attaching all four fasteners to the legs, flip the top over, center the base on the top and attach the base. Remember the top is only ⅝"-thick, so don't use screws that are too long!

The Wright Finish

Unlike many of his contemporaries in the early 20th century, Wright didn't stress too much about the finish on his Prairie furniture. While Gustav Stickley preferred a rather dark, heavy finish on many of his pieces, Wright settled instead on a pleasant, lighter mocha finish for his Prairie furniture pieces.

I found an off-the-shelf stain that adequately matched that philosophy. I wiped on a coat of Olympic Colonial Oak gel stain (available from Lowe's), then wiped off the excess to leave an even, warm-brown color.

A few coats of spray lacquer in a can (Deft semi-gloss Clear Wood finish in a spray can from Lowe's), sanding lightly with 320-grit paper between coats and the table was finished.

While Wright might not approve of the application I've chosen for his design, I think he'd be happy with the way it looks. Now where is that remote?

Start with the main top glued-up and trimmed to finished size. The spacer and doubling material also are solid white oak, cut to width and thickness as given.

Now flip the top upside down and mark the corners ¼" in from each edge. By holding the spacer pieces at this offset you will create the recess for the shadow line.

A note here on wood movement: Because the top is solid wood, it will move across the width with seasonal changes in humidity. If you attach the spacers and doubling across the ends of

the top with glue, they will likely break or shift with this movement. Because of this, I didn't use glue and simply pinned the pieces in place. I used a few extra pins, but because of how thin the pins are, they're more likely to bend slightly with the wood movement, rather than tear the top apart.

Attach the spacers, mitering the corners. I used ½" pins at this point, holding the pieces ¼" in all the way around the top.

The doubling is next and it's important to align the doubling flush to the

Nothing says "classy" like bringing out a full tea service on a tray table. This tray table lifts off its base. Butler not included.

PROJECT

19

Butler Tray Table

BY JIM STUARD

When we set out to build a tray table, we thought we'd come across plenty of examples in the historical record. Truth be told, there weren't many. This form probably originated about 100 years ago, in the Victorian era. A time when showing all of the trappings of wealth included having the butler bring out the good tea service for afternoon tea. Having the head servant emerge with everything in its place and setting it on the table base would appear most impressive.

Ellipses and Squares

The top is a rectangle set inside of an ellipse. The wings touch at the four corners of the rectangle.

Begin by cutting out all the parts according to the cutting list. Next, cut the wings to shape as shown in the illustrations and photos. Then put the wing parts in place against the rectangle and, using masking tape, attach the wings to the top so they pull up tight.

Mounting the Wings

Mark the hinge locations 4" in from each corner and transfer the location to each wing with a knife. The barrels of the hinges don't align exactly with the wing joint, so use the template in the illustrations on page 140 to locate the hinge recesses. Rout the recesses on the table side first; then, with a spacer, rout the wing side. There is some chisel work involved in fitting the hinge's spring mechanism to the top and wings. After this is done, attach all of the wings and test the fit.

You will notice that after mounting the wings, all four can't fold up at the same time. Routing a roundover profile on the edges of the top and wings will fix this. Rout a ⅜" profile on the top and a ¼" profile on the bottom. After this is done, remove the wings. Use a scroll saw or jigsaw to cut the handle holes using the pattern on page 143, sand and rout with a ¼" radius. Finish sand the top and wings and then set them aside for finishing.

The Pierced Stretcher

The stretcher on this table is strictly for show, and the turned ball centerpiece discourages people from putting anything on the stretcher, including their feet. Rough-cut the stretchers to size,

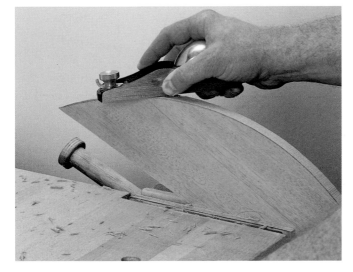

If you're making this table, cut out the wing patterns on pages 143 and 145. Make copies of the wing pattern halves and tape them together. Glue the patterns on the appropriate wings and cut out the oval-shaped wings. Next, clean up the edges of the wings with a block plane and prepare for mortising the hinges.

If you are going to change the size of the top, you'll need to use an ellipse-marking jig.

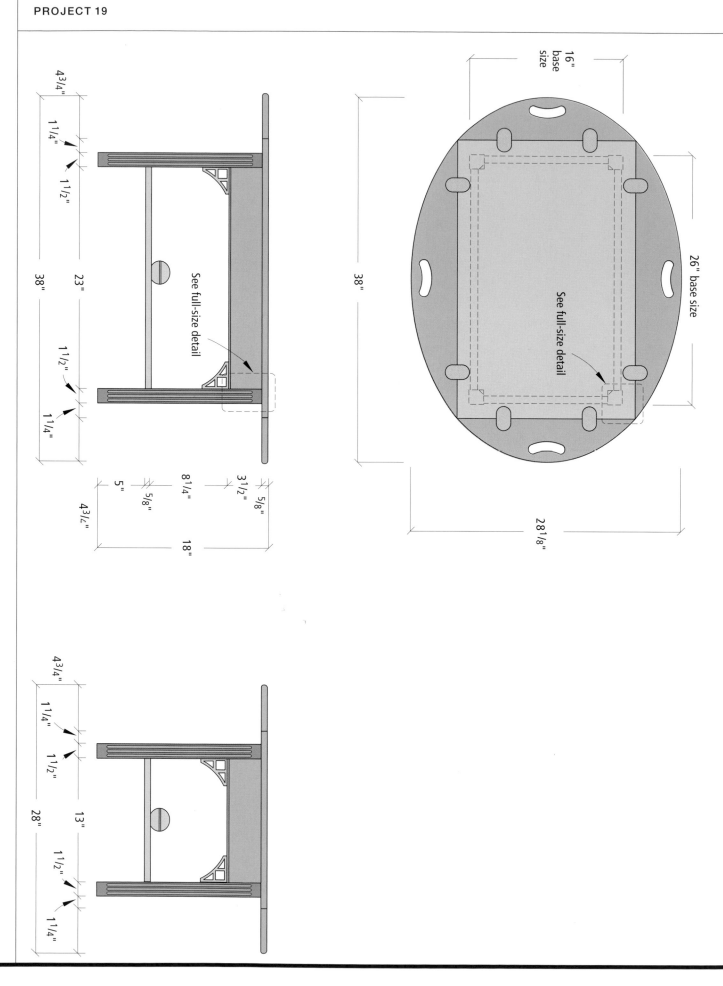

BUTLER TRAY TABLE • INCHES (MILLIMETERS)

QUANTITY	PART	STOCK	THICKNESS	(mm)	WIDTH	(mm)	LENGTH	(mm)	COMMENTS
1	top	Mahogany	5/8	16	18 1/2	47	29	737	
2	short wings	Mahogany	5/8	16	4 1/2	114	18 1/2	470	
2	long wings	Mahogany	5/8	16	4 3/4	121	29	737	
2	short aprons	Mahogany	3/4	19	3 1/2	89	14 1/2	368	
2	long aprons	Mahogany	3/4	19	3 1/2	89	24 1/2	622	
4	legs	Mahogany	1 1/2	38	1 1/2	38	17 3/8	441	
2	stretcher halves	Mahogany	5/8	16	4	102	30	762	
8	brackets	Mahogany	1/2	13	2 3/4	699	2 3/4	699	
1	tray foot stock	Mahogany	3/4	19	1/2	13	24	610	
1	center ball	Mahogany	2	51	2	51	3 1/2	89	

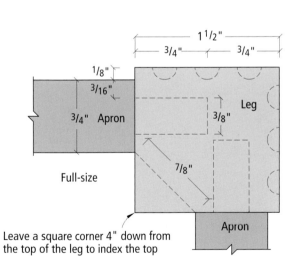

Full-size

Leave a square corner 4" down from the top of the leg to index the top

Detail plan of table base corner

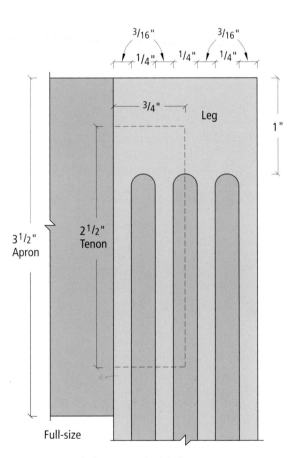

Full-size

Detail elevation of table base corner

then use the pattern on page 143 to lay out the angled half-lap joints on the pieces. I cut the half laps with a hand saw and a rabbet plane, but a straight edge and a router would work fine. After cutting the half laps, temporarily attach the stretcher pieces together with a screw.

Next, make two copies of each stretcher pattern. This gives a left and right, and the cross hairs in the center give a good indexing point. Tape the pattern pieces together and affix them to the stretcher blank. Remove the screw and cut the stretchers out using a scroll saw or jigsaw.

Precision is important here because there is little room for error when fitting the stretcher to the legs later on in construction. Take your time and do it right. Once the stretchers are cut and sanded, glue them together. Lastly, turn a small ball for the center of the stretcher. Drill a $1/2$" × $3/8$"-deep hole in the center of the stretcher and a deeper hole in the ball. Attach the ball with a dowel after finishing.

Fluting the Legs

Use a router in a table to flute the legs. Set stops at each end of the fence and

Make a jig to rout the hinge mortises. Use the pattern on this page to make a jig for routing the mortises. Be sure to fit the jig to the correct of hinge that you are using. If you use a bearing-on-top bit, make sure that you use material thick enough to accommodate the bit and bearing when you make the jig.

Full-scale drawing of router hinge jig

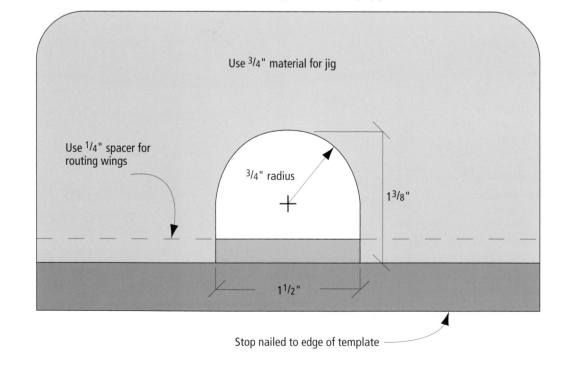

Use $3/4$" material for jig

Use $1/4$" spacer for routing wings

$3/4$" radius

$1^3/8$"

$1^1/2$"

Stop nailed to edge of template

measure (include the bit width) from the mounted bit to the stop. The distance should be 1" less than the length of the leg. This gives a 1" space at the top and bottom where there is no fluting. Using a ¼" round nose bit, the first setup is ³⁄₁₆" from the bit to the fence and ⅛" up. The second is centered on the leg. The photo below details the setup necessary to complete this procedure. The diagram on page 139 shows you the location of each flute.

To complete the legs, first set the jointer fence at a 45° angle and cut a chamfer on the inside corner, away from the outer fluted sides. Set the depth of cut so there is an equal amount of width left on each remaining bevel. See the full-sized diagram on page 139 for details.

Begin the stretcher layout by marking the centers of each stretcher piece along the length and across the middle. Drill a small hole through each center and place a small finish nail through both pieces. Place this assembly on a 60° angle and mark both pieces at the edges where they touch.

Beading the Aprons

The bead at the bottom edge of the aprons will cast a shadow line that separates the aprons from the corner brackets. After beading the aprons, cut ⅜" × 2½" × ¾" mortises on the legs in the locations shown in the diagram. Then cut the ⅜" × 2½" × ¾" tenons on the ends of the aprons. Now check the fit with the mortises in the legs.

Assembly and Finish

The base can now be dry assembled to get the finished size of the stretcher. Set the base upside down and lay the stretcher onto the bottoms of the legs, spaced evenly on all four legs. Mark the joints where they meet the legs. Cut the excess off and sand the ends until the stretcher fits snugly between the legs. Bore holes in the stretchers and legs for a dowel as shown in the photo above

Once you get the angle correct, cut the half lap. First I used a hand saw to define the edges, then I used a rabbet plane to hog out the waste.

This is how you create a drop-cut flute: With the router running, hold the leg firmly and gently lower it onto the bit with the end of the leg against the first stop (which isn't visible behind my right hand). Run the leg across the bit to the other stop and lift it straight up. Now rotate the leg 90° and repeat the process. Reset the fence to rout the flute down the center of the leg. Use a test piece first; then run the center flute on each leg.

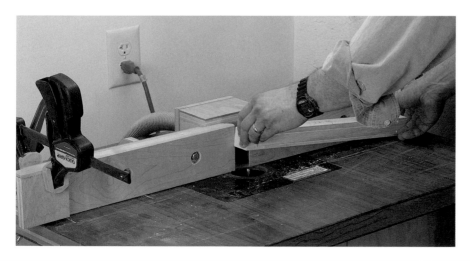

I beaded the aprons using an old Stanley No. 45 moulding plane. The bead is a standard ⅛" and can also be made with a beading bit in a router table.

After fitting the stretcher, lay out and drill dowel centers so that the stretcher will attach 5" up from the bottom of the legs.

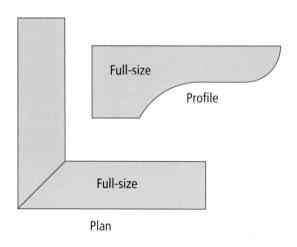

Full-size
Profile

Full-size

Plan

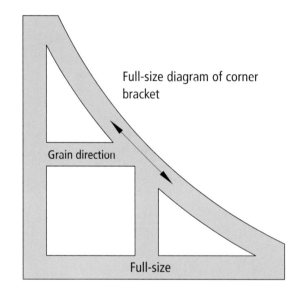

Full-size diagram of corner bracket

Grain direction

Full-size

right. Glue the base together and clamp. While the glue dries, make eight copies of the corner bracket pattern, which is shown at right.

Lay out the brackets according to the pattern and cut their corners square with a miter saw. Note the grain direction for strength. Affix the patterns to your wood with spray adhesive and cut them out on the scroll saw or coping saw. Sand and attach the brackets with small brads and glue.

Now build the tray's feet, which keep the tray centered perfectly on the base. First cut 45° miters on the ends of some ¾" × ½" stock (called "tray foot stock" in the cutting list) and cut them to 2" lengths. Using the foot pattern below,

scroll saw left and right mitered pieces for each foot. Place the top and base upside down on a blanket. Center the inverted base on the top. Nail two of these corner pieces together and attach them to the top at the inside corner where the long apron meets the leg. Leave a little clearance so the top won't get stuck.

Start the three-step finishing process with a thinned-down red aniline dye. Why red? This will accentuate the red that is already in the mahogany. Your goal is a bright reddish or pink color when dry. So don't be shocked if your table suddenly looks like it belongs in the circus. Rag it on, preferably with cheese cloth (it doesn't leave lint on

the surface). Wipe any blotches down with a clean rag lightly soaked with the thinner used for your dye. Next, reduce some neutral grain filler with oil-based mahogany stain to the consistency of heavy cream. Rub the stain/filler mixture across the grain leaving a fairly heavy coat. Let it stand for a few minutes until the thinnest part of the application starts to dry. Rub the excess stain/filler out across the grain and finish rubbing lightly with the grain. Apply three coats of clear lacquer, sanding between coats. And now it's tea time.

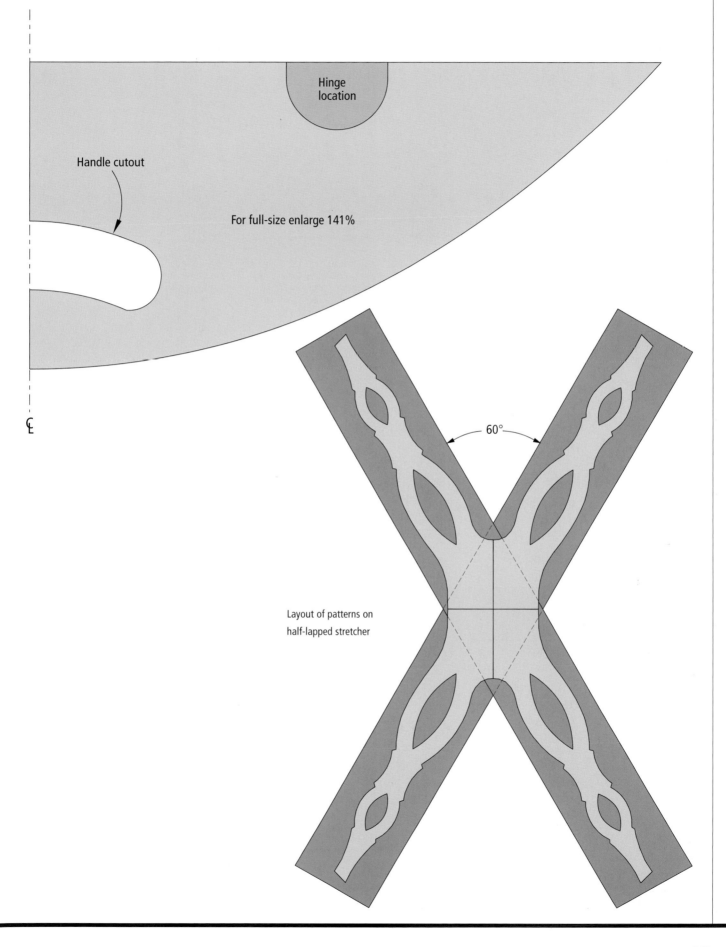

Hinge
location

Handle cutout

For full-size enlarge 141%

℄

60°

Layout of patterns on
half-lapped stretcher

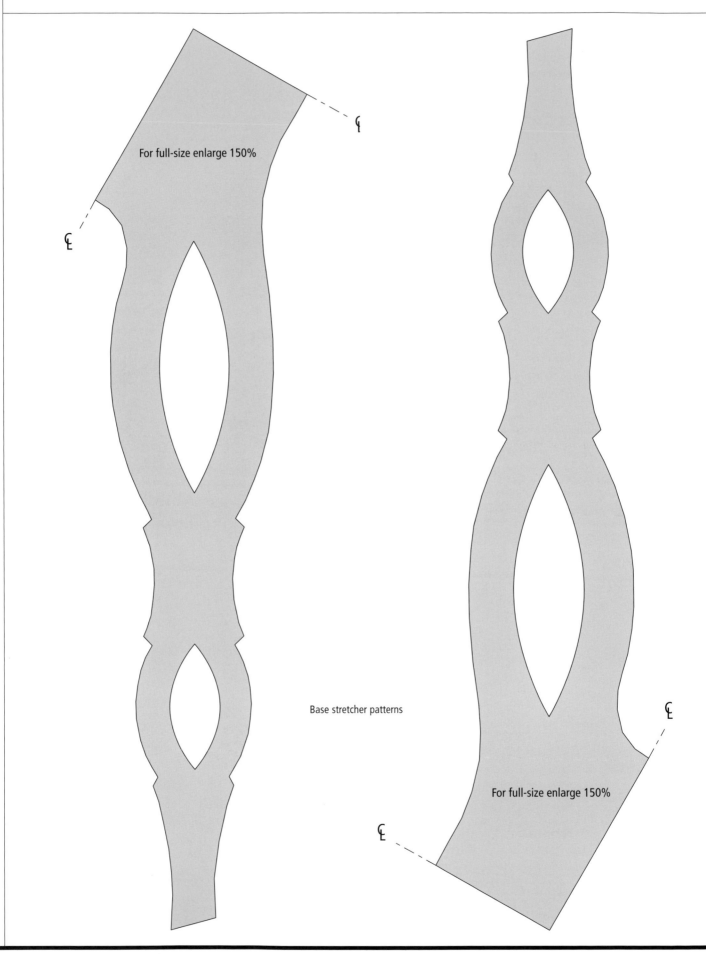

For full-size enlarge 150%

Base stretcher patterns

For full-size enlarge 150%

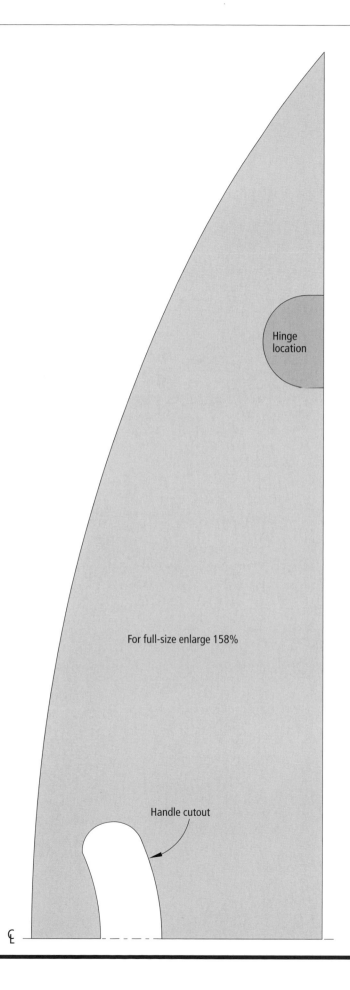

Hinge
location

For full-size enlarge 158%

Handle cutout

One table or three — how you use these sleek tables is up to you.

Plywood Nesting Tables

BY DAVID THIEL

If you've been looking for an excuse to buy a nice table saw blade — or at least get your old one sharpened — this is the project. While these tables are simple to build, precision and a sharp saw blade will make the difference between a relaxing weekend project or a frustrating exercise in gluing up miters.

I made these tables using three sheets of plywood. I ripped each sheet down the middle and glued the two pieces from each sheet together to make a 1½"-thick slab. Then I beveled the front edge and glued thin solid-wood pieces to cover the slab's plywood edges. Finally, I cut the legs and top for each table from the slab and biscuited the pieces together. This method allows the grain on the top to continue uninterrupted down the legs.

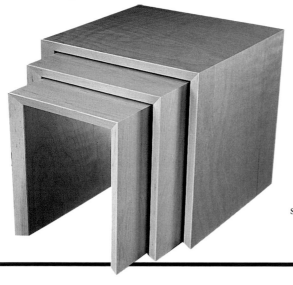

Make a Slab

Start the nesting tables by ripping three sheets of plywood in half. Rip them just under 24" in width. You won't need all that width, but it will come in handy later. As for the lengths, using the full 96" is a little wasteful, but it does make gluing the two halves together easier.

After ripping the sheets, determine which three faces are most attractive and mark these as the outsides of the tables. Next glue the pairs together. To keep the sheets from sliding around during glue-up, pound a nail into each slab about 1" from the ends. Stack the three pairs together, then clamp across the stack using stout wood cauls to spread the pressure.

After the glue is dry, square off one end of each slab. Then cut the slabs to 68", 62½" and 55" in length. Don't pitch the fall-off pieces, they'll be useful later.

Next, rip each slab to 23" wide to give you one flat edge. You could run one edge over a jointer, but the adhesive in plywood is murder on high-speed steel knives. When you have one square edge, set the table saw's blade to bevel at 33° and rip the three slabs to 21⅝", 20⅝" and 19⅝" wide respectively. Again, be sure to save the fall-off.

Homemade Veneer

You're now ready to run some solid lumber to cover the plywood edges. I used soft maple edging on my birch ply tables.

Run out six lengths of ³⁄₁₆"-thick solid wood for the edges. To plane wood that thin, you will need to put an auxiliary bed board over the bed of your planer because most planers aren't designed for wood that thin.

With the strips ready, it's time to glue them to the slabs. Go find the fall-off from the bevel cuts and grab a couple other sturdy solid strips. Use the fall-off as a caul for clamping. By gluing the edges on the slabs with the bevel facing up, gravity is on your side. I also cheated just a little by tacking the edge strips in place with a few small brads at either end. Once again, the extra inch in length will be cut off, so the nail holes won't show.

Glue the edging to the three slabs, then trim the edging flush to the plywood. I used a router with a flush-cutting bit for the back edges, and I used a jack plane to get the beveled edges nearly flush. Then I used a random orbit sander to flush the edges perfectly. To soften the edges, I used some 120-grit paper wrapped around a block of wood.

Make Your Miters

The tables slip inside one another with a ¼" gap between each, so accurate cutting and spacing is very important. To make the mitered corners and still maintain

PLYWOOD NESTING TABLES • INCHES (MILLIMETERS)

QUANTITY	PART	STOCK	THICKNESS	(mm)	WIDTH	(mm)	LENGTH	(mm)	COMMENTS
4	sides*	birch plywood	3/4	19	22	559	22	559	
2	tops*	birch plywood	3/4	19	22	559	22	559	
4	sides*	birch plywood	3/4	19	22	559	20 1/4	514	
2	tops*	birch plywood	3/4	19	21	533	18 1/2	470	
4	sides*	birch plywood	3/4	19	20	508	18 1/2	470	
2	tops*	birch plywood	3/4	19	20	508	15	381	
6	veneer edges	birch/maple	3/16	5	2	51	96	2438	

All sizes are finished components, not cutting sizes.

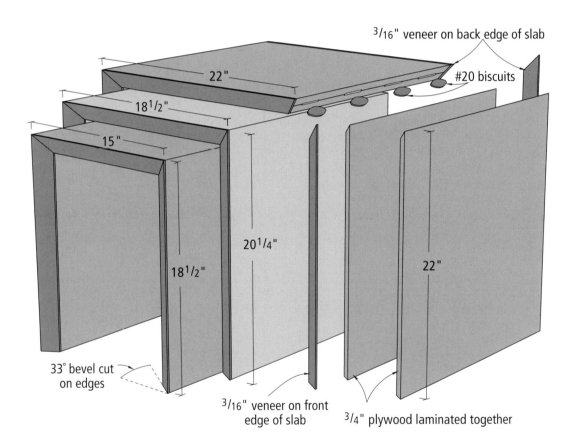

3/16" veneer on back edge of slab

#20 biscuits

22"

18 1/2"

15"

20 1/4"

18 1/2"

22"

33° bevel cut on edges

3/16" veneer on front edge of slab

3/4" plywood laminated together

the grain pattern on the tabletops, first crosscut the three slabs into three parts. Use the table saw with the blade set to 90°. Start by marking the middle of each slab and cut the top section from the middle of each slab, allowing the excess length to remain on the leg sections.

You're now ready to do the precision cutting, and you'll see quickly why a sharp blade is important. Start with the largest top (22" × 22") and set the blade

bevel to exactly 45° and the rip fence to cut the miter exactly to the width of the top. If you have a left-beveling table saw you're in luck as the inside of the table is on the tear-out side. If you have a right tilt, that sharp blade is important. Make the first bevel cut on one end, then spin the top and make the cut on the opposite end. Again, with a right-tilt saw you have the extra difficulty of the first miter trying to slide under the rip fence.

Adjust your cut for any variance and consider adding an auxiliary fence that fits tightly to the table surface. Repeat this with all three tops.

You're now ready to make the miter cuts on the legs. Start with the 22"-high legs and work through the 20 1/4"- and 18 1/2"-high legs, then trim the extra 1" off the 90° end to achieve the perfect height. Check the spacing between the tables by "dry-nesting" as you go.

Spacers underneath the slab allow the solid-wood edging to hang over to evenly cover the edges. It doesn't take a lot of pressure to clamp the edges. Too much pressure will force the front edge caul to slide.

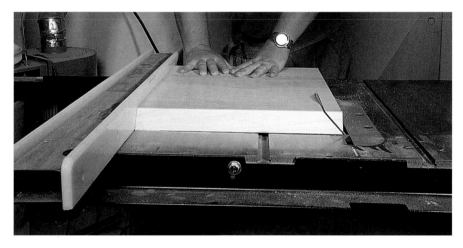

The first miter cut on the center slab (on a right-tilt saw) will balance the fall-off piece on the blade. Be aware of possible kickback of the scrap piece.

Unless your rip fence is tight to the saw's table, the miter will have a tendency to slide under the fence during the second cut (on right-tilt saws). Recheck your measurements to accommodate this, or, you can add a tight-fitting auxiliary fence to the standard rip fence.

Assembly

The hard part is done. The rest is biscuits and clamps. I used four No. 20 biscuits for each miter joint. With the biscuits cut, the fall-off pieces from cutting the slabs to length come into play. You'll stick them between the legs while gluing up the miters. It makes glue-up much easier. First check the internal dimension between the miters on each tabletop. Try to be as exact as possible, then cut spacers from the fall-off pieces for each table.

Finish sand the interior faces of each table and the beveled front edge of each piece before assembly. Put glue on the miters and biscuits and glue the tables. Pay careful attention to the miter joint where the top and legs join. Unlike the hardwood edging, you only have about $\frac{1}{16}$" of veneer to sand to match the joint.

With the tables assembled, sand the outer faces, taking extra care with the mitered joint. You're now ready to finish. I chose to add a few coats of clear finish to the tables, but any number of stains to match an existing décor will work well.

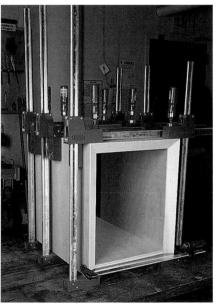

Enough clamps and careful adjustment during glue-up will ensure tight miters and an evenly spaced opening from top to bottom.

Don't hate me because I found some 20"-wide curly maple.
It was a lucky accident, and, it was a good deal.

Great Danish Modern Table

BY DAVID THIEL

Mill the Wood

First, mill all your material to ¾" thickness. The schedule includes four blanks for the legs that will yield one leg per piece. If you're being thrifty, the pieces will interlock and save material, but orient the grain so it follows the path of the lower part of the leg. Use the pattern on this page to lay out the legs.

Cut the Legs

Use a band saw or jigsaw to cut the legs to shape. Use double-sided tape to hold the four legs together and sand the edges at the same time.

Soften all the edges (except the ends of the end stretchers and the tops and bottoms of the legs) using a ¼" roundover bit. Then mark the dowel locations as shown in the diagrams and drill the holes.

Sand the Project

Sand the entire base through 220 grit, then glue the legs to the side stretchers, seating the dowels in the holes to leave ¾" of the dowel exposed. Then glue the end stretchers between the two side pieces.

Lay Out and Finish the Top

Now lay out the top. Bend a strip of ¼" material along the edges of the top to mark the gentle curve, then cut the top to shape. For an interesting effect, I routed the edges of the top with a ½" roundover. I cut this detail on the bottom of the sides and the top of the ends. I then marked a line 1" in from the edges and used a random-orbit sander to further roll the edge details toward the 1" line.

I finished the table with natural Danish oil, then fastened the top to the legs using figure-eight table fasteners placed parallel to the side stretchers. This way the fasteners will move if the top piece moves.

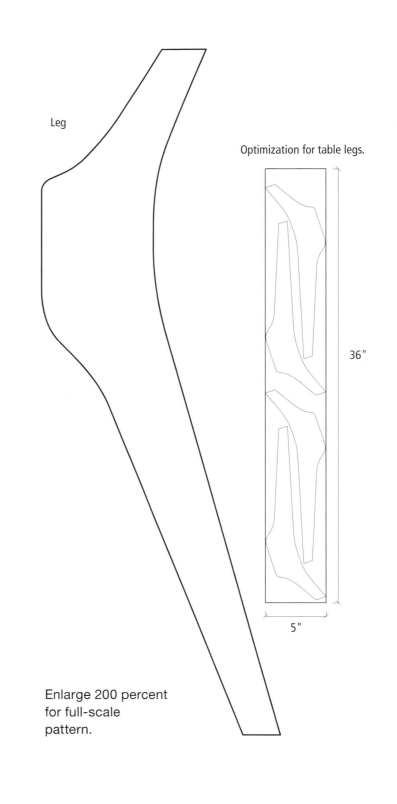

Leg

Optimization for table legs.

36"

5"

Enlarge 200 percent for full-scale pattern.

GREAT DANISH MODERN TABLE • INCHES (MILLIMETERS)

QUANTITY	PART	STOCK	THICKNESS	(mm)	WIDTH	(mm)	LENGTH	(mm)	COMMENTS
4	legs	walnut	3/4	19	5	127	14 1/4	362	
2	side stretchers	walnut	3/4	19	2 3/4	70	36 1/2	927	
2	end stretchers	walnut	3/4	19	2 3/4	70	10 1/2	267	
16	dowels	maple	3/8 D	10	1 1/2	38			
1	top	maple	3/4	19	20	508	60	1524	

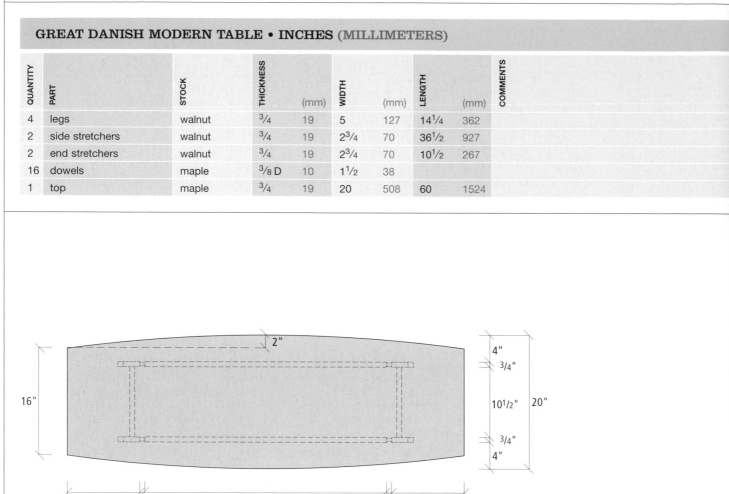

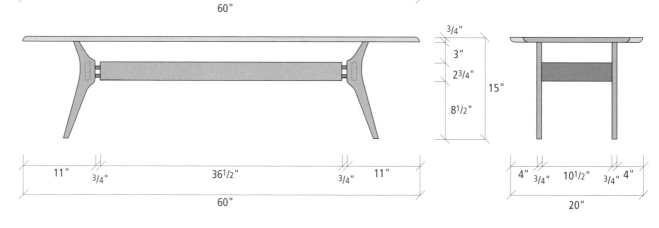

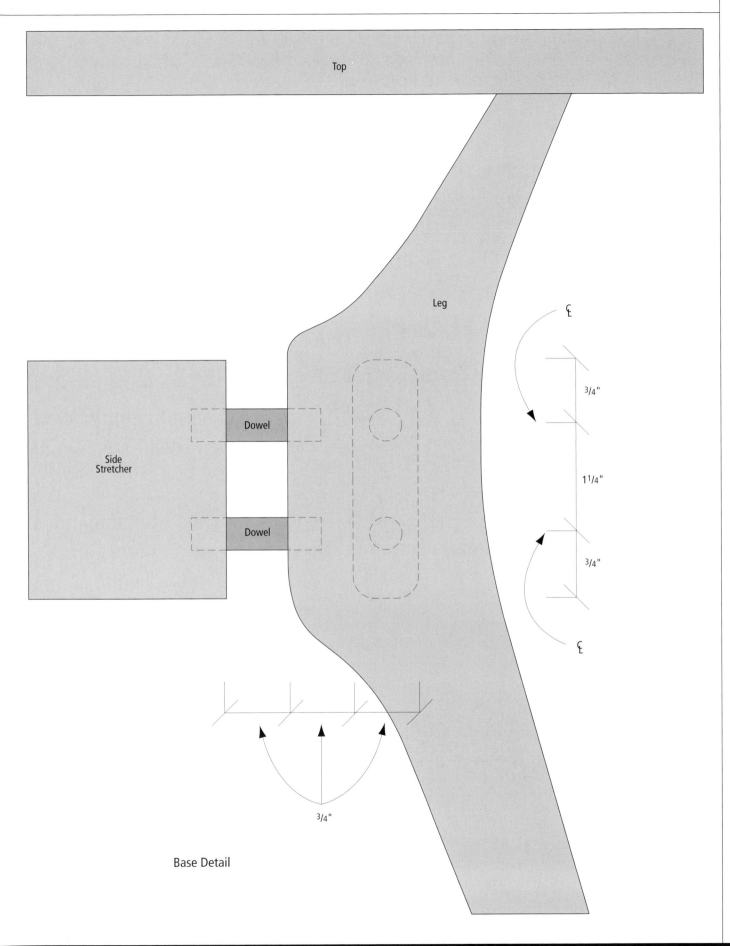

Top

Leg

Side Stretcher

Dowel

Dowel

3/4"

1¹/4"

3/4"

₵

₵

3/4"

Base Detail

One of the first "how-to" projects to ever appear in
Popular Woodworking Magazine.

Maloof-style Table

BY DAVID THIEL

One of the earliest "how-to" projects in
Popular Woodworking (which at the time
was called *Pacific Woodworker*) had the
distinction of being a table by renowned
woodworker Sam Maloof. While the
article was not an actual step-by-step
explanation (indeed, there weren't even
dimensions offered), the process for
constructing the distinctive table base
was described. Using that article, I built
this Maloof-style table. And while this
isn't a weekend project, it's not a particularly difficult piece. More importantly,
this table will remind you of why you
love to work with wood.

If you're concerned about copying
another person's design, sign the work
as your own and keep in mind what
Maloof said in his book, *Sam Maloof,
Woodworker,* when asked about those
who copy his furniture:

"This reminds me of an anecdote
about Hamada, the Japanese potter.
When someone asked Hamada if imi-
tations of his work bothered him, he
replied, 'When I'm dead, people will
think that all of my bad things were
made by the other potter, and they will
think that all of his good things were
made by me.' "

Starting at the Post
The first step is roughing out and shaping
the base's center post. The post measures
3" × 3" × 23", and unless you're very lucky

you'll have to glue up a couple of boards to achieve this dimension. Using 1¾"-thick material, I was able to glue up two 3"-wide pieces with room to spare.

If you've ever tried to glue two flat pieces together you know that glue works like butter and the wood wants to slip. Drill two dowel holes on the matching faces and use dowels as indexing pins during gluing so you won't fight with your pieces.

Next run the post down to 3" × 3". For now, you should leave the post longer than the finished 23" to allow for fitting. The first milling procedure is to use a dado stack to cut grooves the length of the post on all four faces.

Forming the Inside Curve

With the post grooved to accept the leg tenons, make cove cuts on the four corners so that the shape flows into the legs. I accomplished this with a ¾" cove bit. This bit is a necessity. There is no other tooling that provides the control given by a router and bit set up in a router table.

As shown in the photo, the location of the cove cut is critical to how easy it will be to assemble the base and how good it will look. Use two passes of increasing depth to put less stress on your router.

Quite a Joint

With the post essentially complete, it's time to make the legs. You will be making four duplicate leg sections, each made of three pieces. The templates for the three pieces are shown on page 159.

Cut the pieces to rough size, being careful to mark the 45° angle location exactly. On each leg's top and center

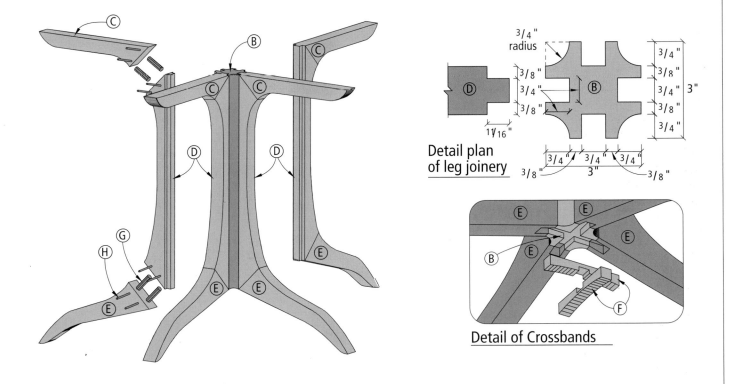

Detail plan of leg joinery

Detail of Crossbands

MALOOF-STYLE TABLE • INCHES (MILLIMETERS)

QUANTITY	PART	STOCK	THICKNESS	(mm)	WIDTH	(mm)	LENGTH	(mm)	COMMENTS
1	top	walnut	⁷⁄₈	22	42	1067	42	1067	
1	post	walnut	3	76	3	76	23	584	
4	leg tops	walnut	1¾	45	2½	64	13½	343	
4	leg centers	walnut	1¾	45	2¾	70	23	584	
4	leg bottoms	walnut	1¾	45	3½	89	14½	368	
2	cross bands	maple	¾	19	¾	13	5	127	
16	dowels	maple	½	13	2	51			
32	dowels	maple	⅛	3	2	51			

Center the grooves. The ¾" × ¾" grooves must be centered in the width of the post to make the fit (and the sanding) acceptable. A careful setup with a dado set makes this quick work.

Make careful coves. Getting the cove cuts to align with the edges of the leg centers makes sanding and the final finish easier. If anything, allow the cove cuts to be a hair wider than necessary so that the sanding to fit occurs on the leg centers, not in the cove cut.

pieces you still have a flat edge to use as a guide to cut the angles on your table saw, or miter saw. On each leg's bottom you'll need to make the cut with the band saw or a hand saw and sand the face flat. These are critical joints that determine how flat your table will sit, so pay special attention to making them meet correctly.

With the pieces roughed to shape, make the two rabbet cuts on the leg centers to leave an ¹¹⁄₁₆" × ¾"-wide tenon. Check the fit with the grooves in the post. It should be a hand-tight fit.

Next sand the leg pieces to match the templates. A spindle sander is great for this step, but a drum sander chucked in your drill press will work, too. When you sand the shapes, leave a couple of inches to either side of each joint wide of the line. The joints should be shaped to match after the leg pieces have been glued together to ensure a smooth transition.

Lay out the locations for the ½" dowels as shown in the top photo on the facing page.

Clamping Ballet

The glue-up of the leg components is tricky, but the lower photo on the facing page shows a method that worked well for me. Next, look to the diagram for the locations of the ⅛" dowels used to pin the larger dowels. Drill completely through the leg and dowel, but use a backing board to avoid tear-out on the exit side. Then add some glue to the 2" dowel lengths and tap them into place so the dowel protrudes on both sides. When the glue dries, sand the dowels flush.

Use a ½" roundover bit with a bearing guide to ease all the edges of each leg — except the tenon edge and the top edge. Be careful while routing because the grain is likely to change direction, especially at the joint, and tear out.

After routing, glue the legs to the center post. Definitely dry-fit the base assembly, clamping the legs in place. Make sure the base sits flat without rocking and mark the center post to cut it to length to match the legs. After that, glue and clamp the base.

Dowel the legs. Use dowels to join the leg tops and bottoms to the leg center. I used ½" dowels, which were later pinned through the side of the legs with ⅛" dowels. A self-centering doweling jig like the one shown in the photo takes some of the measuring out of this step.

Strength and a Decorative Touch

Before sanding, there is one detail Maloof adds to his sculpted-base tables that adds strength, as well as a nice touch.

The half-lapped maple cross pieces are added to provide strength across the base, tying the opposing legs together with the center post. Chisel the ¾"-wide by 5"-long grooves for the pieces to a depth of ½" at the center of the "X" and allow the bottom of the groove to level out into the legs. This leaves the trench about ⅝" deep at the ends of the grooves.

Next, cut the half-lap joint in the two maple pieces and fit them into the two grooves. Then drill four ⅛" pilot holes, ½" in from the ends of the pieces. Then drill ⅜" × ⅜"-deep holes to allow the screw heads to recess into the maple. After inserting the four No. 8 × 2" flat-head screws, plug the holes with ⅜"-diameter walnut plugs.

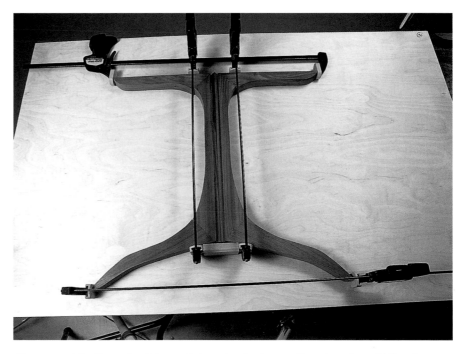

Clamp carefully. Properly gluing and clamping the leg sections is awkward. The clamp arrangement shown here glued two leg sections at the same time with only four clamps. The block between the leg bottoms kept the clamps from sliding on the sculpted leg.

The half-lapped pieces of maple are shown in place, shaped, screwed and plugged. The process was time consuming, but the finished appearance is dramatic.

After that, the rest is rasping and sanding. Maloof's pieces are known for their contours and smoothness of transitions. I spent about six hours shaping and sanding the base through to 220 grit. It was worth the effort.

It seems silly, but the most visible part of the table took the least amount of effort. The 42" square/round top was made of four ⅞" × 11" walnut boards. I didn't want to use more than four boards for the top, so I had to buy 8/4 lumber to get the width I needed — the result was that after resawing the boards on the band saw I had some nice ¾" walnut for another project.

While Maloof makes no bones about using sapwood on his tops as long as it's stable, I prefer a more consistent appearance — though I did leave a little sap as a nod to Maloof the master.

The top was edge-glued using six No. 20 biscuits per joint. To shape the top, mark a point 2" in from each corner and locate the center of each edge. Bend a strip of ¼" maple across the center point of each edge in toward the 2" marks and mark the curve for the top edges.

Complete the top (except for sanding) with a ¼" roundover on the top and bottom edges.

To finish the table, I used Sam Maloof's line of finishing products offered through Rockler. These reproduce the poly/oil and oil/wax formulas mentioned in "A Maloof Finish" at left.

A Maloof Finish

Mix one-third semi-gloss polyurethane varnish, one-third pure tung oil and one-third boiled linseed oil. You can substitute linseed oil with a third tung oil if it is polymerized (pure tung oil dries too slowly). Apply this mixture three times at one-day intervals.

For a final coat, heat a 50/50 mix of pure tung oil and boiled linseed oil (or 100 percent polymerized tung oil) in a double boiler. Grate solid beeswax and add it to the heated mix until it is the consistency of heavy cream (about two double-handfuls of wax per gallon of mix). Let cool. The wax in the cooled mixture will stay in suspension and has a good shelf-life. This is applied a minimum of three times, vigorously rubbing in the mixture each time.

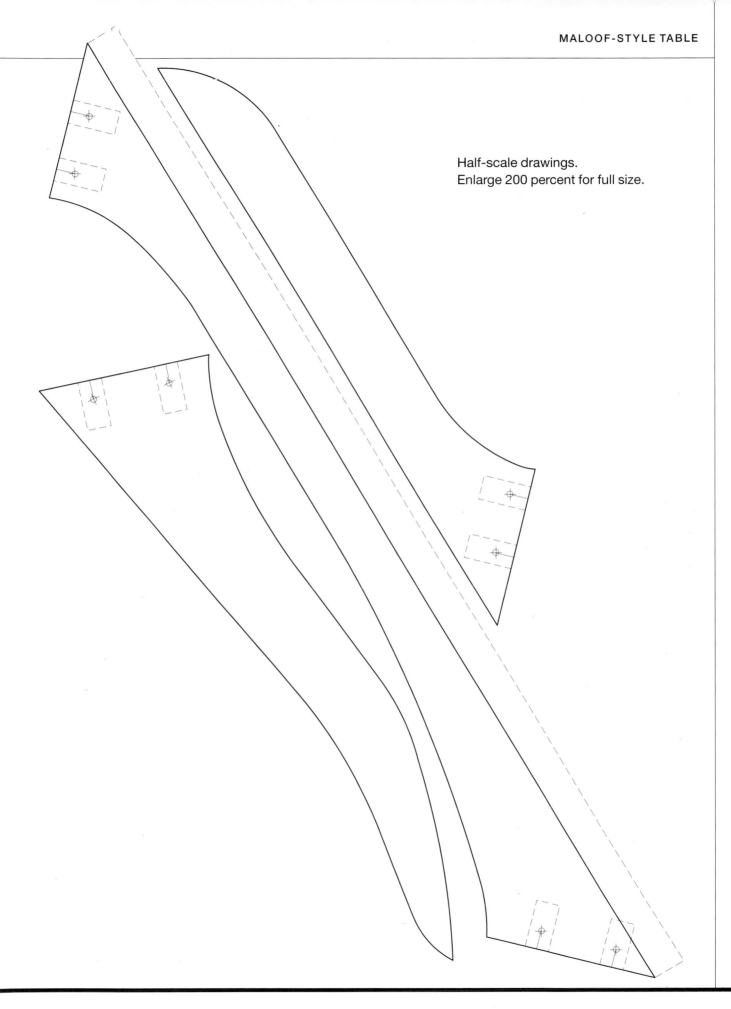

Half-scale drawings.
Enlarge 200 percent for full size.

Construction of this table is simple, strong and it looks good too. Then spend time with family playing chess or checkers.

Game Table

BY GLEN HUEY

Back in the day, gentlemen would sit for hours at the local barbershops and while away the time discussing the day's events and playing checkers. Hours might be spent sliding pieces from square to square.

Jumping the opponent's checkers was the way to clear his pieces from the board and to reach his back line where one would utter those fateful words, "king me". The king, two stacked checkers, possessed new powers that would allow it to move in new directions. With those added powers came a better chance at clearing the board.

Removing all of the opponents checkers would make one the winner. It would allow him to obtain the local title or possibly begin a heated argument that went on for days by itself.

What could be better than to bring those long passed days back into your home with the building of this game table? The time spent with family members playing at this table will bridge many gaps and start many a conversation about life.

It All Starts at the Top

The tabletop is the most important part of this table. That's where we begin. Select the material for the frame and make a 45° cut on both ends of the pieces leaving 23" of length at the long side of each piece. Cut all four pieces the same length.

The 23" figure comes about due to the size of the game board. The board is 18" square and using the stock for the

frame at 2½". To wrap the board with this stock you need to have pieces for the frame at 23". If you choose to change the board size remember to adjust the frame size as well.

With the frame pieces cut to length you'll need to use the pocket-screw jig to drill two holes per end on two of the pieces (see top left photo page 162).

Putting the frame together is as simple as driving the pocket screws. Place a clamp on the piece that is accept-

ing the screws so it won't move. Position the pocketed piece against the clamped frame member and drive the screws to make the connection. Repeat this step for each corner and the frame will come together.

For extra reinforcement I added screws to the corners (see lower left photo page 162), then cut plugs from matching stock to fill the countersink area. Anytime during the project add a small amount of glue to the holes and

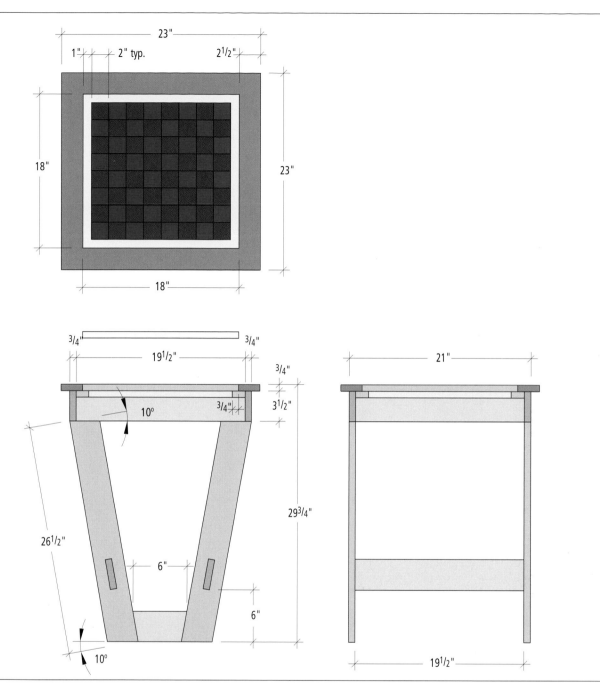

GAME TABLE • INCHES (MILLIMETERS)

QUANTITY	PART	STOCK	THICKNESS	(mm)	WIDTH	(mm)	LENGTH	(mm)	COMMENTS
4	board frame	oak	3/4	19	2¹/2	64	23	584	
4	board supports	poplar	3/4	19	1¹/2	38	19¹/2	495	
1	board	plywood	3/4	19	18	457	18	457	
2	inside fit aprons	poplar	3/4	19	3¹/2	89	19¹/2	495	
2	outside fit aprons	poplar	3/4	19	3¹/2	89	21	533	
4	legs (pre-miter)	poplar	3/4	19	3¹/2	89	27	686	
2	leg connectors	poplar	3/4	19	2¹/2	64	6	152	
2	stretchers	poplar	3/4	19	3¹/2	89	19¹/2	495	

Set the angled cut flat to the jig and drill the holes perpendicular to the cut end. The remaining pieces will accept the screws and no holes are required.

When driving the pocket screws, it's best to clamp whatever you can to the bench. This helps to ensure a tight, flush fit when the screw is tight.

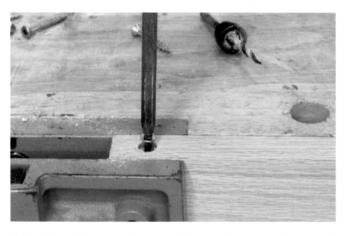

Drill a hole with a tapered countersink at each corner, four in total, then add a screw to help to hold the corners of the frame tight.

Attach the board supports using screws.

tap in the plugs.

Next, prepare the stock for the board supports. Each piece has a mitered 45° cut at each end made at the miter saw. These pieces are attached to the inside edge of the frame with ¾" lying on the frame and ¾" sticking into the center area to catch the game board when it is positioned. Attach the support pieces with #8 × 1¼" wood screws. Be sure to use the tapered countersink for these holes too.

A Strong Leg to Stand On

The apron for the table is built to snugly fit around the support pieces. The best method to gather accurate sizes is to use the support frame to align the apron. Two pieces are the inside-fit aprons. These pieces are cut to the same length as the support pieces. The two outside-

fit aprons will extend past the support pieces and cover the ends of the inside-fit aprons. Return to the pocket-screw jig to cut two holes per end on the inside-fit apron pieces.

With the holes cut connect the apron pieces with the pocket screws. The assembled apron should just slip over the support pieces and allow the top to fit into the apron. Don't make the connection of the top to the apron just yet. You'll want to separate the two assemblies before you are finished with construction.

The legs are started at the miter saw. Set the saw for an 80° cut or 10° off of a square cut of 90°. Position the material for two legs at the saw and cut the angle at what is to be the top of each leg. Leave the saw set at that angle for the next set of cuts on the legs.

Set the top apron assembly on one

side and position the angled cut on a leg against the bottom edge of the aprons. Pull a measuring tape from the bottom edge of the apron and mark at 25½" down the leg. This is where the second cut of the leg is placed.

Making that second cut is a snap. Position the leg material so that both legs are flush at the top end and cradled into the saw tight to the fence. Slide the two pieces, making sure that they stay aligned, into position to make another angled cut at the mark (lower right photo on facing page). It is important to have the cuts angled the correct way. When this cut is complete you'll have a parallelogram shape to the legs (both cuts angle in the same direction). Repeat the steps for the second set of legs.

Next, add pocket-screw holes to the top end of each leg and align them with

Fit the apron parts to the board supports.

Use pocket-hole screws to assemble the apron parts.

After cutting the leg connectors to length, attach them to the legs. Make two of these leg assemblies.

Using a miter saw, cut a 10° miter on both ends of each leg. These cuts should be parallel.

the bottom edge of the apron making sure that the edge of the leg lines up with the side of the apron. It doesn't really matter which opposing aprons you select to attach the legs to since the apron is square, but I attached the legs so the end grain of the outside aprons sat on the leg top — there may be additional support with this choice.

Add the legs to one side of the table, then cut the leg connector to fit in position. This connector also cuts at the same angle as the legs. Make the cut on one end, then flip the piece, measure the distance between the legs at a mark that is 2½" above the floor and make the second cut at that point. In this scenario you'll have the cuts set at opposing angles. Place two pocket-screw holes at each end and attach the connector to the legs. Repeat the process for the second

leg assembly and you're ready for the stretchers.

The stretchers have square cut ends and pocket holes, two at each end, that allow you to attach them to the legs. Position the stretchers to the legs with the screw holes facing inside the table. I like these stretchers to be centered in the leg. To accomplish this easily I cut a scrap at the miter saw to the appropriate width, 1⅜" for this example, placed it at the front edge of the leg, pulled the stretchers tight to the back of the scrap and set the screws to make the connection. The base is complete.

Making the Game Board

Cut and fit the piece of plywood that is the game board to the opening in the table. This piece should be a loose fit so it can be removed if necessary. You see,

you can also have a different game on the bottom of the board.

To mill this board use your jigsaw to cut close to the layout lines and then hand plane to bring everything into shape. Remember that if you're cutting across the grain of the plywood it is best to score a line with a sharp utility knife before cutting. That way as you cut to the line the top veneer of the plywood will not splinter.

Once the game board is fit you are ready to complete the table. Add the plugs to the top frame if you haven't already, install pocket-hole fillers into any hole that is easily visible and sand everything to 150 grit. Use 100-grit sandpaper to knock off any sharp edges and move to the finishing stage.

The game board is a checker board and to make your own board you need a few additional tools. Gather a utility knife, framing square (or square of some kind) and a roll of painter's tape that is 2" wide. Of course you'll need two or three different colors of acrylic latex paint.

To begin the board you'll need to layout the lines that define the checker squares. Find the center of the board and draw a line across the entire piece. Next, move each way in 2" increments each time, drawing a line as before. You should end up with eight squares and 1" of space on either edge which will be the outside border of the board.

Rotate the board 90° and repeat these steps for the opposing lines. Make sure that you continue the lines clear to the edge of the plywood piece. These will become important after the first layer of paint. You now have the sixty-four spaces for the checkerboard.

Paint Makes the Square

Add painter's tape to the outside edges of the squares which protects the borders from the first paint color. Traditionally, black and red are the colors of the checkerboard, but there is no reason you couldn't choose different colors. I selected black for the first layer. Whatever color you decide upon, make the first layer the darker of the two.

Apply the paint in a light coat moving from side to side on the board. When that coat is dry (you can speed it along with a hair dryer), add a second coat of the same color, brushing in the perpendicular direction. This coat completes the first layer of paint.

Remove the tape from the borders. See those lines for the layout? Stretch the tape from end to end aligning it with the lines. Apply tape to every other section as shown. Rotate the board and add tape in the second direction as well.

Now you need to remove the tape from any areas where the tape is double layered. Align the rule or straightedge to the tape and use a utility knife to cut the tape on all four sides of each square that needs to be removed. Carefully peel away the tape to expose the black painted surface below. Each square will be two thicknesses of tape.

Attach each leg assembly to the bottom of the apron assembly using pocket screws.

Lay out the location for the stretchers and attach them to the legs.

Once the necessary areas are removed it is time to add paint. For this layer you need the second color and two coats will be needed to cover the exposed areas. Begin by brushing on one coat of paint moving from top to bottom. The second coat will be applied moving from side to side. This process provides better coverage. After the second layer is dry you can peel all remaining tape to expose the painted checkerboard.

To complete the painting you will need to apply tape around the outer edge of the checkerboard. The tape will be the barrier that will prohibit paint from touching the completed squares. I elected to paint a third color — one that will show favorably against the oak of the frame. You can also decide to allow the border to match the second color added to the checkerboard.

The completed board fits into the frame of the top. All that's left to complete the project is to apply paint to the base (I used black and added a layer of an oil/varnish finish for protection) and to apply two coats of Watco's Special Walnut finish to the oak.

Set this game table in your home and rekindle the past with a rousing game of checkers.

Measure and mark the game board itself, using the table frame as your guide.

To lay out the checker grid, start from the center and measure out. It's much easier.

After taping off the 1" border, a base coat of black paint is applied to the whole board.

Tape is first stuck down in one direction, skipping every other space. This pattern is repeated in the other direction, then the tape is trimmed and removed where doubled.

Two coats of red paint are then applied over all the exposed squares. Again, alternate directions between coats to hide brush strokes.

With the paint dry, the tape is removed, and the checkerboard pattern is revealed. I re-taped the board to add a third contrasting color to the bare wood border.

I used Danish Oil to finish the frame and painted the base black.

Harvesting a backyard cherry tree pays tribute to master woodworker and furniture designer George Nakashima.

PROJECT
24

Nakashima-inspired Table

BY STEVE SHANESY

Most of the lumber used by George Nakashima was sawn from the log under his supervision, stacked in the order in which it was cut, then stickered and left to air dry before kiln drying. At his disposal then were thousands of boards which were sawn "through and through," retaining each board's waney or "free" edge and unique shape. And because the logs were not sawn for grade, which is when the log is turned time and again during the sawing to avoid defects like knots and splits, these "defects" were

retained and often became an important feature in the use of the board.

Needless to say, most woodworkers don't have easy access to wood that has been processed this way. But I had the opportunity when a black cherry in my backyard fell prey to a hard, late frost and succumbed. Within a few weeks I engaged the operator of a Wood-Mizer portable band saw mill and had the log sawn where it fell. The going rate for this work is about 45 cents a board foot. About 18 months later, having stacked it carefully for air drying, I was ready to start working it. Now if you don't have access to lumber like this, you could always make a rectangular top.

From my boards I selected a shorter one that came from the top of the log where the tree began to branch. This area is referred to as a "crotch" and usually yields nicely figured material. But this part of tree also has a lot of stress in the lumber and often wants to split during drying. True to form, a wide check

occurred on the end. Never mind, I decided, I'll work with it. The grain was just too pretty to toss in the scrap box.

The 17"-wide board was also cupped starting at the heart's center. To flatten the board, even if I had a jointer or planer that wide, would have sacrificed too much thickness. However, sawing lengthwise along the heart, splitting the board in two, rendered two relatively flat pieces. It was at this point that I decided to the use an open spline detail of contrasting walnut to join the pieces back together. The decision made the technical necessity of splitting the boards an interesting design element.

After the top was separated I smoothed and flattened the pieces using a Performax 22"-wide belt sander. When done, I routed a $\frac{1}{2}$" × $\frac{5}{8}$"-deep groove in the edges to be joined, and then I cut a walnut spline that was $1\frac{7}{16}$" wide. That left a $\frac{3}{16}$" gap when the top was glued back together. Before gluing I used a block plane to make a slight chamfer on the top edges of the open joint.

Working the Free Edges

Needless to say, the bark had to be removed from the edges of the board down to the sap wood. With dry wood, the bark pops off quite easily. You can use just about any tool from a chisel to a screwdriver to knock or pry the bark off. Just be sure you don't gouge the surface you want to eventually display. To further prepare the rear edge of the top,

NAKASHIMA-INSPIRED TABLE • INCHES (MILLIMETERS)

QUANTITY	PART	STOCK	THICKNESS	(mm)	WIDTH	(mm)	LENGTH	(mm)	COMMENTS
1	top	cherry	1	25	25	635	43	1092	
2	panel ends	cherry	1	25	16	406	32	813	
4	panel build-up	cherry	$5/16$	8	3	76	32	813	
4	panel build-up	cherry	$5/16$	8	5	127	32	813	
2	leg	cherry	2	51	2	51	31	787	
1	beam	cherry	$2^7/8$	73	$23^7/8$	606	$32^1/2$	826	

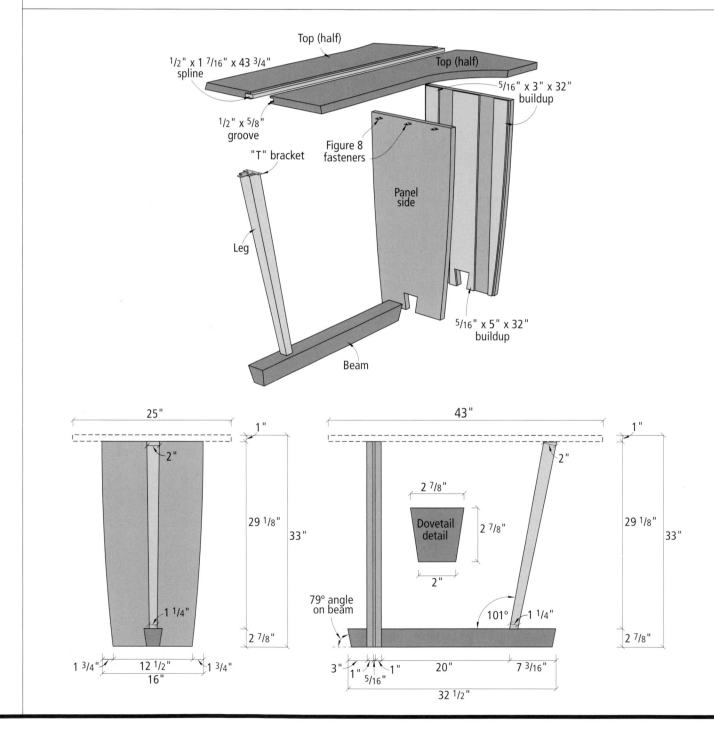

Mark the outline of the dovetail to be cut in the center of the bottom edge of the panel end using a trim piece of the actual beam. With the dovetail shape already cut on the beam, an accurate layout is assured.

Cut the dovetail sides using a saw without a back because the cut is nearly 3" deep. Also, make sure when starting the cut that the saw is properly aligned on both faces of the panel. Make the cut slowly until you've established the saw kerf following the layout line.

sand it by hand with 120-grit paper. On what I considered the front edge, I used a gouge to make small facets in the surface to give the edge a more interesting visual and tactile surface. Afterwards I sanded the edge lightly.

I moved on to the area of the big check on the end of the board. The inside surfaces of the crack were rough and needed smoothing. While I didn't want to make the edges look like a polished surface, neither did I want the torn fibers and rough surfaces. My solution was to use 100-grit C-weight sandpaper to get into the crack anyway possible. At this point, except for final sanding of the top and ends, the hardest part of the job was completed.

The Base

The base is very simple to construct, even easier than a conventional table with legs and aprons. A slab end, a dovetail shaped beam and a tapered, angled leg is all there is to it.

To make the slab end I started with two panels that were about an inch thick each. My plan was to glue them together as a sandwich with a $5/16$"-thick build up in the center that, when set back from the edge, created a reveal that mimicked the spline detail on the tabletop.

To do this, I first made a template of the gently curved convex taper for the slab edges. I then penciled the shape onto the individual pieces and cut the shapes on the band saw. Next, I used the panel's edge to transfer the shape to the build-up pieces to make the reveal. These were band sawn and the face edge cleaned up with a hand plane. I cut one additional piece of buildup to use in the center of the panel so that when cutting the through dovetail for the beam I'd have solid wood through and through.

Next I glued up the panels by first gluing and nailing the build-up to one piece, maintaining a $5/16$" setback at the edges, then gluing the second panel to it. I was careful not to apply too much

After sawing out the bulk of the waste with a coping saw, chisel the remaining waste. Make certain your cuts are perpendicular to the face. After cutting halfway down, turn the panel over and work from the other side to avoid tear out.

Each edge of the leg panel has a slight bevel detail that's made with a hand plane or a spokeshave.

The tapered leg is joined to the bottom beam with two ½" dowels. Although the spacing is tight, two dowels can be used. Use a doweling jig for alignment and, depending on placement, make sure you don't drill too deep.

glue to prevent a lot of squeeze-out in the reveal.

While the glue was drying I started making the hefty beam that ties the panel and leg together. I didn't have any stock thick enough to make the 3" × 3" blank size, so I glued up three pieces of 1" stock. After it dried I cleaned up and squared two opposing edges on the jointer then planed the remaining two. Next, I sawed the blank to the dovetail shape, sloping the sides to an 8° angle. At this point I sliced off a small piece of one end that served as a template for marking the cut to be made in the bottom edge of the panel.

After marking the centers of the template and panel bottom edge I cut the sloping slides of the dovetail using the ripping teeth of my Japanese pull saw. Next, I removed most of the waste

with a coping saw, then chiseled the edge flat. I found the fit of the beam just a bit tight so I pared the sides of the panel dovetail opening until achieving a fit that went together with just a slight amount of force. I then removed the beam and made the 11° bevel cuts on the ends. To complete the work on the panel I put a slight bevel on the panel edges. A hand plane was the tool of choice for this chore.

The leg that supports the other end of the table is simple enough to make. I started with a blank that was 2" square. I wanted the leg to taper from top to bottom so I penciled lines to follow on the band saw. After cutting, I cleaned up the edges with the jointer.

The leg cants at a 101° angle, so I chopped the bottom edge at 11°. To determine the length, I simply set the

leg on the beam with the bottom edge seated evenly and the side touching the top edge of the panel. I made the mark there and made the final 11° cut on the top of the leg.

The leg is joined to the beam using two ½" dowels. First I drilled dowel holes into the bottom of the leg; then, after inserting dowel centers, I marked the dowel locations in the beam. It then was a simple task to drill the holes.

To assemble the base I used polyurethane glue because of its superior bonding characteristics in gluing non-long-grain to long-grain joints. I first glued the beam to the panel making sure the beam and panel were square. After this dried, I finished up gluing the leg to the beam using a band clamp with a little assistance from a pipe clamp to maintain the desired angle.

Transfer the dowel hole locations using dowel centers. A slight tap on the top of the legs drives the center point of the dowel center into the beam. Then drill the holes.

To clamp the tapered leg in place, use a band clamp. The pipe clamp is essentially used to maintain the leg in the right position. The "T" bracket is later screwed to the top of the leg and is used to secure the leg to the underside of the top.

Fastening the top to the base was a snap. On the top edge of the panel end I used three figure-eight fasteners, setting them flush. For the leg, I used a common "T" shaped bracket that I screwed down to the top of the leg, then up into the top.

To finish, I sanded everything to 150 grit and broke all the sharp edges. Next I mixed equal amounts of Olympic brand Early American and Red Oak oil stain and combined seven teaspoons of this blend with a pint of boiled linseed oil. The diluted color won't blotch the cherry but will give the wood a nice color to start. Time will enrich the color more, encouraged by the linseed oil, which speeds the photochemical reaction that occurs naturally in cherry. After wiping away all excess oil, I let the pre-finish dry for two days. I completed the finish with a clear top coat of lacquer, although any clear coat will work fine.

I was quite pleased with the outcome of the table. Realizing this style may not be everyone's cup of tea, but I think most woodworkers would have to agree on one thing. Using the free edge of boards sawn straight off the log and showcasing "defects" in the lumber clearly celebrates the material we all enjoy using so much. It instantly reminds us of just where all the wonderful wood we use comes from.

If you can rout a mortise for a hinge,
you can handle the inlay on this table.

Federal Inlay Table

BY GLEN HUEY

This highly decorative table will test and improve your inlay skills. It is based on a Massachusetts piece from 1805 that displays many of the characteristics of cabinet makers from that area and period.

The finely turned legs with reeded detail lead up to a scalloped-edge tray. From there you move up past he exceptional figured panels toward the drawer front that boasts of mahogany crossbanding and band inlay that matches the top.

When you finish this table, not only will you have added to your inlay expertise, you will have created a piece that will be treasured to many generations to come.

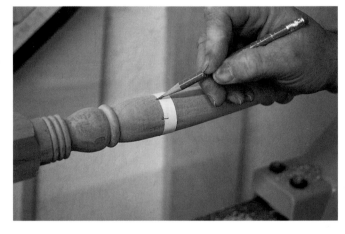

Turn the lower portion of the legs according to the plan. To create the reeds, wrap a strip of paper around the largest diameter and mark the overlap. Remove the paper, trim it to that mark, then lay out six equal spaces. Rewrap the paper in the same place and transfer the six marks to the turning.

How you cut the reeds on this project depends on the lathe you use. The jig I have is an L-shaped bracket that my trim router sets into. Adjust the point of the bit so it's at the center of the lathe's drive spur. Run the cut the length of the post, stopping before touching the bead at the top and bottom.

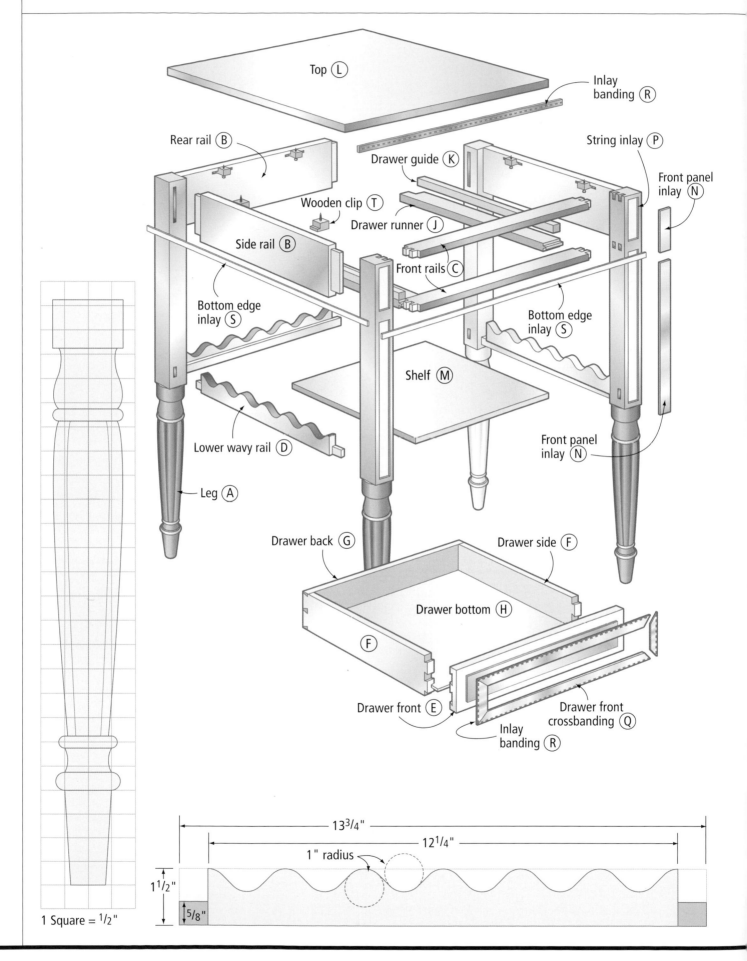

Top (L)

Inlay banding (R)

Rear rail (B)

Drawer guide (K)

String inlay (P)

Front panel inlay (N)

Wooden clip (T)

Drawer runner (J)

Side rail (B)

Front rails (C)

Bottom edge inlay (S)

Bottom edge inlay (S)

Shelf (M)

Lower wavy rail (D)

Front panel inlay (N)

Leg (A)

Drawer back (G)

Drawer side (F)

Drawer bottom (H)

F

F

Drawer front (E)

Inlay banding (R)

Drawer front crossbanding (Q)

1 Square = ¹/₂"

13³/₄"

12¹/₄"

1" radius

1¹/₂"

⁵/₈"

FEDERAL INLAY TABLE • INCHES (MILLIMETERS)

LETTER	QUANTITY	PART	STOCK	THICKNESS	(mm)	WIDTH	(mm)	LENGTH	(mm)	COMMENTS
A	4	legs	mahogany	1½	38	1½	38	27½	689	
B	3	side and rear rails	mahogany	¾	19	4¼	108	13¾	349	¾" TBE
C	2	front rails	mahogany	⅝	16	1½	38	13¾	349	¾" TBE
D	4	lower wavy rails	mahogany	½	13	1½	38	13¾	349	¾" TBE
E	1	drawer front	BE maple	⅞	22	3	76	12³⁄₁₆	310	
F	2	drawer sides	pine	⁷⁄₁₆	11	3	76	13⅝	346	
G	1	drawer back	pine	⁷⁄₁₆	11	2⅜	61	12³⁄₁₆	310	
H	1	drawer bottom	pine	½	13	11¾	298	13⅝	346	
J	2	drawer runners	pine	⅝	16	1⅝	41	13¼	336	⅜" TOE
K	2	drawer guides	pine	⅝	16	¾	19	12¼	311	
L	1	top	mahogany	¾	19	16½	419	16¾	425	
M	1	shelf	mahogany	½	13	14¾	375	14¾	375	
N	1	front panel inlay	BE maple	¾	19	4	102	24	610	
P		string inlay	ebony	⅛	3	⅛	3	7 LF	2134	
Q		drawer front crossbanding	mahogany	³⁄₁₆	5	¾	19	3 LF	914	
R		inlay banding				⁹⁄₃₂	7	5 LF	1524	drawer and top
S		bottom edge inlay	tiger maple	³⁄₁₆	5	¼	6	4 LF	1219	
T		wooden clips	pine	½	13	⅞	22	4	102	

TBE = tenon both ends; TOE = tenon both ends; LF = linear feet; BE = bird's eye

SUPPLIES

Rockler, rockler.com

2 - 36" traditional inlay banding, #18812

Horton Brasses, horton-brasses.com

2 - 1½"-dia. Sheraton antique-finish knobs

with bolt fitting, #H-46

Mark and cut the mortises for all the rails. Also, you can see the finished carving from the previous step.

To cut the tenons on the side and rear rails, first define the shoulders as shown, then come back and cut the cheeks.

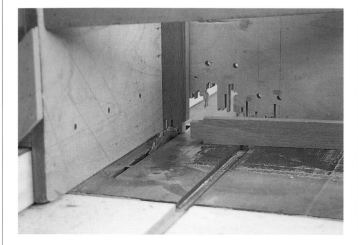

To create the twin tenon on the front rails, make the shoulder cut on the $5/8$" sides only. Using a tenoning jig, make the cheek cut for both edges and reset the jig to remove the waste between the tenons.

This is the finished twin mortise-and-tenon joint used for both front rails. Cut the mortises in the back edges of the bottom front rail to accept the drawer runner tenons.

For the wavy rails around the tray, begin with a $1/4$" cut on the face of the piece, then make a second cut on the opposite face with the fence set $1/2$" away from the blade.

Reset the fence to $1/4$", then raise the blade to remove the $7/8$" waste up to the second cut make. This produces an L-shaped profile.

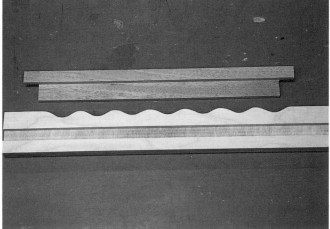

Make the cheek cut that leaves the necessary $1/4$"-thick × $3/4$"-long tenon on the ends of the lower rails.

Make a pattern of the wavy design with a piece of $1/4$" plywood. Cut a groove into the plywood so that the stock snugly fits into the groove.

Assemble the table in steps. First, glue the side rails to the legs, then, when dry, glue the front and rear rails. Before you assemble the rear rail, cut the slots for the wood clips near the ends of the piece. (See step 17.)

Fit the stock into the groove in the pattern, with the ends of the stock located at the top of a wave. With a ¼" beading bit set to the correct height, make the cut, creating the wavy design. You should make this a climb cut or move against the rotation of the bit.

Notch the corners of the shelf so it fits around the legs.

Mill the shelf to size and make a ¼" × ¼" rabbet on all edges. Slide the piece into the area, allowing the front edge to rest against the back side of the front legs. Mark where the edges of the leg meets the shelf. Repeat this process on all four sides of the shelf. When complete, extend the marks to form the area that needs to be removed so that the shelf fits between the legs.

Prepare the drawer runners and guides and make the tenon on one end of each runner. Remove the tenon at the front leg and cut a notch at the rear leg.

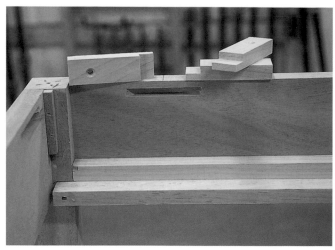

Glue the mortise and tenon, slide the runner into place, hold tightly to the front rail and nail into the rear post to secure. Glue and nail the drawer guide into place even with the two posts.

Use a biscuit joiner to cut the slots for the wooden clips. Set the cut to begin " down from the top edge. Cut a ¼" slot, Make the wooden clips for the top. Secure with No. 8 × 1" wood screws.

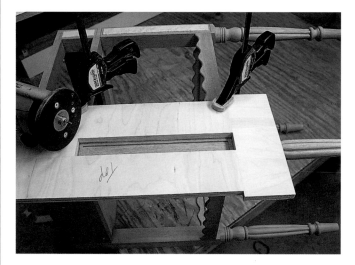

Make a template for cutting the inlay by using ¼"-thick plywood and biscuit joints. Compensate for your router's guide bushing when sizing the template. Mark the edges of the inlay template carefully.

Following the directions with the inlay kit, cut the material for each of the front panel inlay areas and glue in place.

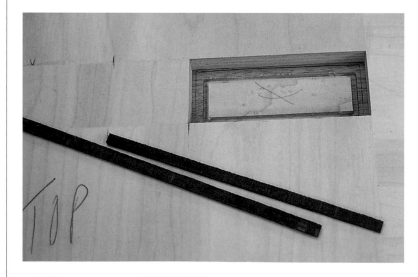

Place the template back at the layout marks created earlier. Carefully cut a ¼"-deep groove around each inlay for the ebony string inlay. Mill the string inlay to size and glue it down. When dry, sand the inlay smooth.

Cut a 1/8"-deep × 1/4"-wide groove on the front and both sides, even with the bottom edge of the rails. Cut an inlay of tiger maple to fill the groove and glue it in place. The front should overlap the sides to hide the end grain.

Begin building the drawer by laying out the dovetails on the drawer front. Cut the lines down to a line scribed 7/16" from the inside of the drawer front. Over cut toward the center of the interior face of the front. A front this size has two full tails, one pin and two half pins.

Using a Forstner bit, cut away some of the waste, then clean the area with your chisels.

Set the front onto a side piece with the inside even with a line scribed 7/16" from the end of the side and mark with a sharp pencil. Remove the waste area with the chisel and test the fit.

Lay out the back piece so there are two full pins and one half pin at the top. Cut those pins, removing the area of the tails. Set the back onto the side and transfer the marks from the back to the sides and shown. Then remove the waste, leaving the tails.

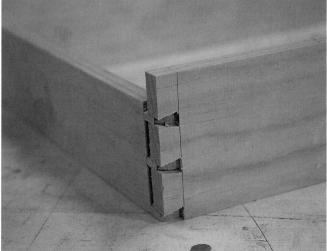

This is how the side tails fit into the drawer back's pins.

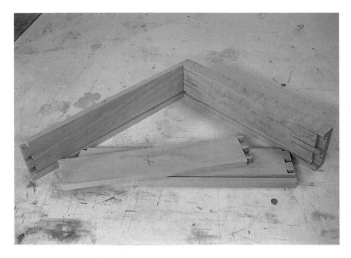

With the dovetails complete, cut a ¼" groove that is half the thickness of the drawer sides for the bottom.

Cut the drawer bottom to size so the grain runs across the drawer and bevel three edges — the two end-grain ends and one other edge — to fit the groove. Make a ⅛" cut into the drawer bottom, just to the inside edge of the back piece.

With the drawer apart, set the saw blade's height to ¾" and cut a rabbet in the front on all sides, creating the shoulder for the crossbanding.

Cut the crossbanding on the band saw, noticing the grain direction, and fit to the drawer front with mitered corners. Use cyanoacrylate glue to bond the banding to the drawer face.

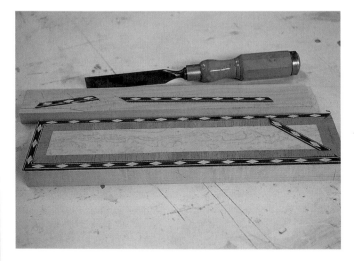

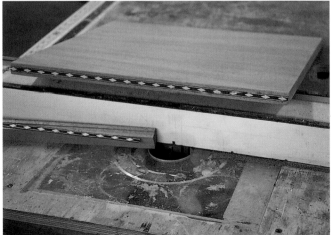

Repeat the process to install the decorative banding.

Using a ⁵/₁₆" straight-cut bit in the router table, run the front edge of the top, creating the groove for the decorative inlay. Glue the strip in place.

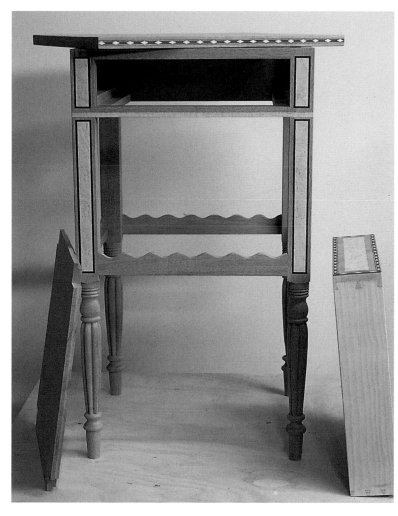

Tip: To set the depth of the biscuit joiner, cut a scrap to the thickness necessary, set the piece against the blade that is extended, then bring the fence tight to that scrap. Make sure the tool is unplugged!

Sand the table completely, then you're ready to finish. The finish I use is an oil/varnish mixture. Three to four coats give a good sheen and protection. Then a coat of past wax seals the deal.

Install the knobs by drilling the location with a $3/32$" bit through the front. On the inside of the drawer front, drill a $5/8$" hole $1/2$" deep using a Forstner bit to recess the nut on the inside. Complete the process by redrilling the first hole using a $3/16$" bit. Cut the know shaft to size and attach the knob.

Learn inlay techniques while building this beautiful accent table for your home.

PROJECT
26

Baltimore Card Table

BY GLENN HUEY

A beautiful demilune side table always catches your eye. Some of these tables also open into an equally attractive and more functional four-legged round table. The table here is a inspired by an original attributed to Levin S. Tarr (1772-1821) and built between 1795-1810 in Baltimore, Md. The original is now part of the Colonial Williamsburg Collection of Southern Furniture in Williamsburg, Va.

The ornamentation on card tables from Baltimore varies quite a bit, but the construction details and design are consistent. Tarr's table has all the construction details common to post-revolutionary Baltimore card tables. These features include the half-round shape, a laminated apron, two rear swing legs that overlap the ends of the front rail when closed and a dovetailed rear apron. Oak and/or yellow pine are the secondary woods used in construction.

On my table, the inlay has been simplified and some of the inlay was purchased rather than hand-fit, as in the original. This saved time without affecting the overall grace of the piece.

Because of the detail involved in this table I've focused on the inlay work and swing legs.

A comfortable level with basic woodworking skills is advised for building this piece.

Shaping the Apron

The apron, which is built up using rows of pine blocks, is a detail faithful to the original. It's a stable way to make an accurate curved shape. Begin by cutting a half-circle template from a piece of $\frac{3}{4}$"-thick medium density fiberboard (MDF) that's 18" × 34". The finished diameter of the template is $33\frac{1}{2}$". To make the circular cut I used an auxiliary table that clamps to my band saw's table. This setup lets me insert a $\frac{1}{4}$"-diameter guide dowel at $16\frac{3}{4}$" from the blade.

A matching diameter hole is made in the MDF board centered on one long edge and set in $\frac{3}{4}$". This allows the hole to not be precisely at the back edge. The resulting shape will be larger in circumference than a half-circle, which is fine. Save the falloff pieces for later in the project.

Now divide the template into 10 pie-shaped wedges to help align the pine blocks. To lay out the wedges, start with a line at the pivot point running parallel to the back edge. Then get your protractor out and divide the top into 18° sections. You should end up with a center line perpendicular from your base line.

Next, cut your pieces of yellow pine to size and trim the ends at 9°. The $1\frac{3}{8}$" dimension is the height of the blocks. The blocks are located on the template with the center of the block flush to the edge of the template. Glue the pine blocks onto the template around the outer edge.

When the glue on this first row has dried, use a bearing-guided flush-trim router bit to sculpt the front face of the blocks to the template. Then repeat the process with the second row of yellow pine blocks (staggering their location) and rout the face again. Repeat the steps for the third row.

With the bricking complete and the outside curve routed, carry the line from the template that marks the back edge of your apron (the true half-circle location) up the sides of the apron. Then move back to the band saw and reposition your center pin to $15\frac{5}{8}$" from the blade to shape the rear surface of the apron.

Next, head to the table saw and carefully make two cuts. The first is to separate the apron from the strip of MDF template still attached. The second is to rip the apron to its 4" width.

Then clamp the apron to the miter saw so that you can make 90° cuts exactly at the lines marking the back edge of the apron.

Making the Apron a Frame

To join the curved front apron into the frame of the table, the rear apron is dovetailed to the curved front apron at both ends. Lay out the dovetail pins on the just-cut ends of the front apron. Define the pins with a backsaw and remove the waste material, keeping the bottom of each tail area at a right angle to the apron end. Transfer the pin layout onto the rear apron and cut the tails. Once fit, glue it in place.

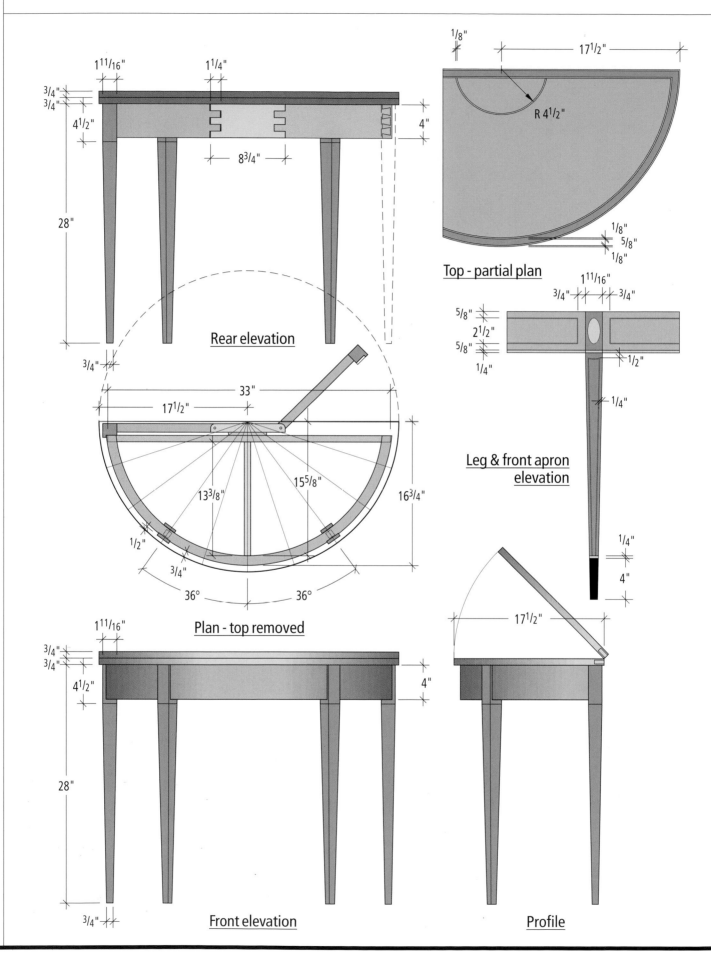

Rear elevation

Top - partial plan

Leg & front apron
elevation

Plan - top removed

Front elevation

Profile

BALTIMORE CARD TABLE • INCHES (MILLIMETERS)

QUANTITY	PART	STOCK	THICKNESS	(mm)	WIDTH	(mm)	LENGTH	(mm)	COMMENTS
32	blocking pieces	yellow pine	1 3/8	35	1 1/2	38	5 3/16	132	
1	rear apron	poplar	3/4	19	4	102	33	838	dovetails BE
4	legs	mahogany	1 11/16	443	1 11/16	443	28	711	
1	medial stretcher	poplar	3/4	19	4	102	13 3/8	340	
1	fixed rear rail	poplar	1	25	4	102	8 3/4	222	
2	swing rails	poplar	1	25	4	102	14	356	cut to fit
1	swing rail spacer	poplar	3/8	10	4	102	5 1/2	140	
2	tops	mahogany	3/4	19	18	457	36	914	half round
2	legs string inlay	maple	1 1/2	38	1/16	2	24	610	shop-made
2	cuff inlay	maple	1/4	6	1/8	3	24	610	shop-made
2	top edge inlay	maple	1 1/2	38	1/8	3	36	914	shop-made
1	top stringing	maple	1 1/2	38	1/8	3	36	914	shop-made
1	veneer inlay	madrone burl			8	203	10	254	
10	table top clips	poplar	3/4	19	7/8	22	2 1/2	64	

BE = both ends

SUPPLIES

ROCKLER

rockler.com

2 - oval inlays 1 1/4" × 2 1/2" No. 18440

1 - mahogany veneer, 36" × 96" No. 13953

1 - inlay bushing and bit No. 83642

DOVER INLAY MFG. CO.

doverinlay.com

1 - apron banding, 1/16" × 1/4" No. 356

LONDONDERRY BRASSES LTD.

610-593-6239 or

londonderry-brasses.com

2 - card table hinges No. H-34

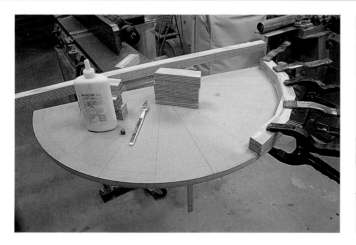

I have oriented the grain on the blocks so the quartersawn edge is to the front. This helps reduce the movement of the face when complete.

Make your first cut to remove the template piece. Hold the apron as tight as possible against the fence during this step. Then reset the fence to the finished height of the apron, rotate the piece to the opposite edge and make your second cut.

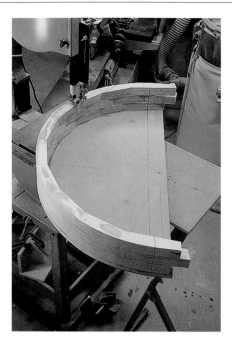

To trim the ends of the apron, patience and accuracy are required. I clamped the apron to my miter saw, carefully checking the squareness of the end mark to the blade before making the cut.

Set the template and bricking onto the guide pin and make a slow, steady cut using a ½" skip-tooth blade. The resulting apron thickness is slightly over 1" thick, completing the curved apron.

Finally, cut a medial stretcher that fits snugly between the rear and front aprons. Attach the stretcher with screws and plug the front screw holes.

The front legs have a bridle joint at the top that straddles the front apron. To add strength, the bridle joint also slips into a dado cut in the face of the apron.

I used a template to locate the front leg dado in the apron. The center of the legs actually falls on the 36° arc from the center of the top, where the first level of bricking was laid. Place the template (shown above) into position and clamp, making sure that the inside edges are tight to the apron. Use a dado or planer router bit with a top-mounted bearing to cut away the material to a depth of ³⁄₈" in the apron. Do this in both front leg locations.

Tapering the Legs

To make the tapered legs, first rough cut the lumber to size. I prefer using the jointer to taper the legs. It gives me nearly identical tapers on all the pieces.

Draw a line on each leg 4½" down from the top. Draw a second line at the center point of the total length of the

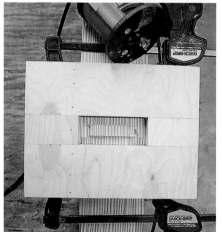

I make my routing template using ½" Baltic birch plywood. Rather than cut out and clean up a hole, I make my template from four pieces and hold them together with biscuits. This method leaves an accurate opening that is 1⁵⁄₈" wide x 4" long.

taper, measuring up from the foot. Set the jointer to cut at a depth of ³⁄₁₆". Then run each face of each leg flat on the jointer starting at the foot. Stop the cut at the half-way mark, carefully lifting the leg from the knives.

Flip the leg end-for-end and take a second pass on each side by holding the foot and the stop point of the first cut flat on the infeed table. This will cause the top of the leg to "pop a wheelie" over the knives and start the tapering cut at the 4½" mark.

Mounting the Legs

Select the legs that will be the front legs and lay out the area to create the bridle joint to attach the legs to the apron. Measure down 4" from the top of the leg and ⁵⁄₈" from the front face. Remove about ⁹⁄₁₆", leaving about ½" at the rear of the leg. You'll need to fit this notch to

your apron making several cuts at the band saw and finishing with sharp chisel.

The rear legs attach to the swing rails with the more traditional mortise-and-tenon joint. Cut the ¼" × 3" × 1"-deep mortises on the inner face of each of the rear legs.

Preparing the Leg Inlay

The inlay work on this table starts on the legs. Using the miter gauge on your table saw, make a cradle that will hold each leg in position and level to the table saw top. Install a dado blade to cut the ¼"-wide × ⅛"-deep dado for the cuff starting 4" up from the foot of each leg. Cut all four sides of all four legs.

The next inlay to prepare for is the banding that runs across the front of the front legs, on the outside face of the rear legs and along the bottom edge of the apron.

To cut the recess for the banding on the legs, load a ¼" straight router bit into the router table. Set the fence 3¾" from the bit and set the bit height for ¹⁄₁₆". Make the cut. Because the leg tapers just below the cut, it's important to keep the face side flat against the table during the cut.

The next step is to cut the string inlay groove along the length of the legs as shown in the photo above right. For the scalloped stringing at the tops of the legs make a simple arched pattern that will act as a guide for your router bushing, as shown above. It's a good idea to mark the beginning and ending edges of the router base for reference.

Cut and install the stringing. I cut the necessary thickness at the table saw and ripped the width at the band saw. It helps to install a zero-clearance throat plate at the band saw. Add the glue spar-

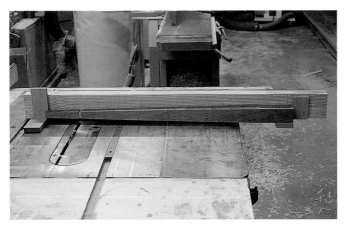

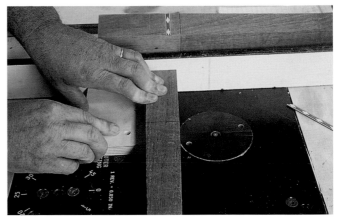

My miter gauge cradle isn't fancy, but it is accurate. It needs to hold the centerline of the leg parallel to the saw table during the cut. Don't worry about how high off the table the cradle holds the leg. Adjusting the blade height will set the cut's depth perfectly.

Holding the top of the leg against the fence and the face side toward the table (remember that the face side of the rear or back legs is the side facing outward, opposite of the mortise) make a pass over the bit, cutting the thickness of your inlay.

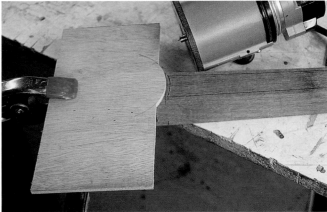

Install a 1/16" bit in the router table and set the fence 1/4" from the bit. Set the bit to cut 1/8" deep. Run the cut on two edges of the face, from the 4 1/2" line at the top of the leg into the area that was cut for the cuff.

Start the scalloped stringing cut by inserting the bit into one side of the existing cut and move toward the opposite side until it just enters the second side cut. Keep the bushing against the pattern.

ingly into the cut, start the stringing at the top, and gently force it into position. Sometimes I use a larger piece of dowel as a rolling pin to help. Also, cut and fit the 1/4"-wide and 3/16"-thick cuff. I like to miter its corners for appearance.

Oval Inlay

The last inlay pieces are the two ovals at the top of the front legs. You need to build a simple three-piece U-shaped cradle that will hold the leg steady. Another piece of plywood is cut out for the oval pattern and makes a fourth side to create a box. Use an inlay bushing and bit (I've included information on one in the Supplies box on page 73) to cut the oval inlay recesses on the legs.

The cradle supports the leg from underneath. The top piece with the oval template is clamped to the box, centering the cut between the top of the leg and the lower edge of the apron as well as the middle of the leg. Note that the orange-handled clamp serves to keep the leg positioned lengthwise in the cradle.

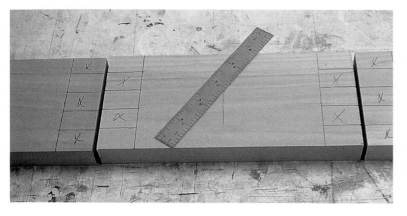

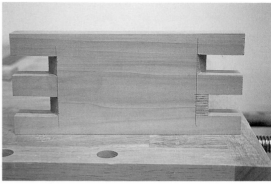

To mark out the knuckle spacing, set one end of a ruler (at zero) on one side of the board and set the 5" mark on the opposite edge of the board. Then transfer each of the inch marks to both ends of the center rail and one end of each swing section.

To allow enough room for the swing rails to open, on the back side of the center rail draw a line ¾" behind the shoulder cut at the saw. With a hand saw cut small cuts to that line while maintaining the front edge shoulder. With the cuts made, chisel away the waste.

With the length of the two swing legs determined (¼" beyond the apron corner) you're ready to lay out the tenon location on the end of each piece. Then cut the tenons and the corresponding mortises in the legs.

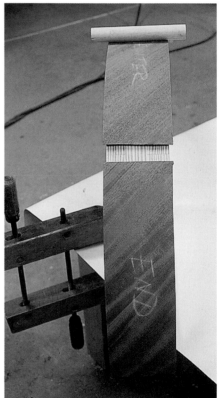

To trim the purchased oval inlay to fit the leg recess, use double-stick tape to attach the inlay onto a scrap piece of wood. Place the same pattern used to cut the recess into position over the inlay and again, using the inlay kit as directed, cut the inlay to match.

Carefully remove the cut piece of inlay from the scrap, apply the glue and install. Place a piece of wax paper over the inlay, then cut a small oval scrap to act as a press over the wax paper and inlay. Clamp the scrap in place over the inlay until the glue dries.

Knuckle-joint Legs

The knuckle joint at the rear of the table is one of the magical parts of this project. While closed, the table looks like a solid demilune table. The knuckle joints and swing legs allow the table to open into a stable, full-size table.

Begin the twin knuckle joints by cutting the three pieces to size that create the mechanism. Scribe a line 1¼" in from the ends, and begin by laying out five equal spaces. Mark the blocks as shown to designate the waste areas. Mark the top edge of all three pieces to ensure they go back in position.

With the oversized veneer panels you should not have trouble placing the veneer panels on the apron. Make sure to roll the panels to smooth any small air bubbles. I use a section of dowel rod for this step.

At the table saw set the blade height to the 1¼" line and make the cuts that define the joint's fingers. Cut on the waste side of the line and nibble away the waste.

With the fingers all cut, the fixed rear rail needs to have 45° back-cuts made in

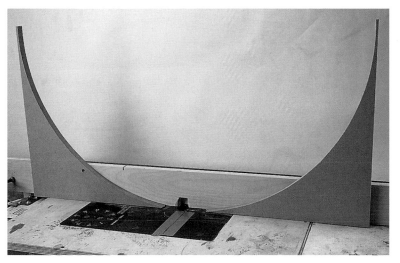

To rout the grooves for the apron stringing, attach the template scraps to a sacrificial fence on your router table. Attach them so that the apron just fits inside the pair. Install a $^1/_{16}$" straight bit set to an $^1/_8$" height and mark both sides of the bit width on a piece of tape that extends about 5" from the bit. Mark a line that is $^3/_4$" from each end of all the panels of the apron. Set the fence $^5/_8$" from the bit and you're ready to rout.

After marking the legs at the meeting point of the apron, remove the legs from the swing rail. Use a router and straight-cutting bit to remove as much of the material as possible. Don't cut past the lines. Finish up any remaining material with a sharp chisel.

With the template secured, install a $^5/_8$" straight-cutting bit with a $^3/_4$"-outside diameter bushing into the router and remove waste material to create the recess for the edge banding.

To cut the veneer sections, simply make a first cut on the end of the veneer strip, then slide the veneer out about an $1^1/_4$" and make a second pass. This creates the first piece of edge band veneer. You will need 22 or more pieces of this curved edge banding.

This is the edge of the table that everyone will look at, so take your time fitting the veneer sections. Hold each piece in place after fitting to accurately match the next piece to it.

the notches to allow the fingers on the swing rails to open correctly.

Round the outside edge of the fixed rail and the inside edges of the swing rails. I used a quarter to draw the circle and rounded over the edge with the sander.

Position the pieces into place against a tall straight fence on your drill press leaving a small space between the ends of each set of fingers. Use a $^3/_{16}$"-diameter drill bit to drill for the steel-rod hinge. The hole should be $^3/_8$" from the

end of the fingers and $^1/_2$" in from the outer edge.

To determine the final length of the two swing legs, clamp the knuckle assembly to the rear apron, and mark and cut each swing leg $^1/_4$" longer than the apron corner at each end. This is the outside edge of the leg. Then lay out the tenon for joining the swing rails to the rear legs.

With the mortise and tenons made on the swing rails and legs, add the swing-rail spacer centered on the inside

face of the fixed rail with glue and brads. Set this assembled section aside for now. Don't attach the legs to the swing rails or the knuckle assembly to the table yet, there's still some work to do on the apron section.

Apron Veneer

Now it's time to veneer. The front of the apron is veneered from a single sheet of mahogany veneer. I followed the pattern on the antique table and oriented the grain at 45°. Roll out the veneer and

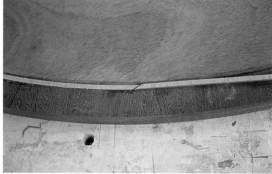

To cut the string inlay on the top, install an $\frac{1}{8}$" bit and the bushing from an inlay kit without the additional spacer, and run the groove guided by the top template that's still in place. This groove runs around the entire top edge.

Clamp this template in place, and follow the direction on the inlay kit to cut the area and the matching inlay.

mark the three pieces on a 45° angle. I made the panels $\frac{1}{2}$" oversized to allow for trimming. Lay out and cut the panels for the apron with a utility knife.

Apply a generous amount of contact cement on the apron and panels. When the cement is ready, carefully place the panels onto the apron. Use a flush-trim router bit to trim the edges of the veneer. To help make a clean cut, work in the direction of the veneer grain. Carefully trim the ends with a straightedge and a sharp knife.

Apron Stringing
To cut the recesses for the stringing on the apron faces I used the scrap pieces from the MDF apron template to set up a jig on the router table, which should still be set up for the stringing on the legs.

With the jig in place (see photo, next page), plunge the apron onto the bit and spin the assembly in the jig to the opposite line. Repeat this process on each panel. Reposition the fence to $3\frac{1}{8}$" and make the same cuts, creating the string inlay line for the bottom of the apron.

To complete the work using this jig, install a $\frac{1}{4}$" straight bit, reposition the fence and cut the bottom edge of the apron for the banding inlay.

Next it's back to freehand routing to connect the recesses you just cut. Install the $\frac{1}{16}$" bit into a trim router along with a small bushing to act as a pilot. Clamp

a straightedge into position that's long enough to allow the bit to begin in one of the string lines. I mark the edges of the router base plate to help me with this cut.

Using contact cement, install the banding along the bottom edge of the apron. The banding I've listed in the Supplies was somewhat expensive and there are alternatives available from Rockler for significantly less.

Cut to size and fit the shop-made string inlay using wood glue. Here you will need to take your time to install the inlay. A little glue goes a long way in that small line. Roll the inlay into the groove with a section of dowel.

With everything dry and set, carefully use a scraper to bring the inlay flush to the veneer surface.

Fitting the Legs
Assemble and clamp in place the swing leg assembly, then pull the rear legs tight to the apron while leveling the top edge, and mark the area on the leg that is to be cut away to a depth of a $\frac{1}{4}$". I used a router to remove the waste. Then glue the legs to the swing rails and attach these to the table.

Now make the final connection of the front legs. Add glue to all surfaces of the bridle joint, clamp in place until set, then finish with a #12 × $1\frac{1}{4}$" wood screw from the inside of the leg.

Cut and fit glue blocks into the corners of the table. These will need to be cut on a slight angle to ensure a secure fit.

The Top & More Details
Set up and cut the half-round pieces for the tops at the band saw as you did the template in the first step. Cut the top halves oversized by placing the pivot hole at $17\frac{3}{4}$" back from the front edge of the top and centered in from side to side. The pin on your circle-cutting jig should also be at $17\frac{3}{4}$".

To begin the detail work on the top, first create a half-circle template guide to rout the recess for the edge banding. The template is made the same way you cut the top pieces. Start with a 17" × 35" blank and use a $16\frac{7}{8}$" location on the pin. Once the template is cut to half round, it's necessary to cut the back edge to achieve the $\frac{7}{8}$" area at the rear of the top. The goal here is to have a $\frac{7}{8}$" setback showing on all sides of the top once the template is in place.

Attach the template with double-stick tape at the edges of the tops and two screws (located in the area that is to be covered with a veneer inlay). You're now ready to rout the recess for the veneer.

Use patience to set the depth of cut to the veneer thickness. This has to be worked in a couple passes. Be sure to keep one pass with the $\frac{3}{4}$" OD bushing tight against the template. Leave the

Here I have changed the bearing on a flush-trim bit to allow for a ¹⁄₁₆" cut. You need to run the top and bottom of both the top and the sub-top.

The hinge I used allows the joint to remain loose when moving. This gives the joint space to move without rubbing the two parts of the top together.

template in place (we'll need it again shortly).

To ensure the edge banding will accurately follow the curve of the top, you need to make another jig and head back to the band saw.

Start with a scrap piece of plywood that is 4½" wide and 18" long. Locate a pin hole at one end, place the circle-cutting jig pin in the 16⅞" hole, then make a swing cut on the piece, creating a small radius on the jig.

Next, with strips of veneer cut to 4", lay one strip onto the plywood, lay a second piece of plywood on top of that to keep things flat, and with the veneer extended, make a pass on the end (see photo at center left).

To trim the veneer pieces, use a sharp utility knife and straightedge to match up the edge of the cross banding while fitting the pieces to the top. Work around the entire top and number the pieces as they are fit. Remove the pieces and apply the contact cement. When ready, carefully apply the edge band to the top. Press the pieces for a tight fit. Allow the adhesive to dry, then trim the veneer flush to the outside edge with your router.

Stringing and More Inlay

To complete the inlay work on the top there are more string inlays and another veneer insert. Start with the string inlay

that separates the veneer edge banding you just attached from the main top (see photo above left). When you need to join two pieces of the stringing, do so with a scarf joint, as shown.

Move to the back edge of the top. Remove the top template, then make a 9"-diameter template for the inner inlay (seen only with the top closed). Because we need to re-install this template I mark the center line of the template and a corresponding line on the top.

The inlay piece was made from a section of madrone burl veneer that I had in my shop, again using the template bushing kit. Glue the inlay into position and when dry, replace the template and cut a groove around the inlay for another band of string inlay.

With all the grooves cut it's time to make the stringing and install the pieces in the top. Remember, a snug fit is required on the stringing. Because of the tight radius of the inner circle, it may be necessary to dampen the stringing before installing. Leave it in the groove to dry. It will hold its shape when dry.

All that's left is creating the final bit of stringing on the top's edge. Create the shop-made stringing for the edge and install this with the contact cement. When dry, scrape and sand all the inlay flush with the top.

Completing the Top

The installation of the hinges is all hand work. Lay out the location and hinge shape, and cut the area with chisels.

To attach the top to the base I use a ¼" three-wing slot cutter bit in the router table to make the slots in the apron. I then use wooden clips to attach the top. Space them equally along the front and rear, and place a few along the medial stretcher. The cut should be a ½" down from the apron edge.

Make the wooden clips, which are ¾" thick × ⅞" wide × 2¼" long. Rabbet one end to fit into the grooves and install using #8 × 1¼" slot-head wood screws. Final sand the entire table and you're ready to finish.

The finish begins with black paint. Place tape at the lower edge of the cuff inlay and paint two light coats of acrylic latex paint on the foot of the legs. This will create the ebonized look. Once the paint has dried, apply two coats of blonde shellac, a coat of dark brown glaze and finish with three additional coats of shellac. Let the shellac dry and hand rub the table to a satin finish with steel wool and wool lube. Then apply a few coats of paste wax.

Whether you build this table with or without the inlay details, you should be very pleased with the beauty — and function — of this Southern furniture classic.

Born on a bayou, this sought-after American table is spiced with both French and Canadian influences.

PROJECT
27

Creole Table

BY CHRISTOPHER SCHWARZ

Until recently, Creole-style furniture was a bit obscure, known mostly to a handful of furniture collectors who specialized in pieces made in the Mississippi valley.

But that's changing.

The original version of this 18th-century walnut table sold for $54,625 at a 2003 auction. And other Creole pieces, such as armoires, are commanding prices up to $140,000.

So what is the Creole style? Essentially, Creole encompasses furniture made in the Mississippi valley by furniture makers who were usually French-Canadian. The pieces have lots of French touches, such as cabriole legs, but also have the unmistakable restraint of early American furniture that collectors seek.

This table, for example, looks quite a bit like drawings of 18th-century French furniture from Denis Diderot's "L'Encyclopedie ou Dictionnaire Raisonné" (1751-1780) — but without the banding, inlay, carving and marquetry.

I first saw this table in the magazine Early American Life and was completely enamored. Our project illustrator, John Hutchinson, took a photograph and produced the construction drawings. And 37 hours of shop-time later, this is the result.

How the Carcase Works

At its heart, the Creole table is a typical apron table, with only a few surprises in its construction: The four aprons are secured to the legs with mortise-and-tenon joints, and reinforced with triangular corner blocks.

The dovetailed drawer slides in and out on a classic web frame. The top is attached to the base with screws driven up through the corner blocks.

Hanging on those classic bones are a few shapely French curves. The sinuous legs and the scalloped aprons make the table appear difficult to build, but it's not the curves that will trip you up. If you prepare your patterns with care, the curves will come easily; the real challenge is the overall fit of the parts — but isn't that always true?

Making Patterns

When conquering any complex shape, such as the scalloped aprons, making a template for pattern-routing is a good idea.

There are two patterns for the aprons: One for the side aprons and one for both the front and back. The pattern for the front and back aprons is a mirror image of the left and right sides of the apron. After marking, cutting and routing one end of the apron, you flip the pattern over to do the same to the other end of the apron.

Make your patterns using the drawings or downloadable plans from our web site (click on Magazine Extras to find them).

Putting the Patterns to Work

Begin construction by shaping the legs. This style of cabriole legs has good points and bad. Good: The shape is simple and easy to cut and smooth. Bad: The legs curve toward the inside of the table. This means that you will have to cut the mortises in the legs after you roughly shape things.

I tried different ways to go about this and the following is the least awkward method. Begin by taking the stock for your legs and cutting one long edge so it

CREOLE TABLE • INCHES (MILLIMETERS)

QUANTITY	PART	STOCK	THICKNESS	(mm)	WIDTH	(mm)	LENGTH	(mm)	COMMENTS
4	legs	walnut	2¼*	57	2¼*	57	29	737	
2	long aprons	walnut	⅝	16	8*	102	32	813	¾ TBE
2	short aprons	walnut	⅝	16	7*	178	16½	419	¾ TBE
1	top	walnut	¾	19	20¾	527	36¼	921	
4	corner blocks	walnut	⅝	16	3⅜	86	3⅜	86	
2	web frame stiles	poplar	⅝	16	2¼	57	16⅜	416	
2	web frame rails	poplar	⅝	16	2¼	57	14¾	375	¾ TBE
2	web frame cleats	poplar	⅝	16	⅝	16	13¼	337	
1	drawer kicker	poplar	¾	19	2½	64	16⅜	416	
1	drawer runners	poplar	⅝	16	⅝	16	16⅜	416	
1	drawer	walnut/poplar	3¼	83	15½	394	17	432	

* Slightly oversized to allow for trimming; TBE = Tenon Both Ends

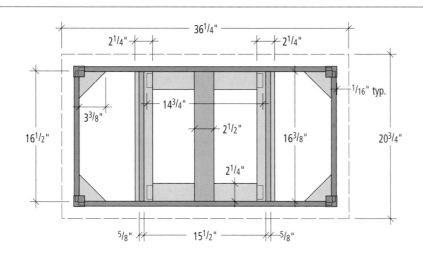

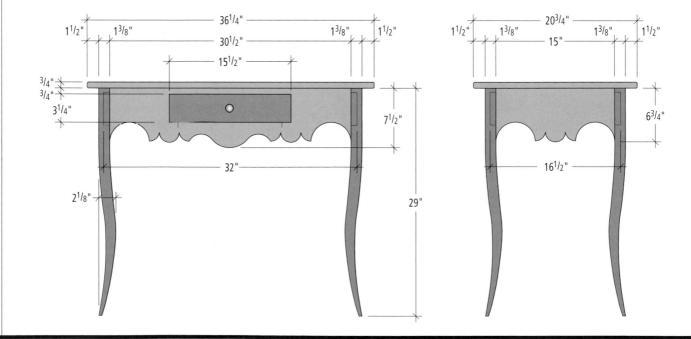

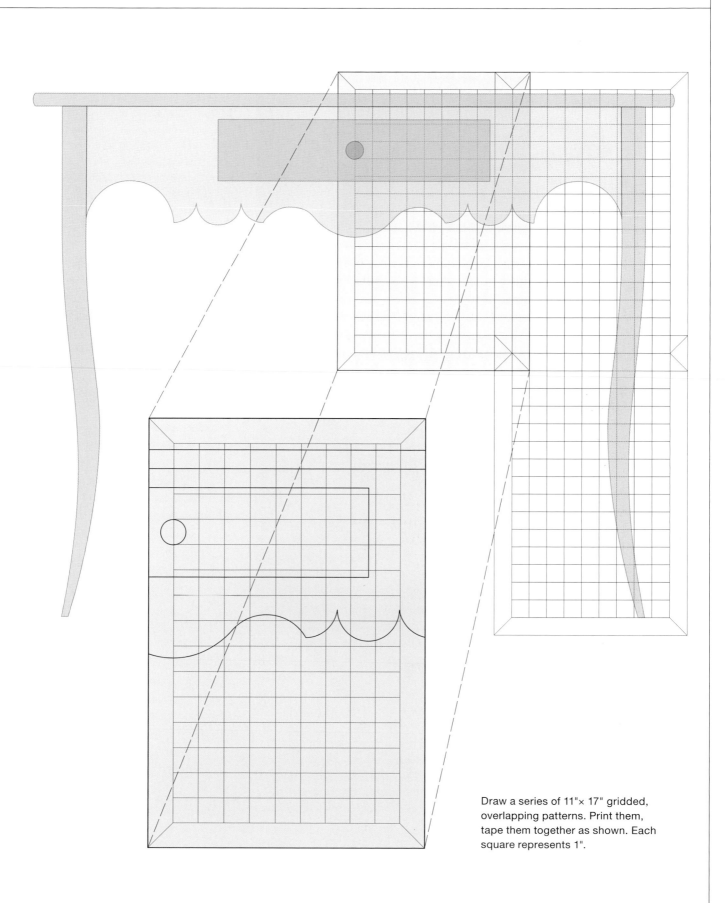

Draw a series of 11"× 17" gridded, overlapping patterns. Print them, tape them together as shown. Each square represents 1".

You can use the scaled drawings to create your own paper patterns, or you can download the patterns from our web site.

Marking walnut is a challenge. After trying a variety of pens, the best was a white ink pen available from an art supply store. The Sakura Pen-touch (gellyroll.com), costs about $2.50. Here's a tip about its tip: A light touch will give you a fine line.

Stop-cuts on the table saw are not my favorite thing. You have to raise the blade all the way to get a cut that ends close to vertical. I have our basket guard raised up here and the saw turned off to show my setup. Use a mark on your fence and the work to indicate when to stop cutting. And don't pull the work back out of a running saw. Turn off the saw.

parallels the grain of the board. Rip out your four leg pieces.

Mark the shape of the cabriole on two faces of each leg. It helps to bundle the four legs as you make these marks, slashing your chance for a disastrous error.

You could band saw out these leg shapes directly, but you would be in for a bit of fussing when you joined the aprons to the legs. That's because the straight surfaces of the legs where the aprons attach are now buried inside your leg blanks. Band saw them out and you'll have a difficult time truing up that surface for joinery.

Don't get me wrong, it's do-able. I made two practice legs this way to try it. A block plane and a try square are all you need, but it's a fussy job. So I made another pair of legs by cutting the straight sections with a table saw. This involves stop cuts: You rip the leg to a certain point and then turn the saw off.

This works quite well.

With the stop cuts complete, remove the rest of the waste with a hand saw or your band saw.

Now cut your mortises on the legs because they are still easy to manage with their long straight edges and faces. I used a ¼" hollow-chisel mortising bit in a mortiser, which is appropriate for the ⅝"-thick aprons. The aprons' tenons are ¼" thick, ¾" long and 3" wide. So start making your mortises 1" from the top of the leg. Set the fence so the apron will set back ¹⁄₁₆" from the legs.

More Nerve Than Skill

Many woodworkers are spooked by cabriole legs. Cabrioles appear daunting because of the curves and the compound shape. Here's the truth: Cutting cabriole legs is easy. Designing a nice-looking leg is hard.

If your band saw blade is sharp and well-tensioned (we like a ¼" skip-tooth blade), the work is easy. Cut the pattern on one face of your leg. Tape the fall-off pieces back in place. Rotate the leg 90° and cut that pattern. Remove the tape and voilà — you're halfway home.

The second half of a cabriole leg — shaping the sawn surface into something sinuous — is easy with the right tool.

Cutting Cabriole Legs

STEP TWO: Turn the leg 90° and cut the same pattern on an adjacent face of the leg. The pieces will begin to fall away as you work, revealing the shape within. It's a bit like sculpture.

STEP ONE: Cut the pattern on one face of the leg (top photo). Save the fall-off pieces (left) and tape them back together (right). Note how I split the white line. Luckily, this is simple because the white line left by the paint pen I used is fairly wide.

Recently I was turned onto a simple and inexpensive tool that is ideal for the job.

Glen Huey, senior editor, convinced me to try out the Shinto Saw-Rasp. It is, in essence, a bunch of hacksaw blades riveted together into a boat-shaped tool. One side is coarse and the other is fine. You can buy this tool with or without a handle. It is a nimble tool and is easy to master, much like a high-quality rasp.

I removed the saw marks from the legs with the Shinto's coarse side and then smoothed things up with the smooth side. After some work with a card scraper, the legs were ready to

finish. I had planned on spending an entire day shaping these legs. The Shinto turned it into a two-hour job.

Speaking of Japanese …

Before you cut the tenons and the curves on the aprons, you need to decide what you are going to do about the drawer front. On the original, the drawer front appears to be cut directly from the apron, instead of using a different piece of wood for the drawer front. If you want to do this, too, you're going to need a couple thin-bladed saws — I like Japanese saws for this.

Here's how I did it: First rip ¾" off the top of your front apron piece using your table saw. Once you cut the drawer front free on its remaining three sides, you'll glue this ¾" strip back to the top of the apron.

Though you could cut out the drawer front freehand, I recommend you clamp a block of wood to the apron as a guide.

With the drawer front cut free you can then tweak the apron to tighten things up if you had problems with your rip cut. You can reduce the width a bit by running the top edge of the apron over your jointer. This is a good idea

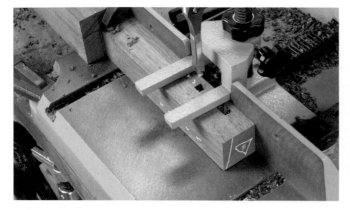

Make your mortises a little deeper than the tenons are long. The two mortises in the legs may end up meeting a bit at one corner, but that's OK. You're not removing material that will ultimately assist in strengthening this joint.

Here you can see the Shinto Saw-Rasp with a handle. Remove the handle and use the tool with two hands — though some cuts are made one-handed. The Shinto is available from a number of catalog companies, including Rockler (rockler.com) and Highland Hardware (tools-for-woodworking.com).

anyway as you'll be gluing the strip back in place shortly and want a clean joint.

Now true up all the surfaces that will be your drawer opening. Chisel out the junk in the corners. Smooth the end grain with a file. Now glue the ¾" strip back onto the front apron.

Fussy but Worth It

Joining the aprons to the legs requires concentration. This joint is highly visible, so gaps are particularly ugly.

Begin by marking the shape of the aprons on all four pieces. This will keep your parts straight as you proceed. Now cut your tenons on your aprons. I use a stack dado set in my table saw for this operation. I guide the work past the blades using a fence on my miter gauge (or the fence on a sliding table). A stop on the fence keeps my cut positioned. This technique is quick — one blade setup cuts both the cheeks and the shoulders of the tenon. And it is safe.

Once you have cut the face shoulders and face cheeks, you can cut the edge shoulders on a band saw.

And Heading Into the Curve

The scalloped shapes on the aprons are a cinch if your templates are made well. The only wrinkle to the process is leaving a little bit of material behind on the aprons to make them robust enough to survive assembly.

The weak spots on the aprons are where they curve dramatically to meet

the legs. By leaving an extra 1¼" of the apron behind you create a place where this weak spot can be clamped without snapping it off (see photo on page 73).

Mark out your strategy for cutting the apron, then cut the scallop shapes. With the rough shapes cut out, I then clamp the pattern to the workpiece and use a router with a bearing-guided pattern bit to smooth out the arcs on the aprons. A laminate trimmer has all the guts you need. However, the tight transition points must be cleaned up by hand.

Cleaning up the corners is easy if you've cut out your aprons carefully on your band saw. A few quick cuts with a sharp chisel will bring the tight corners into line.

Fit for a Fit

Now settle in and fit each joint. Your best friends during this process are a small square, a sharp eye and an old

Once you've cut the ends of what will become your drawer front, connect the two cross-cuts with a rip. A Japanese saw with a curved blade (such as the Azehiki shown here) is ideal. Score your cutline with a sharp chisel, which will make it easier for the saw to follow the kerf. Once you've plunged through the board, switch to a Ryoba saw, which is faster because its blade is longer.

Glue the ¾" strip back to the apron. Make sure you line up the grain as best you can. On my apron, I positioned my cutline so it would run through some straight quarter-sawn grain on the apron. That helped conceal the joint line on the finished piece.

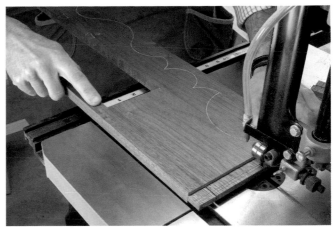

A fair amount of downward pressure ensures accuracy with this technique. If you don't keep the board pressed down flat, it will try to rise up on you. Even a bit of this will result in a too-thick tenon. If you are not sure that you are holding the piece down firmly, make a second pass over the blades.

Trim the edge cheeks of your aprons with a band saw. Then cut the edge shoulders. Cut close. But not too close.

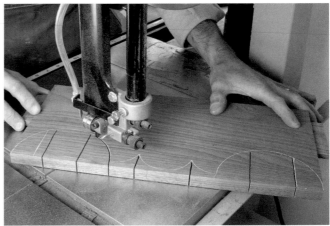

A wide paring chisel makes short work of the waste left from cutting the edge shoulders. Work carefully here and avoid cutting past the shoulder line. If you are skittish, use a 3/8"-wide chisel, which will keep you clear of the shoulders, but it will be a bit harder to steer in the cut.

I place relief cuts at some of the tighter curves. This is efficient because the waste falls away at the same time I need to turn the piece around to cut from the other direction. Note how I've left some extra waste near the tenons to strengthen the apron's curve at that point.

joiner's trick. The square can show you where things are amiss. And your sharp eye? Every time you try the joint, scrutinize the area between the leg and apron. If you can't close this joint with hand pressure, find out what is preventing it from closing. Don't count on the clamps to fix it.

In the end, your best bet is to slightly undercut the tenon shoulders on all the inside surfaces. This "cheat" was handed down to us by 17th-century joiners, who would undercut a shoulder for a tight fit. This approach doesn't weaken the joint much. Most of a tenon's strength is in its

length, according to studies of the joint by the U.S. Forest Products Laboratories. I undercut my interior shoulder with just a pass or two of a shoulder plane.

Before you assemble the table's base, prepare all the exterior surfaces for finishing.

Glue up your base and reinforce it in two ways. One: Add corner blocks that tie together the aprons. My corner blocks are in the shape of triangles and cut from pieces that are 3/4" × 3 3/8" × 3 3/8". I notched the corner blocks around the legs and then glued and screwed them to the aprons.

The second reinforcement is at the point where the aprons meet the legs. I was worried that the weak short grain here would pop off as I sawed or chiseled it.

So I glued a 1/4"-thick backing block behind each curve. The grain of these runs 90° to that of the apron, so they glued well to both the leg and the apron. And because they are so small, wood movement won't (realistically) ever be a problem.

Making the Cut (and Guts)

As with all things in woodworking, if you do enough preparation work, then actual

Because I cut right on my line, there is little material to remove with the router and pattern bit. I clamped the work on top of the pattern and used a bit that has the guide bearing at the bottom of the bit. This allows me to work on top of my bench and prevents me from exposing more of the bit than necessary.

When you glue up the base, the extra waste you left on the aprons comes in handy. Though most authorities on joinery will tell you not to bother gluing the end-grain shoulder area at the bottom of the apron, I think it's essential here. You want all the help you can get when you cut the waste away, and modern PVAs do a better job of gluing end grain than most people realize.

I glued in the backing blocks with spring clamps. One clamp pressed the block to the apron; the other clamp pulled the block against the leg. Here I'm removing the clamps after the glue has dried. With the clamps off, mark the final shape of the apron on the inside as shown.

Having the shape of the apron marked on both the inside and outside of the work helps keep the blade square through the cut.

execution is smooth and quick. Such was the case as I cut the ends of aprons to their final shape with a coping saw.

Once you make the saw cut, clean up your work with a chisel, rasp and sandpaper.

The inside guts of the table are conventional. The drawer rides on a web frame that is attached to the front and back aprons with glue, screws and two cleats. I made the web frame using mortise-and-tenon joints. After I glued up the web frame's joints and allowed them to dry, I glued the frame between the front and back aprons. Then I glued and screwed cleats underneath the web

frame to strengthen the assembly.

You also should install what is sometimes called a "drawer kick." The kick is a single stick of wood between the front and back aprons that is above the drawer. It keeps the drawer from drooping when it is pulled out of the case. I attached the kick to the table base with glue and pocket screws.

My Style of Drawers

When most woodworking magazines describe how to build a drawer for a project, it's usually something like: Build the drawers using the techniques you prefer. While that sounds like the author

ran out of steam, I think it's actually a fair statement.

I've seen a lot of drawers made by a lot of craftsmen. Each one is a little surprise when I pull it out and a reflection of that woodworker's personality.

Here is how I go about it and why. Drawers have a hard life. So if I want a drawer to last 200 years instead of 20, I prefer the dovetail joint for the corners.

I build most of my drawers using ½"-thick poplar for the sides, back and bottom. I use ½"-thick wood for the front that matches the species of the carcase. I join all the corners with through-dovetail joints and then glue a piece of ¼"-

thick veneer (resawn from the piece cut from the apron) on the drawer front and trim it to the size of the drawer opening.

This strategy allows me to stretch my supply of well-figured wood for drawer fronts.

The other detail is how I fit the bottom into the drawer. I plow a ¼" × ¼" groove in the sides and front to hold the bottom. The groove is located ¼" up from the bottom edge of the sides and front. I make the back of the drawer ½" narrower than the sides and front, which allows me to slip the bottom in place.

Here are a couple other details about the bottom: I cut the bottom so the grain runs from left to right in the drawer, so the seasonal expansion and contraction occurs at the rear of the drawer. I also cut a ¼" × ⅜"-wide rabbet on three sides of the bottom that allows the bottom to slide in the grooves cut in the sides and front.

The bottom is secured to the back with a single nail. Be sure to cut the bottom so there's a little expansion room — I make the bottom ¼" narrower overall.

Once I assemble the drawer with dovetails, I glue the drawer front on and trim it to fit the assembled drawer. Then I fit the drawer in the carcase so there is an even gap (about ¹⁄₃₂") all the way around the drawer front. Finally, I clamp the drawer in the table's base and then glue the drawer runners to the web frame so they are snug against the drawer.

Assembling the Top

Tabletops are a bit of a blend of art and science. A bit of effort can result in a top that looks right and is easy to plane or scrape to get it ready for finishing. So choose your boards wisely.

I eased all the edges of the top with a small roundover bit in a trim router. Then I screwed the table's base to the top. I made the clearance holes at the rear corner blocks oval-shaped to allow the top to expand a bit.

Finishing and Hardware

The original table looks redder than I expect natural walnut to. Perhaps it was originally stained or has acquired a

Here you can see how the inside of the table works: Corner blocks reinforce the aprons, a web frame supports the drawer and a drawer kick stops the drawer from drooping. The only thing missing is the drawer runners to guide the sides of the drawer. Those come later.

The two quick-release clamps hold the drawer in position as I glue and clamp the drawer runners to the web frame. Just be careful not to use too much glue. It would be unfortunate to glue the drawer into the case by accident.

patina during the last 200 years. My finish consists of a couple coats of amber shellac, which I applied with a small natural-bristle brush and a rag.

After the shellac dried, I applied two coats of spray lacquer that has a satin sheen. After the finish cured, I rubbed it out with a plain brown paper bag.

The knob is a simple 25mm knob from Lee Valley Tools (item #01A0525, $1.75. 800-871-8158 or leevalley.com).

When complete, the table is quite a spicy charmer. If you want the complete effect in your home, send me an e-mail for a recipe for duck étouffée (or check out the Popular Woodworking blog).

I cut my dovetails by hand. Generally, I have always struggled with the router jigs used to cut dovetails. For me, the hand cutting is something I've done for a long time and am comfortable with. I like to cut my tails so they have a tight opening. I think it lends an old-school look. These tails have ³⁄₁₆" between them.

This two-for-one table adds space for extra players without disturbing anything on the tabletop.

PROJECT
28

Draw-Leaf Game Table

BY GLEN HUEY

I was asked to design and build a gaming table. For me that is a table for playing pinochle or euchre, or a comfortable table for working a jigsaw puzzle with family members. So I set about working to accomplish my task by designing toward card-table dimensions when I stumbled across a television show of the extremely popular "Texas hold 'em" card game. As I looked at the players spaced around the table I questioned the direction I had chosen.

I needed a design that could expand into a larger table. I needed leaves! But table leaves are a constant nuisance. If you need to store them away from the table they take up too much closet space and are always getting dents and dings.

If the leaves store in the table, you need to open it completely to install them.

Then I remembered a seldom-used design that could provide me with exactly what I was searching to find: the draw-leaf or Dutch pull-out table. In this design, the leaves store directly under the main top of the table and extend outward from each end when pulled from the table's base. The main top floats upward as the leaves are extended and will fit flush with the leaf when it is fully brought out. The fascinating aspect of this design is that the leaves may be extended even if the table is being used for the family puzzle. No need to remove anything from the top — just slide the leaves out!

Grab Your Scratch Pad

I began knowing I wanted the table to be 38" wide × 38¾" long and I wanted, for design purposes, a small amount of overhang — 1¼". This works because the smaller the overhang of the table, the wider the leaves will be. Next, I wanted to use a standard 24" for the distance from the floor to the bottom edge of the apron. This allows enough room to get one's legs comfortably under the table. Finally, knowing that the strength of a table is in the aprons, I wanted to use a 5½" apron to provide additional support. This would mean that my table would be 31" high while using two ¾"-thick tops — one for the leaves and one for the main top.

DRAW-LEAF GAME TABLE • INCHES (MILLIMETERS)

QUANTITY	PART	STOCK	THICKNESS	(mm)	WIDTH	(mm)	LENGTH	(mm)	COMMENTS
4	legs	cherry	$1^3/4$	45	$1^3/4$	45	$29^1/2$	749	
2	long aprons	cherry	$3/4$	19	$5^1/2$	140	$35^1/2$	901	$1^1/4$ TBE
2	short aprons	cherry	$3/4$	19	$5^1/2$	140	$34^1/2$	876	$1^1/4$ TBE
1	center support	cherry	$3/4$	19	5	127	$34^1/2$	876	
1	main top	plywood	$11/16$	17	36	914	$36^3/4$	933	nominal $3/4$ plywood
2	leaves	plywood	$11/16$	17	36	914	14	356	nominal $3/4$ plywood
1	fixed top	plywood	$11/16$	17	36	914	$4^3/4$	121	nominal $3/4$ plywood
5	long edging	cherry	$11/16$	17	3	76	40	1016	each makes 2 pieces
3	short edging	cherry	$11/16$	17	3	76	20	508	each makes 2 pieces
4	slides	cherry	$7/8$	22	$1^1/2$	38	$36^3/4$	933	cut to fit for length
1	pierced brackets	cherry	$9/16$	14	$3^1/4$	83	20	508	makes 8 pieces
2	apron moulding	cherry	$7/8$	22	2	51	40	1016	each makes 2 pieces
4	stop blocks	popular	$3/4$	19	$3/4$	19	$1^1/2$	38	
1	locating dowel	popular	$3/4$	19					for top
1	pinning dowel	popular	$1/8$	3					for brackets

TBE = Tenon Both Ends

SUPPLIES

WOODWORKER'S SUPPLY

woodworker.com

1 - Moser's Early American Cherry aniline dye

No. 844-624

Cut the four flutes at the router table. The screw in the end of the leg blank helps to raise the blank from the bit to end the cut or to plunge into the correct position to begin the cut.

Because one cheek of the apron's tenon is barefaced, make a shoulder cut only on the apron's tenon face side of the piece.

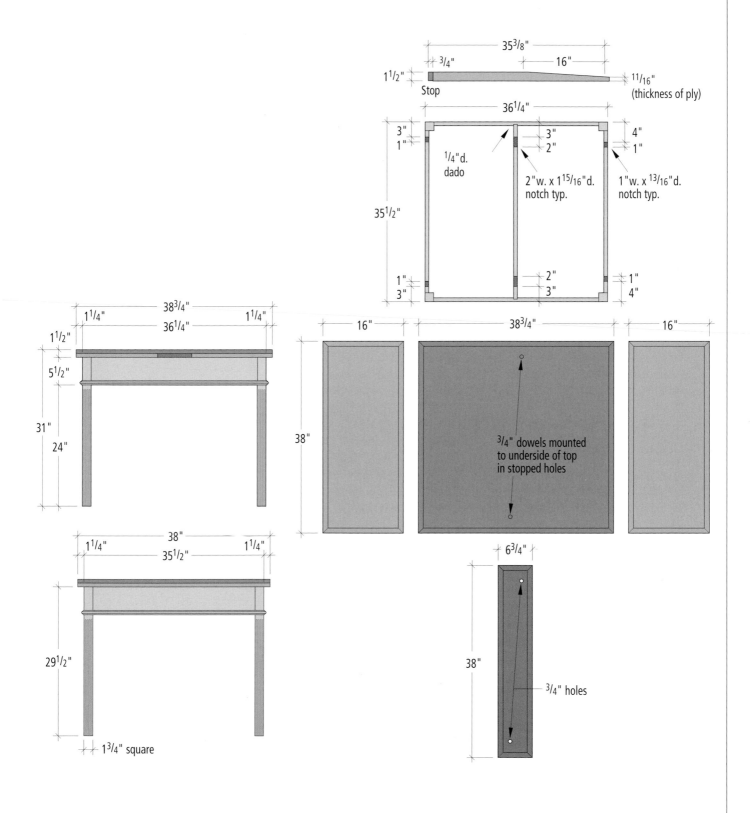

35³/₈"

³/₄" 16"

1¹/₂" Stop ¹¹/₁₆" (thickness of ply)

36¹/₄"

3"
1"

¹/₄"d.
dado

3"
2"

2"w. x 1¹⁵/₁₆"d.
notch typ.

4"
1"

1"w. x ¹³/₁₆"d.
notch typ.

35¹/₂"

1"
3"

2"
3"

1"
4"

38³/₄"
1¹/₄" 1¹/₄"
36¹/₄"

1¹/₂"
5¹/₂"

31"
24"

38"
1¹/₄" 1¹/₄"
35¹/₂"

29¹/₂"

1³/₄" square

16" 38³/₄" 16"

38"

³/₄" dowels mounted
to underside of top
in stopped holes

6³/₄"

38"

³/₄" holes

205

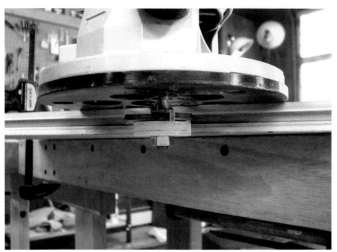

Use a square platform jig made from a few pieces of plywood and a pattern bit to cut the ¼"-deep dado for the center support.

Create the ¼"-deep groove with a router bit and three-wing cutter. Run the cut from both faces of the plywood to ensure that it is centered.

Given these measurements, I determined the sizes of my table's main components. Two ¾"-thick aprons along with the 1¼" overhang on both ends yields a total of 4". If you subtract that from the length of the top when closed, you have 34¾" remaining, which is the measurement of the inside of the base. From that you need to subtract the thickness of the stops (1") and the thickness of the center support (¾") and you have 32", which is the total that the table will extend. Divide that number by two to get the width of each individual leaf (16"). Finally, subtract the 32" from the closed length of 38¾" to get the fixed-top size of 6¾". With the numbers figured, we're ready to build.

A Base From Which to Build

The base is the place to begin with the construction of our table and I always begin with the legs. Not wanting to simply taper these legs, I opted to add flutes to the face sides. First, mill the leg blanks to size and mark the locations of the ⅜"-wide × 4½"-long × 1¼"-deep mortises. We are using a bare-face tenon joint, which means there is a shoulder only on one face of the apron. These mortises are located ⅜" in from the face of each leg.

With the mortises complete, install a ¼" fluting bit into the router and set it so the bit makes only a cut ³⁄₁₆" wide. Place

Cut one end of your long edging stock at 45° and use the falloff, cut to the same angle, to find the exact position.

a line on your fence that is exactly centered with the middle of the fluting bit. I like to use the center of the bit to begin and end each cut rather than setting a line on each side of the bit to use as a starting or ending point.

Now draw a line at ⅞" below the spot where the apron meets the leg. This line will be used to determine the top edge of the fluting. Next, you will need to lay out the locations of the flutes so they are evenly spaced across the face of each leg.

Line up the bit with either of the middle flutes and set your fence.

Make two passes on each outside face of your legs. The first starts at the layout line and continues through the bottom edge of the leg. A second pass is made by reversing the leg and starting at the bottom edge, then stopping as the layout line matches with the line on your fence. This will create the two flutes on the inside of each leg. Next you need to reposition the fence to align the bit with

Place the clamps on the bottom face of the plywood pieces to help protect the panel from damage or staining.

To sand the pieces flush, add pencil lines to the joint of the plywood and edging and when the lines disappear — the surface is level.

Note: Single leaf shown for clarity.

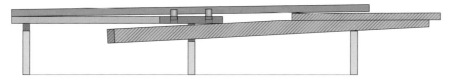

In closed position, extension leaf with attached slide is fully housed beneath floating main top.

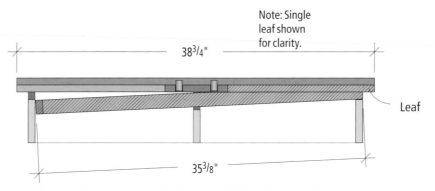

As extension leaf is pulled outward, floating main top pivots upward. Main top is held in alignment with base by attached dowels that ride in holes in narrow fixed top.

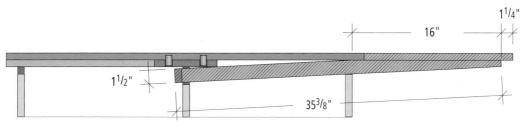

When extension leaf is fully extended, it is flush with floating main top. Main top returns to rest on beveled edge of slide. Stop block, attached to side of slide, contacts center support and prevents overextension.

Layout is the key to the slides and the tapers. First, make a regular pass at the jointer stopping as the cut reaches the 8"-layout line.

Second, reverse the cut and "wheelie" down the area of the first cut while passing the piece over the knives. The cut will not make contact until the 16" line, and will taper the cut the final dimensions.

Set the depth stop at the drill press to leave ³⁄₄" and drill the ⁵⁄₈"-diameter holes into the tapered portion of the slides. Use a tapered countersink centered at each hole to attach the slides to the leaves with #8 x 1¹⁄₄" screws.

The 2¹⁄₄"-long dowels extend down from the top and through the fixed top. The stop blocks at the ends of each slide need to be removable in order to disassemble and finish the table.

either of the outside flute locations and repeat the steps. Afterward, the faces of each leg should have four flutes evenly spaced as shown in the photo on the preceding page. While I've included ample photos in this article to show how to build this project, I've also posted additional photos on my web site that may prove helpful (woodworkersedge.com).

Work on the aprons begins by creating the tenons on the ends. Set the blade height to ³⁄₈" and position the fence to cut a 1¹⁄₄"-long tenon. Because we're using bare-faced tenons you need to make the cut only on the face of the apron. Cut both ends of all four of the apron pieces. Then, without moving the

fence, raise the depth of cut to ¹⁄₂". Roll the aprons onto their edges and make the two cuts at each tenon to define the edge shoulders of the tenon.

Remove the remainder of the waste material on the tenons using the table saw, leaving the ³⁄₈"-thick tenon. At the band saw, set a straightedge fence in position to remove the ¹⁄₂" of material on each side of the tenon. Because these tenons will touch in the center of the leg if left as-is, we need to cut a 45° angle onto each tenon. Make a single pass to cut the back edge of the tenon. Leave the length as long as possible.

The center base's support fits between the long aprons. To install the center

support you need to create a ¹⁄₄"-deep stopped dado located directly at the center of both aprons, into which the center support will slide. The dado is cut leaving ¹⁄₂" of material at the bottom edge of the aprons. This will help you position the piece in the right location and also adds strength by adding support beneath the piece. Square the dado with a chisel to finish.

Now you are ready for some assembly. Add glue into the mortises and on the tenons and slip the joint together. Assemble the base in steps, but remember that your mortises open into each other and the glue can run out the opposite mortise. Allow one set of rails and aprons

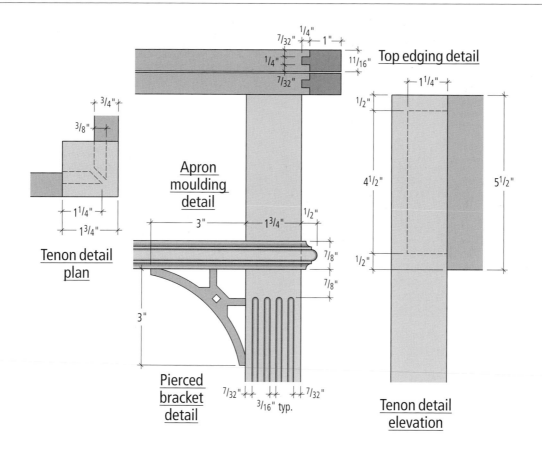

Tenon detail plan

Apron moulding detail

Pierced bracket detail

Top edging detail

Tenon detail elevation

Continuous Grain Tops it Off

Cut the pieces for your top, leaves and the fixed top from a single sheet of plywood. It will look best if you make the grain of the leaves continuous with the main top. Rip the sheet to 36" in width, and then cut (in this order) one leaf, the main top and the second leaf. This will allow you to arrange the pieces so that when the table is fully extended, the grain will run the entire length of the table. Don't forget to cut the fixed top, while you're at it.

Now we need to add the solid-wood edging to the plywood. I elected to run a simple tongue and groove to improve the joint. Use a router bit with a three-wing cutter (Eagle America, 800-872-2511, #199-4622) to make the 1/4"-deep groove in the plywood. To ensure that the groove is centered, I like to make a complete pass from both faces of the plywood.

Create the tongues on the solid stock edging pieces in a series of two-step rabbet cuts on the table saw. Make sure to check the fit. Because I ran the groove cut from both faces, it is likely that the groove will be more than the 1/4"-wide, and you want a snug fit for your table edging. To make things easier, I ran my edging more than double the needed width, then ran the tongues on both edges. I then rip those pieces to the finished size for the edging. I use a 1" finished size (1¼" including the tongue) because it takes the guesswork out of sizing the top plywood pieces.

Carefully fit the edging around the plywood panels, mitering the corners. Slide the edging into the grooves and match the corners of the two pieces. Hold them in position and mark the opposite miter length at the exact corner. Repeat these steps for all four sides of the panels and for all four panels.

Add glue to the groove and to the tongue on the edging, slide the long pieces in place while checking the position, and add clamps until the glue is

dry. Next, assemble the final two pieces of edging per panel in the same manner. Elevate the panel onto a few pieces of scrap lumber to make placing the clamps easy. When the glue is dry, you will need to sand the edging flush to the panels, taking care to not sand through the veneered surface.

The Slides are the Secret

The success of your table rests on the slides. They need to be milled accurately and must be identical for the leaves to slide smoothly and correctly. Mill the stock to rough size and allow the wood to acclimate for a day, then complete milling the slides. This will help keep the pieces stable after cutting them to the final size.

Begin the layout for the slides by making a mark at the top of the side, 16" from one end. At that same end mark the exact thickness of your top (plywood is slightly less than ¾"). This is the amount that the slide has to rise in order for the leaf to be on the same plane as the top when the leaf is fully extended.

Miter the corners of the moulding and use a thin bead of glue. Too much glue and the result might squeeze out onto the aprons, causing finish problems.

Locate the first bracket for the square hole and mark the edges on the scrap below in order to position the remaining brackets for this step.

Draw a line connecting the two points. The small wedge is the waste and can be removed with a tapering jig, but a few years back I began making my tapers at the jointer.

The trick to accuracy and getting the four slides identical at the jointer is in the layout work. First draw a line that is half of the total length of the taper, in our example 8". Next, set the cut of the jointer at exactly half of the total of the taper cut ($^{11}\!/_{32}$"). Don't rely on the tool's gauges for this setup. Make the cut on a scrap piece of lumber and measure for accuracy.

With the layout complete and the machine set, it is a two-step process. Make a normal pass at the jointer up to the 8" layout line and remove the piece. This cuts one half of the taper. Reverse the slide, cut the area away from the knives, then "wheelie" down the previous cut. As you carefully pass the piece over the knives, it is important that you maintain downward pressure on the back edge until the piece makes contact with the outfeed table. Any drop into the knives could ruin your slide. Continue the cut through the knives to complete the tapering of the slides.

Next we need to figure and cut the notches in the aprons and the center support in which the slides travel. Position one slide with the tapered cut

down flat against your bench. Measure $1\!^{1}\!/_{4}$" in from the tapered end and measure the height of the slide at this location. This is the depth of the notches that you will need to cut in the aprons. Take another measurement 19" in from the tapered end that will be the depth necessary for the notch in the center support. In my case the depth was $11^{5}\!/_{16}$". It's OK to be a bit deeper because it's the fixed top that holds the slides when fully extended.

Locate the notch locations using the illustrations on the preceding pages. Note that the 1"-wide notches are in different locations at opposite ends of the table, so the slides nest side by side. The center support notches are 2"-wide to capture both slides.

Cut the notches by sawing two outside lines to define the cut, then make multiple cuts to the bottom layout line. A jigsaw or handsaw will work. Stop short of the bottom line, then break the waste material out with your chisel and pare to the bottom line. Repeat these steps for the four locations in the apron as well as the two areas in the center support.

At this point, the slides are still too long. Position the slides in place on each leaf, with the tapered end flush to the outside edge of the leaf. Mark and then trim each slide where the solid wood meets the plywood leaf, then check the

fit. When closed, the leaf will lay flat on the apron and the slide will extend approximately $^{1}\!/_{4}$" beyond the apron.

Fitting the Top

Set the fixed top, leaves and main top into position on the base with the slides loose, but in position. Get the overhangs set to the correct size, then mark a line on either side of each slide. It helps to center the slide in each notch. To attach the slides to the leaves, use a square to extend the lines of the slides' positions across the leaves.

Use a Forstner bit to countersink the three holes for the screws. Use a tapered countersinking bit to pre-drill for the screws. Add a small amount of glue onto the slide, reposition in place and attach using #8 × $1\!^{1}\!/_{4}$" screws.

Set the leaves and fixed top back onto the base and temporarily attach the fixed top to the base with screws into the aprons. Place the top into position and use a number of spring clamps to hold the top to a leaf on one end of the grouping. Carefully slide the opposing leaf out until the top fits down flush with the leaf. The drag should be snug but if it is too tight, adjust the depth of the notch in the center support. Check the fit of both leaves. Trim the slides for length as necessary and attach the stops that will keep the leaves from being overextended to the slides with

With one pierced bracket complete, fit a scrap into the ¼" hole to locate the position for the remaining brackets. Transfer the design onto the remaining pieces.

The pierced brackets fit into the corners where the aprons meet the legs. Use a small amount of glue and ⅛"-diameter dowels to secure.

screws. These will need to be removed when we begin the finishing steps.

The main top remains loose but is held in position by dowels. Install the dowels by first drilling two pilot holes between the apron and the slide areas (offset them from the center to allow the top to only fit one way) and through both the fixed top and into the main top. Remove the two tops and drill a ¾" hole through the fixed top. Drill a ¾" hole into, but not through, the main top. Slightly taper the exposed end of the dowels with sandpaper to allow an easy fit in the fixed top. Attach the dowels into the main top with glue. As the leaves are extended the top will ride up off of the fixed top. The dowels will keep the two tops in line.

Details Make the Difference

Make the moulding at the bottom edge of the aprons using a profile bit (#841.285.11, cmtusa.com) in the router table. You will need to make two passes per edge to complete the profile. Run the profile on a larger piece, then rip the moulding from the larger piece at the table saw. Sand the apron to #180 grit and miter the moulding corners to fit around the base. Use a thin bead of glue and brads to attach the moulding.

Cut the stock for the pierced brackets into eight triangles so that each leg is

3¼" in length. Set a fence at the band saw that is 3" away from the blade and run each leg through the blade, cutting a small flat area at the ends.

Transfer the pattern from the plans onto the piece. At the mortiser, set up to cut the square hole in the center of the layout by placing the long side of the triangle against the fence. Make sure to place a scrap piece under the cut to keep from blowing out the back side of the cut. Finish the profile at the band saw, then sand or rasp to clean the edges. Dowel and glue the pieces in position where the aprons meet the legs.

I used Moser's Early American Cherry water-based aniline dye to color the wood. Soak the table with dye, allow it to stand for five minutes, and then remove any excess. Once the dye is dry, lightly sand the piece to remove any raised grain or "fuzzies." I sprayed a coat of sanding sealer, sanded the piece thoroughly, and followed that with three coats of lacquer for extra protection.

Because the top slides on the surface of the leaves as they are extended, add a piece of felt to the underside of the main top to prevent scratches.

Start that puzzle with the family or invite your woodworking friends to a poker tournament. You might not come out ahead in winnings, but at least you will be able to show off your new table.

This frame-and-panel project is all about grooves, tongues and ancient proverbs.

Asian Bedside Table

BY CHRISTOPHER SCHWARZ

Building cabinetry can give you a serious case of Zen Buddhism. In fact, the contradictions in woodworking are sometimes amusing — if not always enlightening. Cabinets, for the most part, are more air than wood. To build a piece of furniture is mostly a process of removing wood. And to make a project look as simple and plain as this one does, it is quite a complicated process.

Now before you start worrying that this simple bedside table is too much for your woodworking skills, remember my favorite Bulgarian proverb: "If you wish to drown, do not torture yourself with shallow water."

Frames and Panels

Except for two small pieces of plywood in the sliding doors, this project is made entirely out of solid wood. To account for the seasonal expansion and contraction of the material, the table is built using a series of frame-and-panel assemblies. In a nutshell, all of the frames are connected using mortise-and-tenon joinery. The panels all rest in 3/8"-wide × 3/8"-deep grooves in the frames. After you have milled all the parts using the cutting list and glued up any panels you might need, I recommend you begin by building the doors.

Lightweight but Solid Sliding Doors

The sliding doors on this table run in 1/4"-wide × 1/4"-deep grooves cut into the frame pieces. Once this table is glued up, the doors are in there for good. (You can easily make the doors removable by deepening the grooves in the top rail and increasing the width of the tongue on the top of the doors.) To ensure the doors slide smoothly for years to come, choose straight-grained stock for the parts.

The rails and stiles are joined using mortises and tenons. The plywood panel rests in a rabbet cut in the back, and the slats are merely glued onto the panel.

Begin by cutting your 1/4"-thick × 1"-long tenons on the rails. As you can see

You can see the large shoulder on the door tenon here as I'm dry-fitting the door. The large shoulder makes for a cleaner-looking tongue.

You know, I really should install a starting pin in my router table for making cuts like these. If you take it slow and steady, you shouldn't have any problems. Just make sure you cut against the rotation of the cutter.

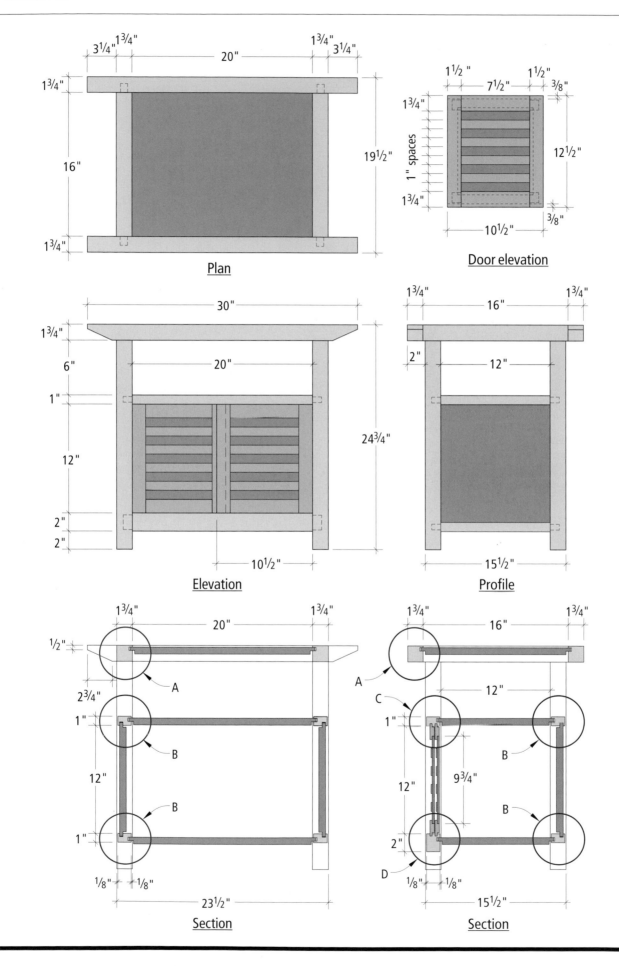

Plan

Door elevation

Elevation

Profile

Section

Section

ASIAN BEDSIDE TABLE • INCHES (MILLIMETERS)

QUANTITY	PART	STOCK	THICKNESS	(mm)	WIDTH	(mm)	LENGTH	(mm)	COMMENTS
TOP									
2	top stiles	maple	1³/₄	45	1³/₄	45	30	762	³/₈" × ³/₈" groove on inside edge
2	top rails	maple	1³/₄	45	1³/₄	45	18	457	1" TBE, ³/₈" × ³/₈" groove on inside edge
1	panel	maple	1³/₄	45	16¹/₂	419	20¹/₂	521	³/₈" × ³/₈" groove; ¹/₂" × ³/₈" rabbet, all sides
BASE									
4	legs	maple	1³/₄	45	1³/₄	45	23	584	³/₈" × ³/₈" groove for side and back panels
4	rails for sides	maple	1	25	1¹/₂	38	14	356	1" TBE, ³/₈" × ³/₈" groove for side panels
3	rails front and back	maple	1	25	1¹/₂	38	22	559	1" TBE, ³/₈" × ³/₈" groove for side panel
1	front bottom rail	maple	2	51	1¹/₂	38	22	559	1" TBE
2	top and bottom panels	maple	³/₄	19	12³/₄	324	20³/₄	527	¹/₂" × ³/₈" rabbet on edges; rest in ³/₈" × ³/₈" groove
2	side panels	maple	³/₄	19	12⁵/₈	321	12⁵/₈	321	¹/₂" × ³/₈" rabbet on edges; rest in ³/₈" × ³/₈" groove
1	back panel	maple	³/₄	19	12⁵/₈	321	20⁵/₈	524	¹/₂" × ³/₈" rabbet on edges; rest in ³/₈" × ³/₈" groove
DOORS									
4	stiles	maple	¹/₂	13	1¹/₂	38	12¹/₂	318	
4	rails	maple	¹/₂	13	1³/₄	45	9¹/₂	241	1" TBE
2	panels	plywood	¹/₄	6	8¹/₄	210	9³/₄	248	in ¹/₄" × ³/₈" rabbet on back of door
8	slats	maple	¹/₈	3	1	25	7¹/₂	191	applied to panel

TBE = Tenon Both Ends

SUPPLIES

ROCKLER

1 pack - desktop fasteners

No. 21650

Micro Fence

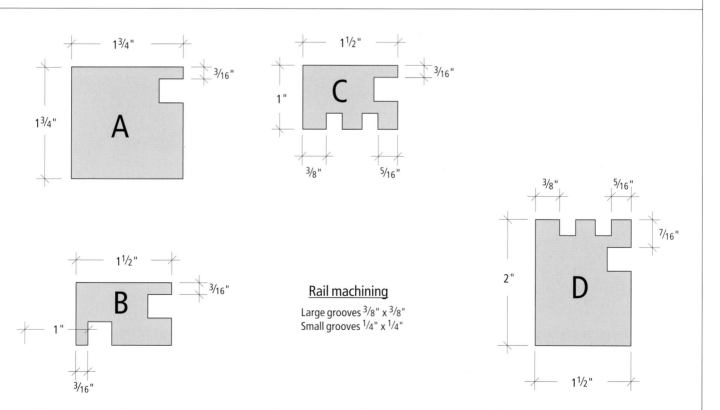

Rail machining
Large grooves ³/₈" x ³/₈"
Small grooves ¹/₄" x ¹/₄"

On the door slats, I cheated. I didn't feel like mortising the really thin stock into the stiles. To ensure your spacing is correct, use a couple of 1"-wide spacers to place your slats. A piece of tape on mine shimmed the spacers a bit to ensure the slats were equally spaced.

Again, when cutting the grooves, you want to move the router in the direction opposite the rotation of the cutterhead. In this instance, this means moving the router from left to right.

in the photo at right, the shoulders facing the outside edges of the door are ½" bigger than the ones facing inside. This makes a cleaner-looking joint when you cut the tongue on the top and bottom of the door. Now cut the matching mortises in the stiles. Glue and clamp the doors.

When the glue is dry, cut a ¼"-deep × ⅜"-wide rabbet on the backside of each door. Square the corners with a chisel. Finish sand the ¼" birch plywood panel and then glue it in the rabbet. When that glue is dry, glue the slats in place spaced 1" apart.

Finally, to complete the doors cut a ¼"-thick × ⅜"-long tongue on the top and bottom edge of the backside of the doors.

The Case

Begin work on the case by cutting ½"-thick × 1"-long tenons on all the rails with a ¼" shoulder all around. Now use your tenons to lay out the locations of the mortises on the legs. You want all of your rails to be set back ⅛" from the outside edge of the legs.

The only anomaly comes when laying out the mortises for the beefy front bottom rail. Its mortises run vertically instead of horizontally. Cut the ¹¹⁄₁₆"-

deep mortises. I used a hollow-chisel mortiser equipped with a ½" bit. As you'll see when you get into it, cutting these mortises is a bit different than in most casework. You'll clamp your work to your mortiser's fence and then move the fence in and out to cut the mortises (except when cutting the mortises for the front bottom rail, which are cut con-

ventionally). Finally, miter the tenons so they fit in the mortises without bumping into each other.

Two Grooves for Every Rail

There are lots of grooves on the rails and in the legs. One way to cut them all is using a ⅜" straight bit and a router table setup. However, I like to see what's going

Quick Tips: Strategies for Ridding Your Joints of Gaps

When you do a lot of mortise-and-tenon work, one of the most frustrating aspects of the joint is getting a seamless fit. Here are a few tricks to ensure fewer gaps.

1. Pay attention to the edge of the board that the mortise is in. If you sand or plane this surface before assembly, chances are you're going to change the angle of the edge, which will give you a gap when you assemble the joint. Before I cut a mortise in an edge, I run it over my jointer slowly to remove any saw marks. After the joint is glued and assembled, I go in and clean up the jointer marks with No.120-grit sandpaper.

2. On highly visible joints, I'll put the tenoned piece in my vise and go to work on it with a chisel. Pare away at the shoulder area around and up to the tenon — but stay away from the edge. You only need to remove ¹⁄₃₂" of material or so.

3. Make your mortises ¹⁄₁₆" deeper than your tenons are long. This stops your tenons from bottoming out in the mortises and gives any excess glue a place to collect.

on when I cut grooves like these. So I used an aftermarket edge guide on my router. I prefer the Micro Fence for work such as this because it allows me to sneak right up on the perfect measurement with its microadjustable knob. Other edge guides are capable of the job, however.

Set your ⅜" straight bit so it will make a ⅜"-deep cut and set your fence so the bit is ³⁄₁₆" from the fence. Now, working from the outside edges of the rails, cut the ⅜" × ⅜" grooves on all the rails that hold the panels (except for the groove in the bottom front rail that holds the bottom panel). To cut that groove, set the distance between the fence and bit to ⁷⁄₁₆" and fire away. See the drawings for more details.

Now cut the grooves in the legs for the panels. Set your bit so it's ⁵⁄₁₆" from the fence and essentially connect the mortises.

Now it's time to cut the two grooves in the two front rails that the doors ride in. Chuck a ¼" straight bit in your router and cut the grooves in the top and bottom rails as shown in the drawings on page 71.

To make the panels fit in their grooves, cut a ⅜"-deep × ½"-long rabbet on the underside of all the panels. You're going to have to notch the corners of each panel to fit around the legs. Cut the notches using a back saw.

Finish sand all the parts for the case and get ready for assembly. Check the fit of the doors in the grooves. A couple passes with a shoulder plane on the tongues made my doors slide smoothly. Once everything fits, glue the side assemblies up. Put glue in the mortises. To allow for wood movement, avoid getting glue in the grooves. You'll want to finish everything before final assembly, so set the side assemblies and the rest of the parts aside for later.

The Top: Still More Grooves

The top is made much the same as the sides. First cut the ½"-thick × 1"-long tenons on the ends of the rails. Cut the mortises to match in the stiles. Get out your router and your fence again, chuck the ⅜" straight bit in there and set the

distance between the bit and the fence to ³⁄₁₆" (this will make the top recessed into the frame). Set the depth of cut to ⅜" and cut the grooves in the rails and the stiles.

Cut the detail on the ends of the stiles as shown in the drawings. I cut it using my band saw and cleaned up the bevel using a plane. Finally, cut a ⅜"-deep × ½"-long rabbet on the bottom side of your panel. Finish sand all the parts and glue up the top frame.

Finish and Fit

Before finishing, apply masking tape to all the tenons and plug the mortises with packing peanuts. Apply three coats of a clear finish, such as clear shellac or lacquer, and sand between each coat. When the finish has fully cured, assemble the case. Apply glue in the mortises, slide the doors in place and clamp it up. Check the case for square across the height and depth of the case. When the glue is dry, attach the top using desktop fasteners (sometimes commonly called "figure-8" fasteners). With a ¾" Forstner bit chucked into your hand drill, cut a recess for the fastener in the top of each leg. Screw the fasteners to the legs. Then screw the case to the underside of the top.

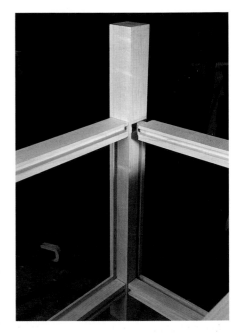

Here's where it all comes together. You can see the grooves for the panels in the rails and legs and the mitered tenons.

Whenever I finish a project such as this, I can't help but look askance at the tiny imperfections (unnoticeable to most people) that come from handwork. But then I try to remember another Zen saying from Ts'ai Ken T'An that should comfort all woodworkers: "Water which is too pure has no fish."

My large shoulder plane is probably one of the most useful tools in my shop. It trims tenons and deepens rabbets better than anything else out there. The original Record 073 (now out of production) sells used for several hundred dollars. I bought my Lie-Nielsen version for $225. Pricey? Yes, but well worth it. When you trim the tongues on the doors, make sure you have something backing up your cut or you will blow out the grain at the end.

Learn to create this classic furniture detail using a template, a band saw and a little lathe work.

Queen Anne Side Table

BY GLEN HUEY

I like the look of the Queen Anne side table shown here mostly because of the elegant shape of the cabriole legs. This table was produced in Philadelphia between 1740 and 1760, but the design of the cabriole leg has been around a lot longer.

Its actual history is a little murky — similar shapes have been found in ancient Egyptian chairs. The shape also is very prominent in traditional Chinese furniture.

The shape has two curves — the upper one is convex and the lower one is concave. It's often given anthropomorphic qualities, evoking an elephant trunk, dragonfly legs or some four-legged animal, leading (not surprisingly) to the frequently seen ball-and-claw feet carved at the foot of cabriole legs.

From a cabinetmaker's point of view, this table is a good introduction to making cabriole legs and it's a piece that can be built in a relatively short amount of time. I chose the basic cabriole turned foot or "club" foot because it also is a good introduction to the leg design.

QUEEN ANNE SIDE TABLE • INCHES (MILLIMETERS)

QUANTITY	PART	STOCK	THICKNESS	(mm)	WIDTH	(mm)	LENGTH	(mm)	COMMENTS
4	legs	cherry	$2^3/_4$	70	$2^3/_4$	70	$28^1/_4$	724	
6	knee blocks	cherry	$1^1/_2$	38	$1^1/_2$	38	2	51	
2	sides	cherry	$^3/_4$	19	$7^7/_8$	200	$11^3/_4$	298	$1^1/_4$" TBE
1	front apron	cherry	$^3/_4$	19	$3^1/_4$	83	24	610	$1^1/_4$" TBE
1	top rail	cherry	$^3/_4$	19	$1^7/_8$	48	$22^1/_2$	57	$^1/_2$" dovetail TBE
1	back	cherry	$^3/_4$	19	$7^3/_8$	187	24	610	$1^1/_4$" TBE
1	front apron extender	cherry	$^3/_4$	19	$1^1/_8$	29	$21^1/_2$	546	
2	drawer runners	poplar	$^3/_4$	19	1	51	$10^3/_4$	273	$^1/_2$" TOE
2	drawer guides	poplar	$^1/_2$	13	$1^3/_8$	35	$9^1/_8$	232	
2	drawer front	cherry	$^7/_8$	22	$3^5/_8$	921	$22^1/_8$	562	$^3/_8$" lip, 3 sides
2	drawer sides	poplar	$^1/_2$	13	$3^5/_8$	921	$11^1/_2$	292	
1	drawer back	poplar	$^1/_2$	13	$2^1/_2$	64	$21^3/_8$	543	
1	drawer bottom	poplar	$^5/_8$	16	11	203	$21^3/_8$	543	
5	wood clips	poplar	$^3/_4$	19	$^7/_8$	22	$2^1/_2$	64	

TBE = tenons both ends; BE = both ends; TOE = tenon one end

SUPPLIES

HORTON BRASSES

3 - Nails, $1^1/_2$" reproduction No. N-7

2 - Drawer pulls No. C-602S

2 - Drawer escutcheons No.C-602SE

WOODCRAFT SUPPLY

1 - Behlen Wool-Lube, 16 oz., No.18Y61

1 - Hock Blonde Dewaxed Shellac, 1 lb. bag No.143155

WOODWORKER'S SUPPLY INC.

1 - J.E. Moser's Water Based Aniline Dye Stain, Early American Cherry, 4 oz., No.W14304

ROCKLER

1 - Sanding sponges, extra fine, No. 23163

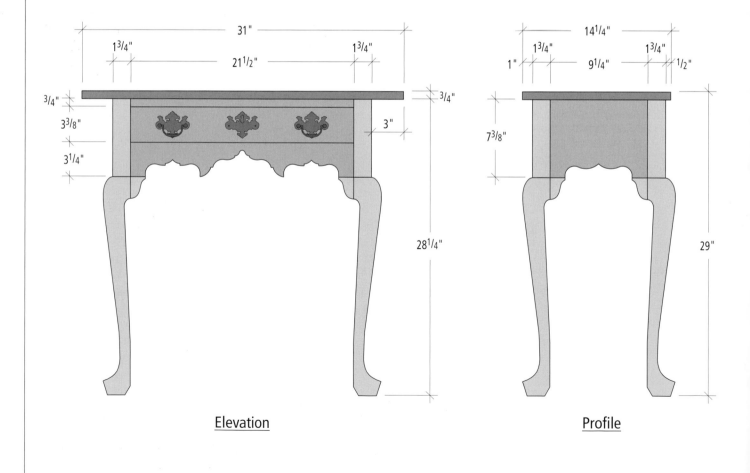

Elevation

Profile

Baby Steps to a Shapely Leg

When taken in small steps, forming a cabriole leg is straightforward work. First you choose the proper leg blanks (to show the best grain pattern), then transfer the pattern to the leg. Most of the material removal is done on the table saw and on the band saw.

The lathe is an important part of the process, but because much of the leg is shaped on the band saw, it's mostly clean-up work.

The last part is creating the details with a rasp, files, scrapers and sandpaper. Don't think of it as carving; it's simple stuff.

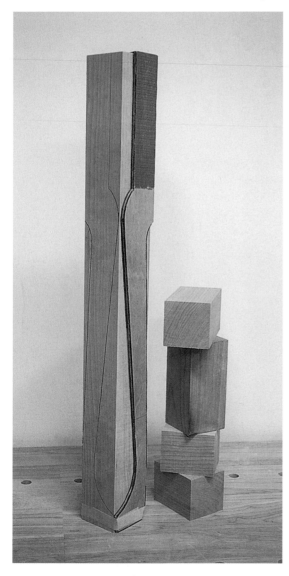

The pattern is the secret of cabriole legs. With the pattern transferred to the "best" faces the legs can be cut to length, but hang on to the scrap pieces for later.

Pattern First

I've included a scaled drawing for the leg on page 223, and that's where you begin. Scale that pattern 400 percent to full size and adhere it to a piece of ¼"-thick plywood. Then cut the pattern out on a band saw.

To ensure good-looking legs, it's necessary to select the best grain orientation on the 2¾"-square leg blanks. Align the blank so that the growth rings run from corner to corner in cross section with the grain terminating at the corner where the knee is located.

Use the pattern to lay out two silhouettes that touch at the knee. With the pattern transferred, cut the legs to length, saving the cutoffs for the knee blocks — the transition from the leg to the apron.

Defining the Leg Shape

The next step is to remove most of the material from the leg blanks to make them look like the pattern. This is done in two stages, using the table saw to shape the leg post and the band saw to shape the curved part of the leg.

At the table saw make two cuts per leg to define the top edge of the knee. Make the cuts at the bottom edge of the leg post just above the knee. Cut only on the two sides that are patterned and cut just deep enough (about ⅞") to reach the edge of the pattern, leaving 1⅞" width of the leg post intact until later.

That's all for the table saw for the moment. Next head to the band saw and cut the outside-facing pattern on one side. Do this in two cuts, starting from the top end of the leg and stopping in the middle. Then cut up from the foot. Leave a small bridge section in the middle uncut to keep the waste piece in place for now.

Leaving the waste pieces in place gives you a stable surface for cutting the second side and leaves the entire pattern visible.

On the outside of the leg (above the knee) there isn't an easy way to leave a bridge, so I complete the cut and use a hot-melt glue gun to reattach the waste.

When the first side is cut, turn the blank 90° and remove the waste on the second side. The second side of the leg can be finished without bridging the cuts.

Once the second side is removed, return to the first side and finish the cuts by removing any connections. Repeat the process on the other three legs.

Turning the Leg

With the leg post and leg rough-shaped, mount the leg onto the lathe. Use the illustration to mark the center of the top and bottom of each leg blank, and mount the first leg on center.

The turning starts at the foot of the leg. Begin by ensuring that the blank turns free and is not making contact with any part of the lathe. At your slowest speed, turn the foot with a gouge to a 2¾"-diameter just to the top edge of the foot (1⅛").

You will need to stop the lathe and remove the waste material at the rear of the foot with a chisel. This will allow you to get your lathe tools in close enough to finish shaping the foot.

Use the point of your skew to mark and define the top of the foot. Then cut the ⅛" pad to a 1¾" diameter using a parting tool. Finally, roll the foot edge to the pad using a skew to complete the shape of the foot. Then go ahead and turn the other three legs to match the first one.

Sanding and Hand Work

The next step is to flatten the top of the foot so that the foot transitions smoothly into the ankle of the leg. While this can be completed with chisels and rasps, I find that a spindle sander speeds the process along.

It's time to shape the legs themselves. I use a Shinto Saw Rasp for the majority of my shaping, along with a few other finer rasps, files and scrapers.

The point where the leg post meets the shaped part of the leg is defined by two crosscuts on adjoining faces. I used a miter gauge on my table saw to make these cuts. Notice that I've used a stand-off block clamped to the lead part of my rip fence to gauge the proper height and to avoid any binding problems during the cut.

On the inner part of the leg a bridge isn't possible, so I use a spot of hot-melt glue to hold the waste piece temporarily in place.

These particular legs have a rather pointed knee so the shaping is basic. I begin by rounding the ankle to a complete diameter and then gradually I move up the leg by transitioning the shape to a square at the knee. By sight and feel you want to move from the roundness of the ankle to the square of the knee area.

This last step will give you the shape you want, but it's still pretty rough. I follow the rasp with files and scrapers and finally sand the leg to a final grit of #150.

Mortising and Post Time

With the legs shaped and the leg posts still at full width, now is the time to choose your best legs for the front of the table.

Determine the most attractive leg orientation, then mark the $\frac{1}{4}$" × $2\frac{1}{4}$" × $1\frac{1}{4}$"-deep mortise locations. They are set $1\frac{3}{8}$" in from the inside of the legs and $\frac{1}{2}$" in from the top or bottom edge.

I used a mortising machine to cut the mortises for the aprons. The front lower apron is a single mortise while the side and back mortises are double mortises (with a $1\frac{7}{8}$" gap) to avoid weakening the leg posts.

With the mortises complete, you can now remove the rest of the material from the leg posts to give them their final shape. Head back to the band saw and cut away the waste at the leg posts. A wide $\frac{1}{2}$" blade works best here. Make

Cut the outside shape of the leg on the band saw, but leave a bit of material (the bridge), which keeps the waste intact until after the second face is cut.

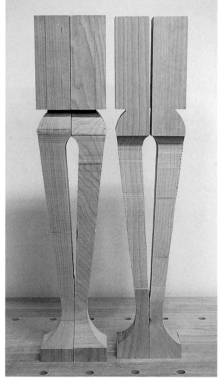

With the waste pieces removed, the four legs quickly assume their classic cabriole shape.

sure to cut the sides in the correct order to ensure a flat surface to support your cuts. Make the cut slowly to eliminate any wandering of the blade. These cuts establish the face sides of the leg posts and should be as neat as possible.

Spin the leg 90° and make the second

cut. The legs are now complete. In the November issue I'll show you how to add the legs and knee blocks to the delicately sculpted table aprons and show you how to add a simple top to complete this heirloom-quality project.

After mounting the leg on the lathe, turn the foot to its finished diameter. It will be necessary to stop the lathe and trim the back of the leg where it meets the foot with a chisel, as shown.

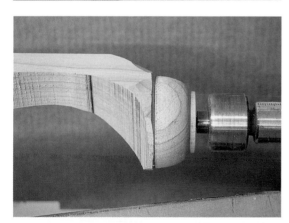

With the foot at its final diameter, cut a slight reveal to separate the foot visually from the leg, as shown above.

Finally, the pad is turned to a 1/8" tall by 1 3/4" diameter at the base of the leg and the foot is radiused to meet the pad.

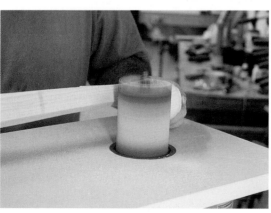

A spindle sander takes a lot of the effort out of the process of smoothing the transition from the leg to the foot.

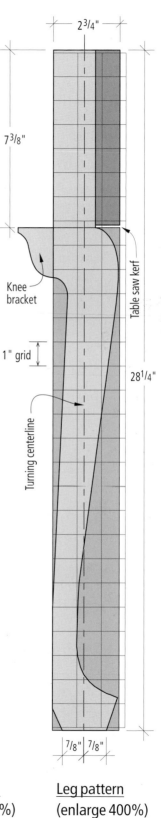

2 3/4"

7 3/8"

Knee bracket

Table saw kerf

1" grid

28 1/4"

Turning centerline

7/8" 7/8"

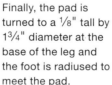

1/2" grid

Knee pattern
(enlarge 200%)

Leg pattern
(enlarge 400%)

There's no getting around some muscle power to shape the legs themselves. Proper tools speed things up, such as this aggressive open-form rasp.

Three Simple Steps on the Band saw

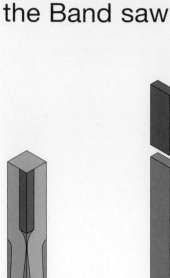

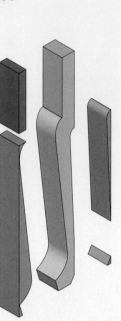

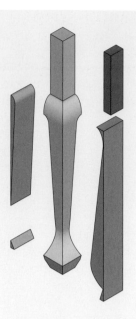

STEP ONE: The first step is to trace the pattern onto perpendicular faces of the leg blank with the "knees" touching. These are outside faces, so choose the best grain pattern.

STEP TWO: Cut the pattern on one face, working in from either end of each section. The pieces are separated from the leg above, but you should leave a small center section uncut to hold the waste in place for now.

STEP THREE: The leg is then rotated to the other patterned face and the waste pieces are cut away. These pieces can be cut away completely. Then go back and finish the stopped cuts on the first face to complete the leg. Most of the work is done, and you can see the leg emerging from what had been a simple stick of wood.

While it might seem logical to finish sizing the leg posts before drilling the mortises, the full width helps support the leg during the mortising process.

After the mortises are complete, head back to the band saw and carefully trim away the waste from the leg posts on the two outside faces of the legs.

Dovetails, Tenons and Finery

At the end of the cabriole legs article, we had completed the shaping of the legs and had made the mortises to accept the back, sides and lower front apron.

The front top rail is attached to each leg with a single dovetail. Lay out and cut a ½"-long × ¾"-deep dovetail into each leg for the front top rail. Then use the completed pin socket to create the tail on the two ends of the top rail.

Next, you need to cut tenons on the back, sides and front apron. Use the mortises cut in the leg posts to size the tenons. Notice that I used double tenons for the back and sides. Because these boards are so wide, the double tenon allows for wood expansion, and avoids cracks or splits in the aprons.

Once the tenons are cut, use the patterns at right to lay out the decorative details on the aprons. This is actually simple work and can be done using a band saw or, if necessary, a jigsaw. Take your time making the cuts, and then carefully sand the profiles to remove the saw marks. It's tempting to gloss over this step, but once the finish is on the table, any leftover saw marks will detract from the final appearance of the project.

Here you can see that I used a Forstner bit to remove the majority of the waste, then I hand-cut the dovetail socket. Transfer these shapes to the rail to complete the joinery on the top rail.

To make the double tenon, first form one complete tenon on the ends, then use a hand saw to divide the tenons. Then chisel out the center.

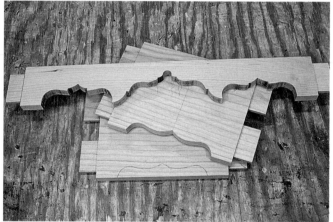

After laying out the pattern for the apron details, use either a band saw or jigsaw to cut out the pattern, then sand the edges smooth.

The front apron extender fits between the front legs and has a mortise on either end that will hold the drawer runners in position.

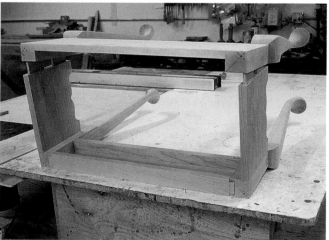

The frame is glued together in stages. Install the sides in the front frame mortises, putting glue only in the front frame. Then place the back frame in position (without glue) to hold everything while clamping the front joints.

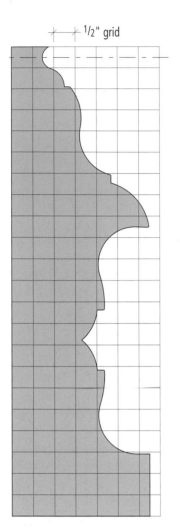

← →| 1/2" grid

Half-apron pattern

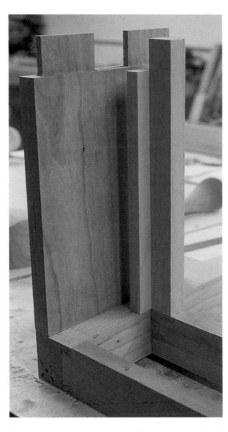

The two-piece drawer guides are installed next. The runner has a tenon on its front end sized to fit into the apron extender's mortises. The guide piece is simply nailed to the runner. Then glue the back assembly in place, leaving the runner/guide loose at the rear for now.

Careful Steps to Glue-up

With most tables it makes sense to glue things up in stages rather than trying to fit everything together at once. It makes it easier to check the fit of the piece without having to hurry.

This table is no exception. First, do a dry-fit on the table pieces to make sure everything aligns properly. Then start the glue-up by first assembling the back apron and two rear legs. Then assemble the front legs, the front apron and the top rail. Set these two assemblies aside and allow the glue to dry.

While the front and back assemblies are in the clamps, use the time to make the front apron extender. The front apron extender simply has $\frac{1}{4}" \times 1" \times \frac{1}{2}"$-deep mortises on each end to receive the drawer runners. It fits between the legs, extending the apron to make it even with the inside surface of the legs. Attach the front apron extender to the apron with glue as shown at left.

The next operation is to attach the side aprons to the front only. Do not glue the back assembly at this point. All you want to do is apply glue in the front mortises and to the front tenons. Slip the sides into place and then put the back assembly in position (without glue), and clamp and square the assembly.

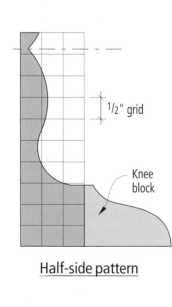

1/2" grid

Knee block

Half-side pattern

Top rail w/ 1/2" dovetail

Side w/ two 1 1/4" tenons

Front apron w/ 1 1/4" tenon

Inside-corner joinery

After the frame is complete, the runners can be leveled and nailed in place to the inside of the leg.

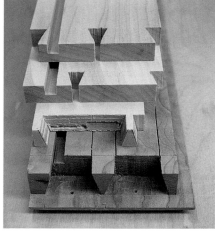

With the frame assembled, measure to double check your drawer dimensions, then mill the pieces. The drawer is assembled with through-dovetails at the back and half-blind dovetails at the front.

Guiding the Drawer

The single drawer slides in the table on wood runners that have side guides attached to keep things straight and smooth.

After the glue in the sides/front assembly is dry, remove the back assembly and make the drawer runner and drawer-guide units. Cut $\frac{1}{4}" \times 1" \times \frac{1}{2}"$ tenons on one end of the runners, which will fit into the front mortises in the front apron extender.

Then cut the drawer guide pieces to length and nail them to the outer side of either drawer runner. Check the fit.

Now glue the back assembly to the sides (glue the front of the drawer runners but leave the back loose) and clamp everything together, again squaring the case.

Let everything dry, then level the drawer runner units from the front to the back of the case on each side. It's also important that the drawer runners are parallel to one another. Otherwise the drawer will rock on its runners. Attach the drawer runners to the rear legs with reproduction nails, as shown on page 227.

Building the Drawer

You're now ready to build the drawer. Start by milling and cutting the drawer parts. I use traditional half-blind dovetail joints at the front of the drawer and through-dovetails at the rear.

The joinery on the drawer is actually one of the more complicated steps in the project, but because there's only one drawer, it's a great chance to practice your hand-cut dovetails.

The drawer front is lipped on three sides (all but the bottom) and overlays the front of the table, as shown above.

Once you have completed the dovetail joinery, cut a $\frac{1}{4}" \times \frac{1}{4}"$ groove into the drawer sides and front to capture the drawer bottom. Then assemble the drawer.

Now mill the $\frac{5}{8}"$-thick bottom to fit the drawer by beveling it on three sides. This will allow the bottom to slide into the drawer groove. You will need to make a relief cut in the bottom (as shown above right), which will allow you to nail the bottom to the drawer back. Mark the height of the relief cut, slide the bottom out of the drawer and make the relief cut. Install the bottom using a single reproduction nail.

Add a Knee

The table base is essentially complete, but the legs are actually missing an important part — their knees. The knee blocks blend the cabriole legs into the apron. When making the legs there's no good way to incorporate the knee blocks into the original shape and material of the legs, so the knee blocks are tradition-

ally added after the legs are shaped.

Even though the knee blocks are additions, it's still a good idea to try for a nearly seamless grain match to help continue the illusion. After selecting the best grain pattern for the knee blocks, there are three steps in making them.

First, cut the knee blocks to size. There are two knee blocks per front leg and one for each back leg. No knee blocks are required at the rear of the table.

Next, align each knee block in place next to the leg and against the rail (or side). Mark each knee block where the curve of the leg terminates at the block, and also where the profile on the apron or sides meets each knee block. Each knee block may have a slightly different fit to the legs, so it's necessary to hand fit each and mark them accordingly.

Finally, trace the profile of the knee block from the pattern on page 63 onto the other side of the block, aligning the shape with the termination marks you carried over from the legs and sides. Then cut and sand to the final profile, and glue the knee blocks in place. The legs are now complete.

To finish off the case, I added square pegs in the legs to add strength and a traditional detail. Mark the peg locations (to intersect the apron tenons in the leg mortises) then drill holes for the $\frac{1}{4}"$ square pegs.

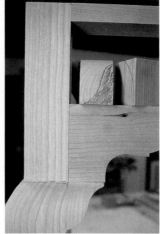

The bottom is a traditional ⁵⁄₈"-thick piece, beveled on three sides to fit the grooves in the drawer sides and front. The back edge overlaps the drawer back and is nailed in place through the relief cut.

The knee blocks complete the shape of the leg and tie the legs to the aprons. Pay particular attention to grain direction when fitting these pieces.

To continue the authentic details on this piece, square pegs reinforce the leg-to-apron joint.

Make the pegs from a harder wood than your table. I used oak pegs for my cherry table and though the finished look is square, I rounded and tapered the leading end of the pegs to make them easier to insert. Apply a bit of glue to the holes and tap the pegs into place. When dry, final sand the entire surface to #180 grit.

Topping it All Off

The top is one of the last steps and while you've spent a significant amount of time getting the legs and aprons perfect, the top is the most visible part of the table.

Because you're likely making the top from more than one board, make sure your wood and grain selection offers the best pattern and color match.

Once the top is milled, glued and has been cut to final size, it's time to form the profile on the edge of the top. Use a ³⁄₁₆" beading bit on the top edge and a ¼" roundover bit on the lower edge to create the profile. Go ahead and sand the top to a finished smoothness with No.180-grit sandpaper.

To attach the top to the case, I used wooden L-shaped clips (sometimes called "buttons") slipped into slots in the aprons. Use a biscuit joiner to cut the ¼" slots into the sides and back, down ½" from the top edge. To make the slot wide

LEFT: Delicate edge treatments with a router give the top a sophisticated profile. Use a ³⁄₁₆" beading bit on the top edge and a ¼" roundover bit on the bottom.

BELOW: Attach the top to the table frame at the rear using L-shaped wooden clips. The tongue of the clip slips into ¼" grooves cut in the aprons with a biscuit joiner.

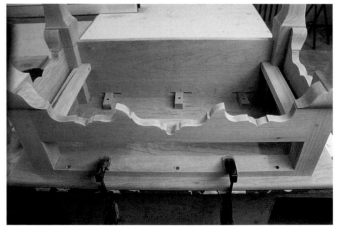

enough at full depth, make two cuts adjacent to one another at each location.

Make the wooden clips to attach the top as shown on page 66. Screw the clips in place on the underside of the top, with the clips located in the center of each slot. To hold the top in place at the front of the case, drive three screws through pre-drilled clearance holes up through the front top rail as shown.

After spending so much time and

care building your table, you want to make sure you devote the same care to your finish.

My preference for adding color to a piece is water-based aniline dye stains. They're much easier to mix and to clean up afterwards, and the water-based dye stains are more light-resistant (less likely to fade in normal sunlight) than the oil- or alcohol-based varieties. They're also easy to apply, whereas alcohol-based stains can sometimes leave streaking.

Water-based dyes can be applied by spraying or brushing with equally impressive results. The secret (if you can call it a secret) is to follow the correct procedure when using either method.

All the fitting and sanding have created a nice piece of furniture, but it still needs a replica finish. Don't try and short-circuit this last step. Even though the piece is sanded, in order to apply a water-based finish, first wipe down the entire piece with a wet rag, then sand again before applying the stain.

Sand and Water Treatment

Begin the process by sanding the entire piece to #180 grit. Don't go any further because it will be time lost and may actually affect the appearance of the finish. Why? Because water-based aniline dye stains will raise the grain on the wood. This makes the surface rough and also affects the absorption of the stain into the wood.

Rather than raise the grain while you're trying to apply an even finish, raise the grain prior to staining by wetting the entire piece with a cloth that is dripping wet. Then let the piece dry and sand a second time with No.180-grit paper to knock down the "fuzzies" that the water raised.

Next, spend a few minutes "softening" any hard corners or edges on the table with a piece of No.100- or No.120-grit sandpaper. Sharp edges are a true sign of an "almost finished" project and will show wear quicker.

Now you're ready to mix and apply the stain. I use Moser's stains and mix them very scientifically — one ounce of powder to four cups of water. That's it. Heat the water until you see small bubbles rising from the bottom of the pan. Place the powder into an opaque container to minimize the reaction to sunlight and add the water when it reaches the proper temperature. Replace the lid and shake the mixture.

When the mixture is cool you can begin coloring the wood. The basic rule of thumb here is to saturate the entire piece. Apply the dye until it runs off of the table. You want to see pooling on the flat surfaces and sometimes this will require an immediate second application of the color.

Once you have given it a good soaking, let it sit for five to 10 minutes and wipe away any excess stain. If you don't have any to wipe away, you didn't thoroughly saturate the piece.

Let the dye dry completely, and sand the table with No.320-grit wet/dry sandpaper. It's easy to sand through the stain around the corners and edges, so be careful sanding these areas.

At this point, if you're coloring a figured wood like the curly cherry used on this table, you may choose to apply a coat of boiled linseed oil. The oil sinks into the grain of the wood and adds depth to the finish. Simply apply a soaking coat of the oil with a foam brush. Let the oil steep for five minutes and wipe the surface dry. Remember to properly dispose of the used rags. Give the oiled piece 36 hours to cure.

You're now ready to apply your topcoat. I used a sprayed-on blonde shellac finish. For use in my HVLP spraying system, I mixed the shellac to a 2-pound cut then sprayed three coats, allowing each coat to dry thoroughly and sanding with No.400-grit paper between coats.

Sand the entire piece again. Here, I like to use a No.400-grit sanding sponge. They don't allow as much heat to build up at your fingertips. Then finally apply an additional two coats of shellac.

Shellac has a shiny appearance when it's applied. I prefer a softer satin finish, and this can be achieved by rubbing out the finish with No.0000 steel wool and Behlen's wool lube.

Here's how: Let the piece dry for 24 to 48 hours, then mix a bit of the wool lube into water, dampen the steel wool and rub the surface in the direction of the grain. After a few minutes wipe the surface with a dry cloth. If the finish looks smooth and satiny, you're there. If not, repeat the steps again. Rub the entire table in the same manner and then give it a coat of good paste wax for added protection.

If you were to choose to brush on the shellac instead of spraying, I would adjust the shellac to a 3-pound cut. Use a good brush (in general, the better the brush, the smoother the finish) and apply two coats of finish. Sand the piece thoroughly and brush on a third coat. Repeat these steps for a fourth and fifth coat, then move to the "rub-out" steps.

If you've followed all the steps correctly, you now have one of the most pleasing examples of Queen Anne furniture sitting in front of you. You've accomplished a complicated piece of furniture in a fairly simple manner — and you've earned your bragging rights. Enjoy!

This unusual splayed-leg table will offer you new challenges (angled tenons) plus a lesson on rule joints.

PROJECT
31

Shaker Drop-Leaf Table

BY STEVE SHANESY

Just about every woodworker will agree that any project with angles other than 90° makes things more challenging. This handsome Shaker-style table with splayed, or angled, legs is no exception. But don't be put off, because it's not as difficult as it looks.

First, keep in mind that virtually all the angles are 4°. Simple enough. As for making the leg-to-apron mortise-and-tenon joint, breathe easy because it's almost as simple as making 90° joints.

All the Angles

Before we start, here's a list of the angle cuts: All apron ends and long edges, including the top edge of the drop-leaf support arm; both ends of the legs; and the cleats for attaching the top. That's it!

There's not a lot of material required for this project, so go ahead and mill the pieces to size, leaving some length for trimming later. Be sure you have some extra pieces to use for setups. I used 1"-thick material for the aprons, but ¾" works equally well (just change the tenon thickness to ⅜").

Keep the leg stock square (don't taper it until after the mortises are cut) and, when cutting to length, cut the 4° angle on the ends.

Use a V-block to simplify the angle cutting, as shown in the photo below left. To determine which corner is up,

first mark the mortise locations on the legs. To cut the angle, bevel the miter saw 5½" to the right and position the leg to the left of the blade with its inside corner (where you will cut the mortises) facing up. Make your cut. To cut to final length, measure and turn the leg so the inside corner is down. Save a short angled scrap from the leg — it will be useful when mortising.

Lay out the mortise locations on a test piece with the angle cut on the top edge. I used an ⅛" setback for the apron to the leg. The mortise starts 1" down and is 3¼" long by ¾" deep.

After mortising, complete the legs by cutting tapers on their two inside faces (the faces with mortises). The taper

Clamp a V-block to a miter saw and bevel the blade to the right 5½". With what will be the inside corner of the leg facing up, make the cut for the top of the leg. Turn the leg end-for-end to cut the bottom end to final length.

Angled offcut piece

Use the angled offcut from the leg when setting the stop block in the mortising jig. Set it in place so the top of the leg is square. By doing so, the mortise will be in the same location on both faces of the leg.

SHAKER DROP-LEAF TABLE • INCHES (MILLIMETERS)

QUANTITY	PART	STOCK	THICKNESS	(mm)	WIDTH	(mm)	LENGTH	(mm)	COMMENTS
4	legs	Cherry	1 1/2	38	1 1/2	38	28 1/4*	718	
2	long aprons	Cherry	1	25	5	127	26 3/4**	679	
2	short aprons	Cherry	1	25	5	127	9 7/8	251	
2	top	Cherry	3/4	19	14 1/4	362	36	914	
2	leaves	Cherry	3/4	19	7 1/2	184	36	914	
2	leaf supports	Cherry	1	25	1 1/2	38	12 1/2	318	

* Dimension is slightly larger than finished size.

** Apron lengths from longest point at shoulder and includes 3/4 " tenons.

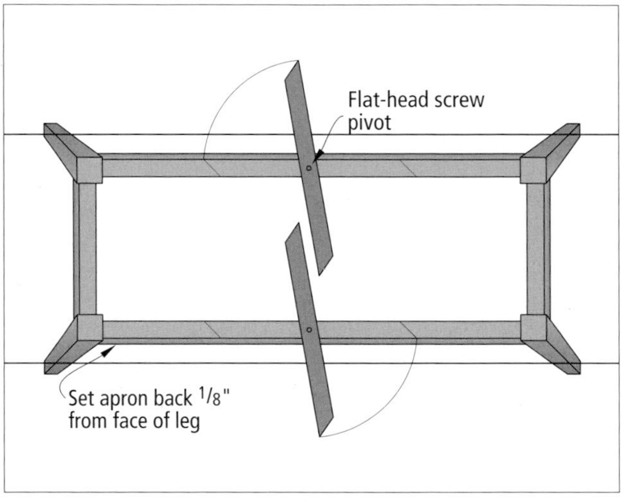
Flat-head screw pivot
Set apron back 1/8" from face of leg

Plan-top removed

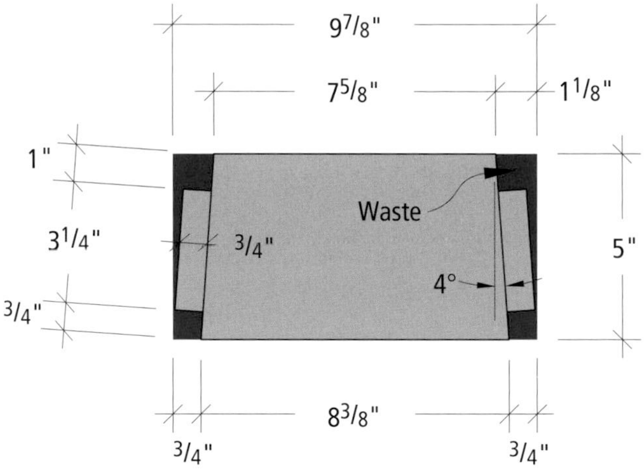
9 7/8"
7 5/8"
1 1/8"
1"
3 1/4"
3/4"
3/4"
Waste
4°
5"
8 3/8"
3/4"
3/4"

Short apron

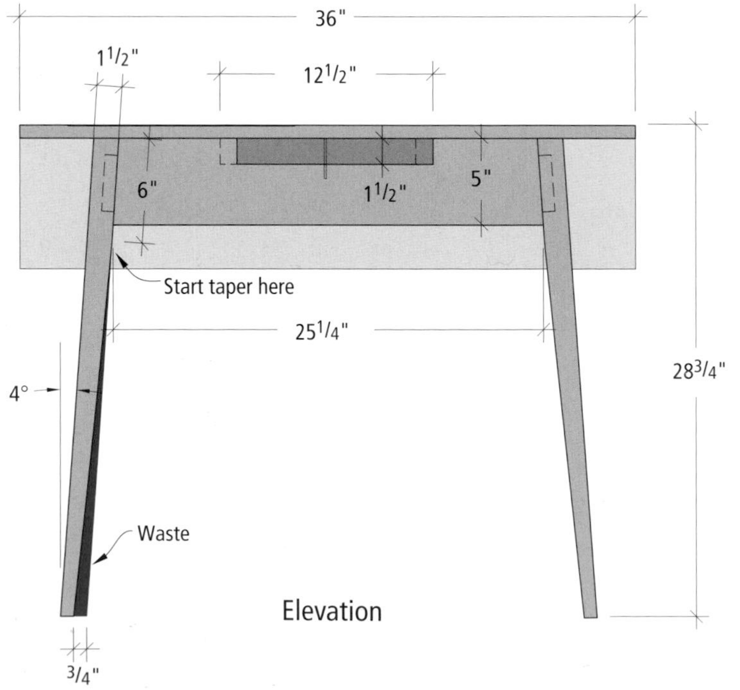
36"
1 1/2"
12 1/2"
6"
1 1/2"
5"
Start taper here
25 1/4"
28 3/4"
4°
Waste
3/4"

Elevation

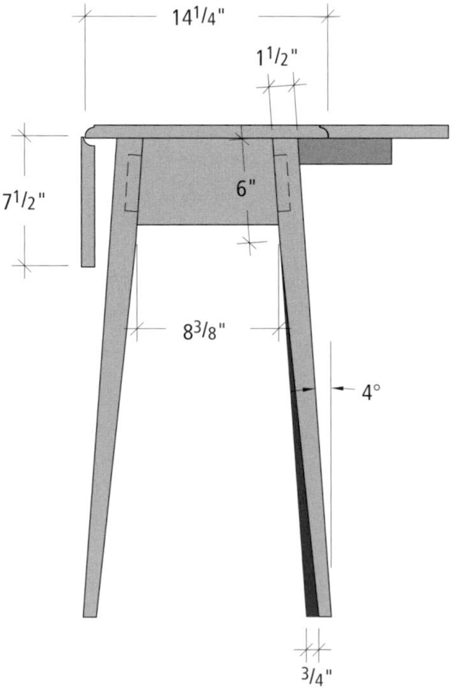
14 1/4"
1 1/2"
7 1/2"
6"
8 3/8"
4°
3/4"

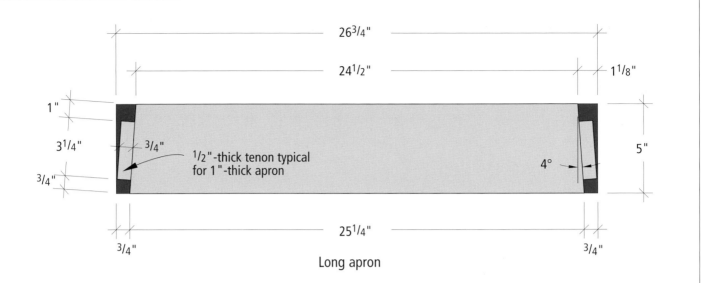

26³/₄"

24¹/₂"

1¹/₈"

1"

3¹/₄"

³/₄"

³/₄"

¹/₂"-thick tenon typical
for 1"-thick apron

4°

5"

25¹/₄"

³/₄"

³/₄"

Long apron

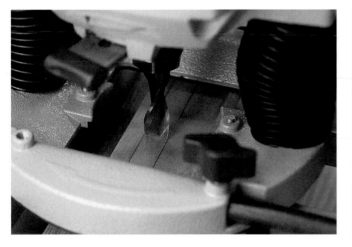

Layout the first mortise to guide you in setting the fence on your router. Using a spiral router bit will cut a clean mortise.

With the leg secured in the mortising jig, plunge-cut the mortise. Don't try to hog out too much material at one time — make several shallow cuts instead.

After routing the mortise, you'll need to square the corners of the mortise using a chisel.

Rough-cut the tapers on the legs. Clean up the cuts using a jointer or hand plane.

With the miter gauge set to 4°, make the first cheek cuts on all the aprons. To make a first cut on both ends of each apron, flip the apron over end-for-end. This will result in these cheek cuts being on opposite sides of the aprons.

Set the miter gauge to the opposite 4° and make the second cheek cuts, using the same steps as before.

Because of the angled cut on the apron ends, the edge cheeks and shoulders are best cut by using a hand saw.

begins 1" down from the bottom edge of the apron. Mark this point. The leg tapers to ¾" × ¾" at the floor — which is one-half its thickness. Mark your taper lines on all four legs. Cut the tapers on the band saw wide of the line and clean up the cut using a hand plane or jointer. Except for sanding, the legs are now complete.

Angled Tenons

Next work on the aprons. Cut them to length as shown in the illustration — don't forget the 4° angle on the ends.

Before ripping the angles on the top and bottom edges of the apron, determine which face will be outside and mark it. When done, the longer edge of the apron will be the bottom edge. To cut the angles, bevel the table saw blade 4°. Now set the fence and place the apron on the saw so the less-acute angle will be the outside. (This depends on whether your saw tilts right or left.) Reset the fence and cut the complementary angle on the bottom edge.

Notch each long apron for its drop-leaf support arm. Refer to the drawings for the layout. Use a hand saw or band saw to make the cutouts. The cut along the length of the notch is square to the face. When making the support pieces, the long bottom edge is square but the top edge is at 4° to match the apron edge. Attach the supports after assembly by screwing them in place, leaving them loose enough to swivel.

Now cut the tenons. Set your miter gauge to 4°, lay the apron against the it and hold the apron end against the table saw's fence. Cut the first cheek. Cut all the cheeks using this setting. Then change the miter gauge to 4° the other side of square, turn the aprons over and make the second cheek cuts. Because of the angled cut on the apron ends, the edge cheeks and shoulders are best cut by hand.

Base and Top Assembly

With the work on the legs and aprons complete, dry-fit the table base. After

Glue up the legs and long aprons to make two assemblies. Note the angled gluing cauls that keep things square for using the clamps.

A crosscutting sled works great for trimming the ends of the leaves and tabletop square.

Take a moment to organize the wood for the best grain pattern and color match. Then cut the wood you need for the top and aprons.

making any adjustments, glue it up. I made clamping cauls with one face at 4° to position the clamps square across the joint. I glued and clamped the base in two operations to avoid the typical panic associated with gluing it up all at once.

Next, glue the stock you need for the top and drop-leaves. Take a moment to organize the wood for the best grain pattern and color match. After the glue dries, trim the pieces to their final sizes.

The Rules of Rule Joints

The traditional drop-leaf table uses a rule joint at the transition between the fixed top and the leaf. It provides an attractive appearance when open or closed. Making the matching inside/outside radius profiles on the leaves and top is not difficult, but properly locating the drop-leaf hinge on the mating parts requires a bit of knowledge and careful set-up (see "Installing Drop-leaf Table Hinges" on page 237).

The edge profiles on the table parts can be made using a hand-held router or a router table. I opted for the router table because it allows for more control.

Some router-bit manufacturers offer matched bit sets to make the mating parts. These sets usually consist of a $\frac{1}{2}$"-radius bit and a $\frac{1}{2}$"-cove bit, each with a bearing guide. If you have one or both bits, the set isn't necessary.

Cut the profile on the table edge first. It has a $\frac{1}{2}$"-radius with a $\frac{3}{16}$" bead on top. Cut the profile in two passes so you don't tax your router. Make the same cut on a scrap piece, too. Next, install the cove bit and mill the mating leaf profile to the dimensions given in the drawing on page 237.

Now turn your attention to the drop-leaf hinges. Before you begin cutting the mortise for the hinges, remember this: Your hinge may be different so base your measurements on the hinges you use.

Place the tabletop and leaves together and upside down on your workbench and gently clamp the three pieces together. Now measure in 6" from the

Rout the roundover profile on both long edges of the tabletop. Note the flat that remains. This will be matched by the flat on the leaves' profile.

Rout the mating profile for the leaves using a cove bit. The bit height should leave a $5/32$" flat to match the mating profile's bead.

When both rule joint profiles are correct they nest together with the top surfaces flush and a $1/32$" gap between the profiles.

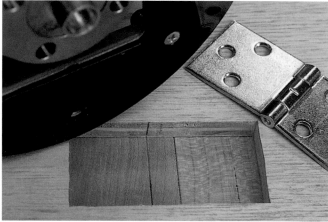

Rout the leaf-hinge mortise using a template and guide bushing. Note the unequal lengths of hinge leaves. The short leaf goes on the tabletop side. Also, use the pencil line on the table surface to align the template. The pencil line on the template edges serve as the center point of the hinge pin.

edge along the rule joint to determine the general location of each hinge.

From the joint edges, make a line $1/2$" back on the tabletop side. This is the pin location on one axis. Repeat this procedure for all four hinge locations.

Now set up a router with a $1/2$" straight bit and guide bushing (mine had a $5/8$" outside diameter). Make a template using $1/2$" plywood with a cutout sized to the hinge and the bushing diameter. In my case, this is the hinge width or length plus $1/8$". After making the cutout, scribe a line on each side edge of the template opening in the exact location of the hinge-pin center. This is not centered because the hinge leaves are

different lengths. The longer leaf is on the leaf side.

Now set the router's depth of cut to include the template thickness plus the required depth for the center point of the hinge pin. It should be about $3/32$".

Using the scrap test pieces for the rule-joint profile setup, test the template by routing the hinge-leaf mortise. Arrange the template so the lines scribed on the template align with the $1/2$" pencil line you marked earlier.

Before installing the hinge in the test pieces, remove some material to accommodate the hinge barrel. Install a $1/4$" fluting bit in your router along with an edge guide. Remove the clamp and the

table leaves. Adjust the edge guide so the bit aligns with the hinge barrel location. Adjust the depth of cut to accommodate the hinge barrel. Now make the relief cut for the hinge barrel.

Install the hinge in your test pieces and check out the movement. There should be no binding, it should be fully closed when on the same plane and it should have a small gap when at 90°. When satisfied, rout the mortises in the three top pieces.

Now install the hinges. Leave one screw out and test the action. If good, insert that final screw.

To attach the tabletop to the base, make cleats that attach the apron sides

and top. The top edge of the cleats must have the 4° angle to match the top apron edge.

To finish the table, I first sanded through progressive grits from No.120 to No.220 grit.

For a clear finish, I used one of my favorite "recipes" when I don't want a heavy film finish. My concoction calls for equal amounts of paint thinner, boiled linseed oil and oil-based varnish.

This liquid is thin enough to rag on and wipe off, and after a couple coats it offers reasonable surface protection compared to an oil finish alone. The finish is especially effective on cherry because the linseed oil accelerates the natural darkening and aging of the wood.

A shallow trough must be made to accommodate the hinge barrel. Use a fluting bit and an edge guide.

Installing Drop-Leaf Table Hinges

Drop-leaf hinge installation isn't intuitive. What seems normal — just placing the hinge barrel where the leaf and top meet, like a door to a stile — is totally wrong. Another wrong assumption is that the correct depth to set the hinges is simply to make them flush with the underside surface.

As with all hinges, the location of the pivot point is the ultimate concern. With the drop-leaf hinge, the pivot point, which is the center of the pin, must be centered on the radius of the matching profiles. In my case, the 1/2" radius of the rule joint requires the hinge pin to be 1/2" down from the top of the radius and 1/2" in from the side.

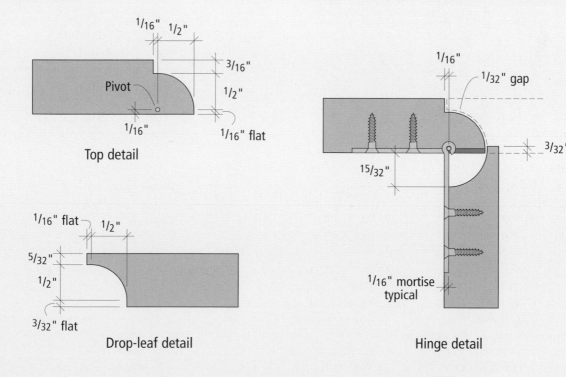

Top detail

Drop-leaf detail

Hinge detail

Squeeze a bit of storage from a place that is usually wasted with a project that's great for an aspiring beginner.

PROJECT
32

Modern Occasional Table

BY JIM STUARD

There is space and need in almost everyone's home for an occasional table. But to sweeten the concept we've come up with a dual purpose for this design. Every family room has those certain items you need only occasionally (is that where the name came from?), but there's never a good place to keep them. You know, the remote control you rarely use, the Scrabble dictionary, or the coasters for when company's around. Well, lift the top off this table and you've uncovered a storage space for those occasionally needed items.

Getting Started on the Legs

Construction begins by cutting out the parts according to the cutting list. Start with the tapered legs. There are many methods for doing this, but the simplest is just laying out the taper on each leg, cutting it out with a band saw and planing the taper with a bench plane.

First determine which sides of the legs will face out, choosing the best figure for those faces. The tapers are on the two inside faces of each leg. To keep the legs correctly oriented during the construction process, place the legs as they will be on the finished table, then hold them together and mark a diamond across the intersection of all four legs at the top.

Next, mark each leg on the inside face (where the aprons will butt against)

at $4^{5}/_{16}$" and $4^{13}/_{16}$" down from the top edge of the legs. The $4^{5}/_{16}$" measurement is the location of the bottom edge of the table's apron, which leaves $^{1}/_{16}$" of the leg protruding above the top, adding a nice

detail. The $4^{13}/_{16}$" measurement is the starting location of the leg taper.

Now move to the bottoms of the legs and, using a combination square, mark a 1" square on each leg, measuring from

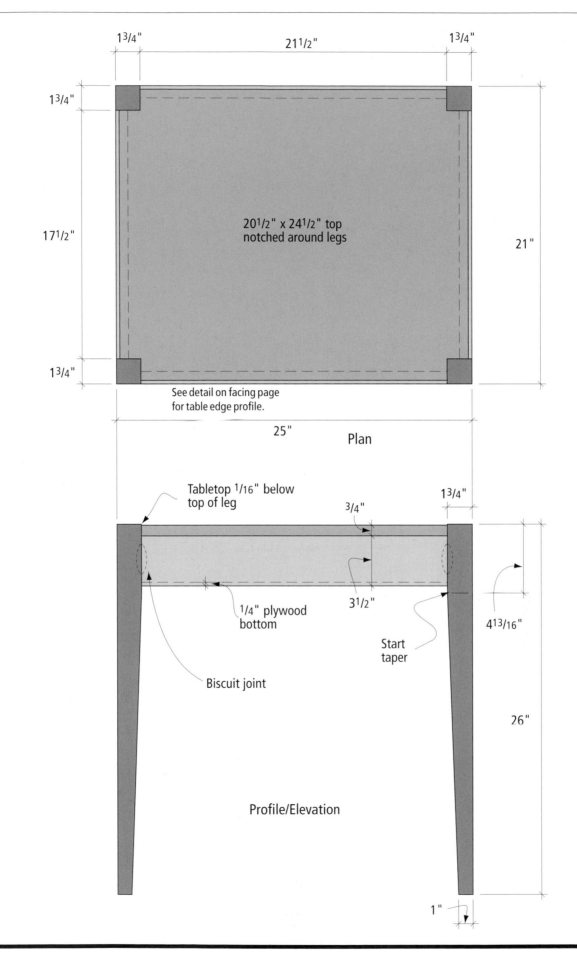

1³/4" 21¹/2" 1³/4"

1³/4"

17¹/2"

20¹/2" x 24¹/2" top
notched around legs

21"

1³/4"

See detail on facing page
for table edge profile.

25" Plan

Tabletop ¹/16" below
top of leg

3/4"

1³/4"

¹/4" plywood
bottom

3¹/2"

4¹³/16"

Biscuit joint

Start
taper

26"

Profile/Elevation

1"

MODERN OCCASIONAL TABLE • INCHES (MILLIMETERS)

QUANTITY	PART	STOCK	THICKNESS	(mm)	WIDTH	(mm)	LENGTH	(mm)	COMMENTS
4	legs	cherry	$1^3/_4$	45	$1^3/_4$	45	26	660	
2	short aprons	cherry	$7/_8$	22	$3^1/_2$	89	$17^1/_2$	445	
2	long aprons	cherry	$7/_8$	22	$3^1/_2$	89	$21^1/_2$	546	
1	top	ash	$3/_4$	19	$20^1/_2$	521	$24^1/_2$	622	corners notched for legs
1	bottom	plywood	$1/_4$	6	$20^1/_2$	521	$24^1/_2$	622	corners notched for legs

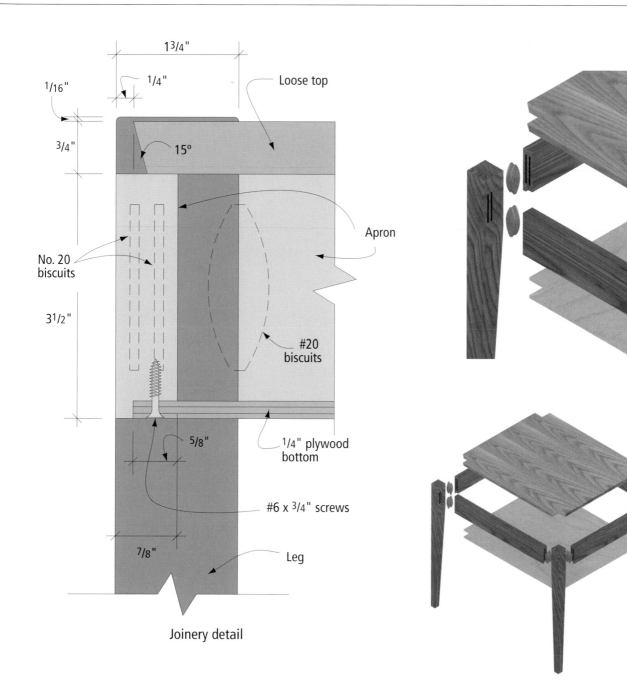

$1^3/_4$"

$1/_4$"

$1/_16$"

$3/_4$"

Loose top

15°

No. 20 biscuits

Apron

#20 biscuits

$3^1/_2$"

$5/_8$"

$1/_4$" plywood bottom

#6 x $3/_4$" screws

$7/_8$"

Leg

Joinery detail

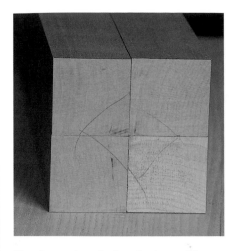

The diamond marked on the tops of the four legs will allow you to always recognize the inside and outside faces of the legs.

To mark the foot of each leg, use a combination square to locate the 1" mark. I used a pen when laying out these measurements so they wouldn't fade or be easily obscured during the clean-up process on the tapers.

the outside corner. This indicates where the inside tapers will end on each leg. Connect the marks from the top to the bottom of the legs, then cut the tapers on a band saw, cutting as close to the line as you can. To smooth out the band saw cut, use a bench plane and a bit of muscle to remove the rough-sawn edge.

The term "occasional table" implies that this table won't be expected to carry a lot of weight. In that spirit, the joinery doesn't have to be extraordinarily strong. Two #20 biscuits in each joint provides plenty of strength for the base. The ¼" plywood bottom screwed in place at the end will add to the base's overall strength.

Set up the joinery by marking each leg 2⁹⁄₁₆" from the top (the center point for the aprons). Adjust the biscuit joiner to space two biscuits evenly in the thickness of each apron and to position the aprons flush to the outside faces of the legs.

After cutting the biscuit joints, set up a router to cut a ¼" × ⁵⁄₈"-wide rabbet in the bottom edge of the aprons for the bottom. With the rabbets cut, start assembling the base by gluing the short aprons between the legs. Dealing with fewer clamps on any procedure makes the glue-up easier.

Check for squareness on each glued-up end by measuring from the top corner of one leg to the bottom corner of the other, making sure the measurements are equal. After about an hour,

glue up the rest of the base, again checking the base for squareness on the sides and across the width and length of the apron. For the loose top to fit accurately, you have to be on the money.

Take the time to wipe off any glue that you see before it dries. The inside of the table gets finished, so you have to keep squeeze-out to a minimum.

Cut out a ¼" bottom to fit the dimensions between the rabbets in the aprons. To let the bottom fit in place correctly, notch the corners around the legs using the band saw. It's easiest if you don't install the bottom until after finishing.

The last construction step is the top. I made mine from quartersawn ash to create an interesting contrast to the cherry base. The top's width was achieved by gluing up four thinner boards. The grain on quartersawn ash is so straight that it's hard to find the glue joints. After the top is glued up and dry, cut it to the same size as the outside dimensions of the table base, which is a bit bigger than the finished size of the top.

Referencing off the table base helps you cut accurate notches in the top. Mark each notch location by laying the top upside down on a clean surface, then turn the base upside down and lay it on the top, flushing the corners. Mark the leg locations for the notches on the underside of the top.

To notch the top using a table saw, clamp a ¾"-spacer board to the rip fence about 3" back from the leading edge of the blade. Set the blade's height and the distance from the fence (including the blade) to the size of your notch and add about ¹⁄₁₆" to the cut to allow room for wood movement.

The top is run on edge against the saw's miter gauge. It's a good idea to add a sacrificial board to the miter gauge as well to add some extra height for support, and to back the top behind the notch to reduce tear-out. The top is pushed up to the spacer block on the fence, then pushed past the blade, holding the top tightly against the miter gauge. The spacer block allows you to properly align the piece for the cut, but keeps the notch (once cut free) from binding between the blade and fence, causing a dangerous kickback. Check the fit of your top. To allow you to lift the top, it needs to be a little loose. Next, cut the bevels on the top's edges by setting your table saw's blade to 15°. Set the rip fence so the cut is almost flush to the top edge of the top, leaving about a ¹⁄₃₂" flat on the edge. This cut will remove about ¼" off the underside of the edge. Repeat this cut on the other edges, then finish sand the top.

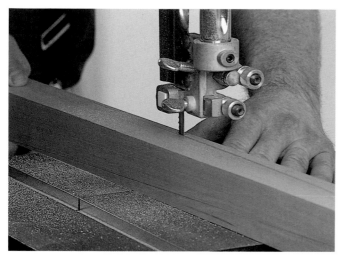

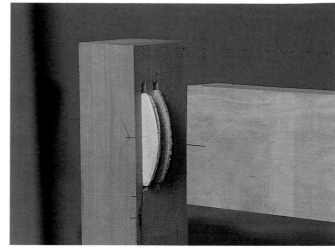

The simplest way to cut the tapers is on a band saw. Cut as close to the line as you can, leaving a little extra to the outside of the line. A bench plane does a nice job of cleaning up the tapers after being band sawn, but there's no sense in leaving too much work.

The double biscuits in the apron/leg joint will provide adequate strength for an occasional table. The biscuits are carefully located to keep the apron flush to the leg, while still providing even strength across the joint.

After sanding the base, apply a mix of boiled linseed oil and stain. The recipe is as follows: Mix ½ teaspoon of Pratt and Lambert Tonetic Cherry Bark stain (S7441) and ½ teaspoon of Minwax (No. 223) Colonial Maple stain with 4 ounces of boiled linseed oil. This gives the impression that the cherry's color is already darkened. The top gets no stain. Apply three coats of clear finish to the base, top and bottom. When the final coat is dry, screw in the bottom with some #6 × ¾" flathead screws.

Notching the top on the table saw can be an easy process. Notice the gap between the top and the saw's rip fence. This is the space left when the top is pushed beyond the spacer block attached to the fence. The gap will keep the notched piece from binding. Also notice that the top is clamped to the miter gauge. This is a good idea to hold everything in place.

This is an elegant and practical drop-leaf table that is at home in a small apartment or a dining room.

Queen Anne Drop-Leaf Dining Table

BY GLEN HUEY

This table is based on a number of New England designs from the latter half of the 18th century. It shares characteristics with many drop-leaf tables.

While the tabletop is just 42", it can be used as a small dining table, a breakfast table or as a table behind a sofa. Also, this table can be easily customized to your specific needs by changing minor aspects of the piece, such as the size or shape of the tabletop, or by using a slipper or trifid design for the foot.

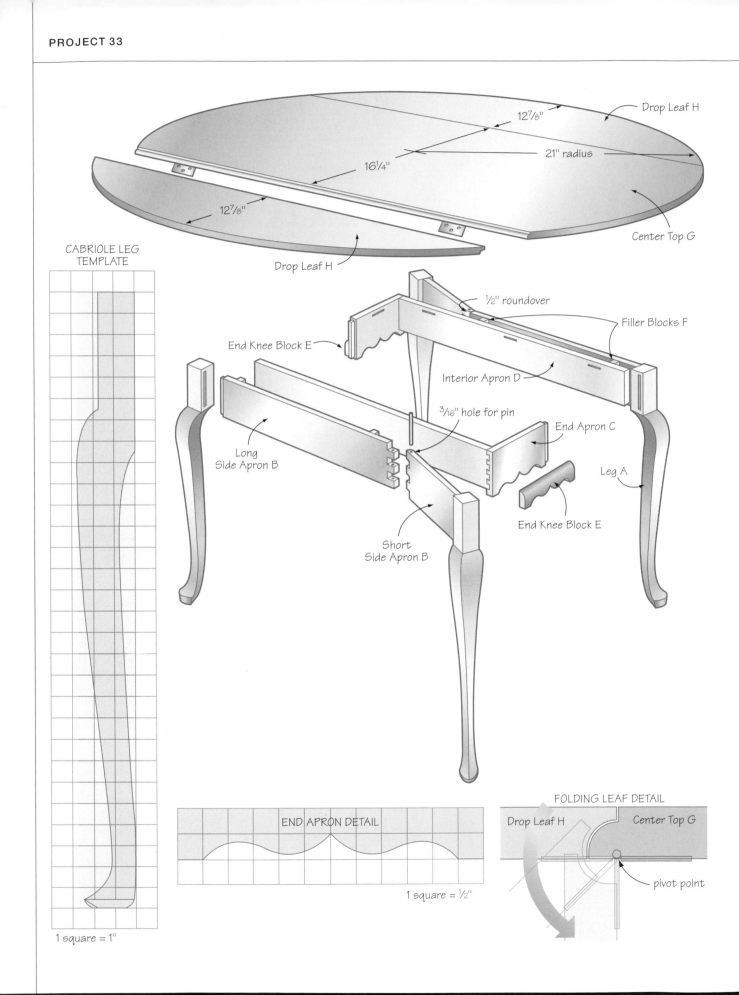

CABRIOLE LEG
TEMPLATE

1 square = 1"

Drop Leaf H

12⅞"

16¼"

12⅞"

21" radius

Center Top G

Drop Leaf H

½" roundover

Filler Blocks F

End Knee Block E

Interior Apron D

³⁄₁₆" hole for pin

End Apron C

Long
Side Apron B

End Knee Block E

Leg A

Short
Side Apron B

END APRON DETAIL

1 square = ½"

FOLDING LEAF DETAIL

Drop Leaf H

Center Top G

pivot point

QUEEN ANNE DROP-LEAF DINING TABLE • INCHES (MILLIMETERS)

REFERENCE	QUANTITY	PART	STOCK	THICKNESS	(mm)	WIDTH	(mm)	LENGTH	(mm)	COMMENTS
A	4	Legs	primary	2³/₄	70	2³/₄	70	29	737	
B	2	Side Aprons	primary	¹³/₁₆	21	5½	140	28½	724	³/₄" TBE rough-cut 4" to 6" longer for hinge joint
C	2	End Aprons	primary	¹³/₁₆	21	5½	140	9³/₄	242	³/₄" TOE
D	2	Interior Aprons	primary	¹³/₁₆	21	5½	140	27¹/₄	692	dovetailed to one end apron
E	2	End Knee Blocks	primary	1	25	1³/₄	45	9	229	
F	4	Filler Blocks	Secondary	⁷/₈	22	1½	38	5½	140	
TABLETOP										
G	1	Center Top	primary	⁷/₈	22	16¹/₄	412	42	1067	
H	2	Drop Leaves	primary	⁷/₈	22	12⁷/₈	327	42	1067	

TBE = Tenon Both Ends; TOE = Tenon One End

HARDWARE AND SUPPLIES

2 pairs	Drop-leaf hinges
No. 8 × 1¹/₄"	Slot-head wood screws
³/₁₆" × 12"	Steel rod

1 Begin by making the cabriole legs as shown in "Shaping the Cabriole Legs" on page 253.

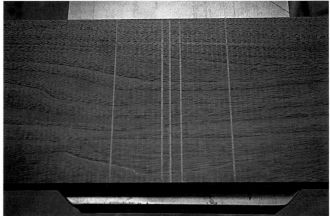

2 Once the legs are shaped, lay out and cut the mortises according to the plan. Begin the process of making the hinged aprons. Make the long aprons with an additional 4" to 6" of length, then move approximately 11" from one end and lay out a centerline. Draw a second set of lines ¼" from the center-line. This leaves enough space to cut apart the two long aprons. Finally, draw a third set of lines 2" from the second set. This defines the fingers for your joint.

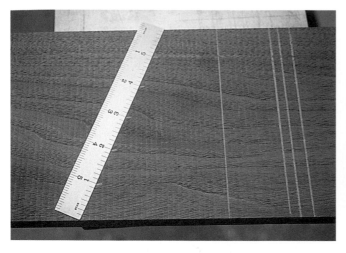

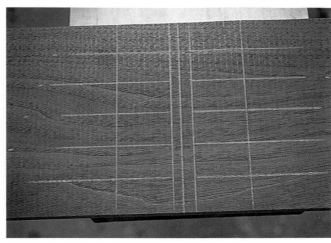

3 Lay out the apron into six equal parts on each side of the group of lines. This is accomplished by setting a rule on an angle at 0" and 6" and marking each inch location.

4 Connect the layout marks to define the individual fingers. Mark an X in the first, third and fifth fingers on one set and the second, fourth and sixth fingers on the opposite set.

5 Set the blade to the correct height and use a miter gauge to remove the X material. Be sure to stay inside the finger lines at each finger. Begin with the longer section of the aprons.

6 Before you cut the short section of the apron, use a 1/2" roundover bit on the end. Remove the back side of the apron. Here I have marked the finger lines on the back for clarity. Then remove the areas as you did on the longer rail.

7 After you have fine-tuned the fit of the fingers, clamp the assembly to a straightedge placed vertically under the drill press, and drill a 3/16" hole completely through the fingers. This allows you to install a steel rod to act as a pivot.

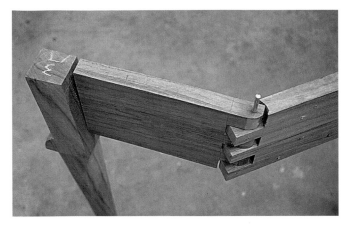

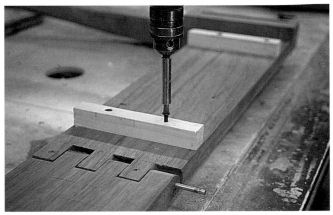

8 With the hinged joint completed, measure and mark 8⅞" from the joint to the end on the short section and 19⅝" on the long section. This is the cutoff of the aprons and where the tenons will be cut to match the mortises on the legs. While the apron is apart, remove enough of the bottom of each slot on the fixed apron to allow the square edge of the swing apron to operate.

9 Lay the long apron assembly on the table, inside up, and install the filler blocks as shown using No. 8 × 1¼" wood screws.

10 Mill the interior and end aprons to size. Cut the dovetail joint and the matching tenon for the leg mortises. Rough out the profile for the end apron and knee block. I used a secondary wood, but suggest you use all primary wood because the interior apron shows when the swing leg is opened.

11 Lay the dovetailed portion of the apron onto the inside of the hinged aprons so that the exterior edge of the end apron aligns with the leg block. Attach into the filler blocks as shown using wood screws.

12 Repeat the process on the second set so you have a pair of identical apron assemblies. Before moving on, this is the time to use the biscuit joiner to cut the slots that will receive the wooden clips.

13 Complete the base of the table by simply sliding the end apron tenons into the leg mortises. If all works well, glue the mortise-and-tenon joints and allow to dry.

14 This is how your completed base should look and operate.

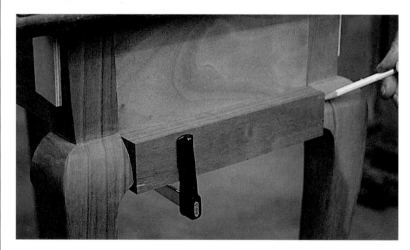

15 With the swing leg firmly clamped to the balance of the base, fit the knee blocks into place and mark the profile that matches each leg on either end of the block.

16 Shape the profile with planes and/or rasps.

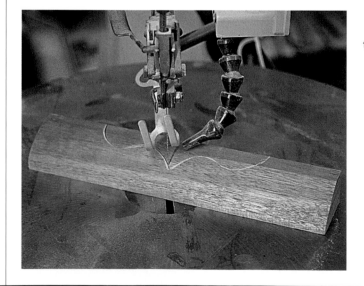

17 After you've completed the shaping, mark the knee block decorative pattern onto the block and make the cutout.

18 Reinstall the knee block and attach it to the apron with glue and screws. Be sure no glue gets on the swing leg area.

19 Keep the sizes of the tabletop to fit the base as you build it. Cut the center top to exact dimensions. Create the rule joint profiles using a 1/2" roundover bit on both of the center tabletop edges and a 1/2" cove bit on one edge of each drop leaf.

20 Lay the center top on the work surface upside down, then determine the hinge location. Mark a line that is 1/2" from the edge and create a groove using a 3/8" straight bit directly over that line. This groove is for the barrel of the drop-leaf hinges.

21 Slide the table leaf into place and lay out the hinge, allowing the longer hinge leaf to extend onto the tabletop leaf. Mark the hinge leaves, and create the mortise so the hinge is flush with the bottom of the table when completed.

22 Check the fit of the tabletop by setting it on the base. This is the place to stop if you would like to have a square table; simply rout your edge treatment. However, I chose to create a round top.

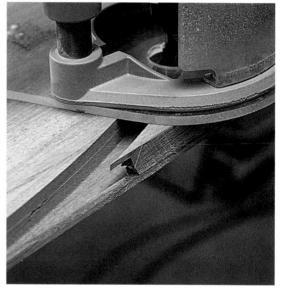

23 To achieve a round top, lay the assembled top inverted on the work surface and locate the center. Using a router compass jig (mine was shop-made) set to the correct size and a plunge router with a straight or up-cut straight bit, rout the round shape from the square top.

24 **ABOVE:** Make the cut in multiple passes, then create the desired edge treatment. I simply knocked off the sharp edge with sandpaper, then final sanded.

25 **LEFT:** This piece was finished with multiple coats of an oil/varnish mix and wax. After the finish has been applied, attach the top to the base with the wooden clips.

Shaping the Cabriole Legs

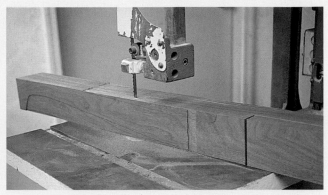

STEP ONE: After milling your lumber to size, mark the centers on both ends of your stock, and lay out the pattern for the leg onto the stock with the rear leg post areas meeting at one corner. (You will achieve the best look if you orient the grain of the leg to run from that corner toward the knee.) Then using the band saw, cut one side profile carefully. Save the waste pieces. Do not cut the leg post block.

STEP TWO: Reattach the waste pieces back into the positions from which they came. I like to use a hot-glue gun for this purpose. It dries in a hurry and also acts as a gap filler to replace the band-saw blade thickness. Cut the leg profile on the remaining side. Remove all of the waste material.

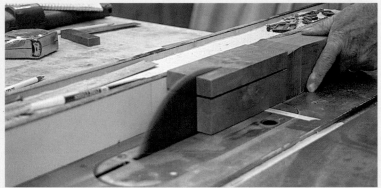

STEP THREE: If you are profiling a Dutch or pad foot, your next step is to turn the foot on the lathe. Mount the blank into position. Check the rotation of the leg prior to turning on the machine. Then use the lathe tools to turn the appropriate shape on the foot as well as on the pad area. If you choose a slipper, trifid or other foot profile, skip this step.

STEP FOUR: Using a saw, raise the blade to the correct height, and mark the front edge of the blade. I use masking tape for this purpose. Then set the fence to just remove the waste of the leg post block and cut to the beginning of the knee profile. Turn the leg a quarter turn and repeat the process. Finish the removal with a handsaw or on the band saw.

STEP SIX: Use common chalk to mark problem areas and finish the shaping with cabinet scrapers until all of the legs are visually identical.

STEP FIVE: Shape the leg with a combination of rasps, planes and riffler files to the profile desired (just off-square at the knee to almost completely round at the ankle).

A classic design with extra stability and an antique finish.

PROJECT
34

Shaker Trestle Table

BY GLEN HUEY

I've built a number of trestle tables in the Shaker style over the years, usually following the style of an original table from one Shaker collection or another. But when I decided to do a trestle table for *Popular Woodworking* readers, I took a second look at some of the designs and decided I could add a feature and come up with a stronger table without sacrificing the simple Shaker lines.

The one shown here is a standard two-pedestal table with a single stretcher tying the bases together. One of the concerns I've always had with this design was the stability of the joint at the stretcher. Anyone who has been to a family dinner at my house knows that a sturdy table is important when everyone starts hungrily reaching for platters of food. To solve the stability concern I doubled-up the hardware from another sturdy piece of furniture — the bed. By using a pair of bed bolts at each joint, this table becomes amazingly stout.

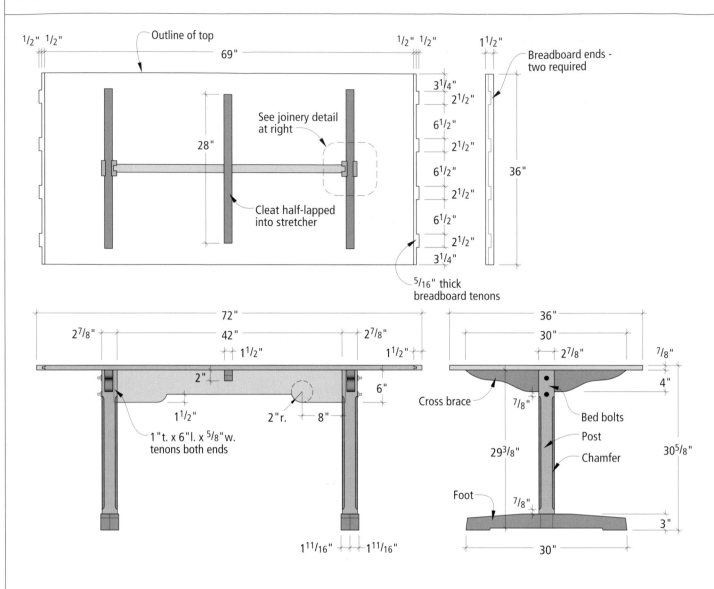

Outline of top

69"

½" ½"   ½" ½"   1½"

Breadboard ends - two required

3¼"
2½"
6½"
2½"
6½"
2½"
6½"
2½"
3¼"

28"

See joinery detail at right

Cleat half-lapped into stretcher

36"

5/16" thick breadboard tenons

72"
2⅞"   42"   2⅞"
1½"   1½"
2"
6"
1½"
2"r.   8"
1"t. x 6"l. x ⅝"w. tenons both ends
1¹¹/₁₆"   1¹¹/₁₆"

36"
30"
2⅞"   ⅞"
4"
Cross brace   ⅞"
Bed bolts
Post
Chamfer
29⅜"
30⅝"
Foot   ⅞"
3"
30"

Painting the Base

A simple coat of paint on the base may suffice for many, but it looked too new and shiny for my taste, so I added an antique finish to the piece.

Begin by staining the piece and applying two coats of shellac. Sand the finish.

Next, mix Olde Century Colors lampblack acrylic paint with fine sawdust particles and paint the mixture onto the base. As the paint dries, wipe with a very wet rag. The wiping will remove paint and dislodge some of the sawdust pieces leaving a "worn" surface.

Once the paint is dry, apply a coat of Maloof's Oil/Wax finish. Simply brush it on and wipe with a clean rag. This step provides a dull sheen to the paint, adding the look of years of polish.

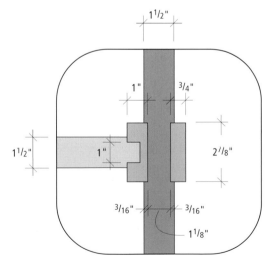

1½"
1"   ¾"
1½"   1"   2⅛"
3/16"   3/16"
1⅛"

SHAKER TRESTLE TABLE • INCHES (MILLIMETERS)

QUANTITY	PART	STOCK	THICKNESS	(mm)	WIDTH	(mm)	LENGTH	(mm)
4	feet halves	poplar	$1^{11}/_{16}$	43	3	76	30	762
2	cross braces	poplar	$1^1/_2$	38	4	127	30	762
2	posts	poplar	$2^7/_8$	73	$2^7/_8$	73	$29^3/_8$	746
1	center brace	poplar	$1^1/_2$	38	2	51	28	406
1	stretcher	poplar	$1^1/_2$	38	6	152	$43^1/_2$	110
1	top	Cherry	$^7/_8$	22	36	914	71	1803
2	breadboard ends	Cherry	$^7/_8$	22	$1^1/_2$	38	38	965
10	top fasteners	Cherry	$^3/_4$	19	$^7/_8$	22	$2^1/_2$	64

*Finished size is 36" long.

SUPPLIES

Ball and Ball
4 - 6" bed bolts No.U60-076

Horton Brasses
4 - 6" bed bolts No.H-73

Olde Century Colors
1 - pint of lamp black acrylic latex paint No.2022
(waterbase) or No.1022 (oil-based)

Rockler
1 - pint of Sam Maloof Oil/Wax Finish No.58669
10 - No.8 × 1¼" slotted screws

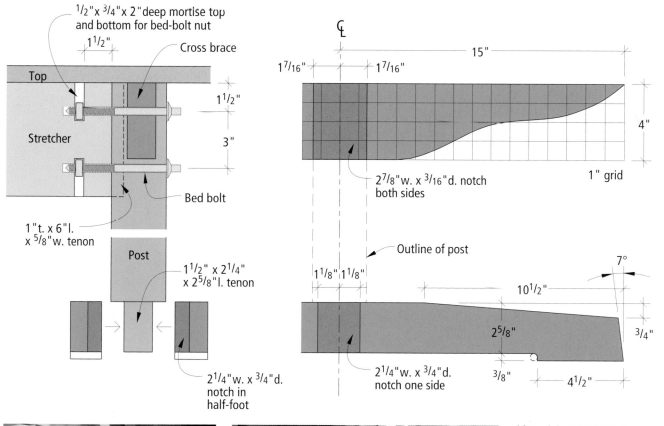

Nibbling away the mortise locations on the leg halves can be accomplished with a flat-tooth rip blade or a dado stack.

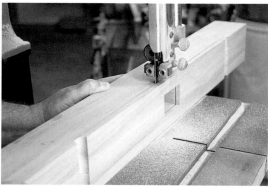

After gluing the halves together, I first drilled two $^3/_8$" holes to define the foot pad and then connected the dots. The rest was simple band saw work.

With the post cut to shape, the first step in forming the tenon is to define the shoulder on all four sides. The miter gauge (hidden behind the work) on my saw works well, while the rip fence allows you to set the shoulder location.

I use a high-sided shop-made tenoning jig to cut the cheeks on the tenon. You could also nibble away the waste like the foot mortise if you don't have or want to build a tenoning jig.

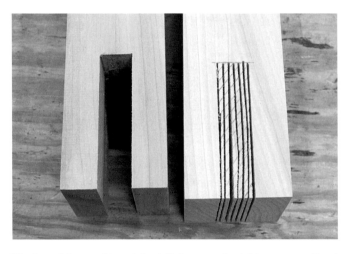

The top of the post is notched 4" deep, so the table saw won't cut it (pun intended). The band saw will and I use staggered cuts to remove much of the wood, then chisel out the excess. Notice the notch isn't centered on the post, but offset by ¼" to one side.

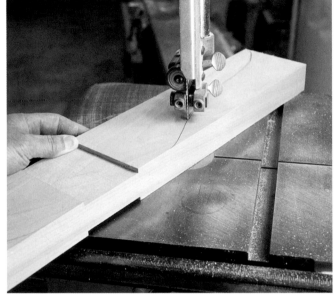

Sculpting a shape on the cross braces isn't necessary to keep the table sturdy, but it does keep it from looking clunky. After transferring the pattern onto the brace, I cut wide of the line on the band saw, then used a spindle sander to smooth the shape.

With the cross braces glued to the posts, they are pegged in position. Clamp them tight and check for square between the post and brace. Note that the pegs are at opposite corners of the joint. This allows room for the mortise (in the next step).

Here's the mortise for the stretcher. I removed most of the waste with a Forstner bit, then chiseled the mortise square.

Getting the holes for the bed bolts straight is important. And the best tool for that task is the drill press. The two $^7/_{16}$" holes are located in 1$^1/_2$" from the top and bottom edges of the mortise.

After clamping the stretcher between the legs and drilling the bed bolt holes into the stretcher I simply dropped the nut into the previously cut mortises and bolted the base together.

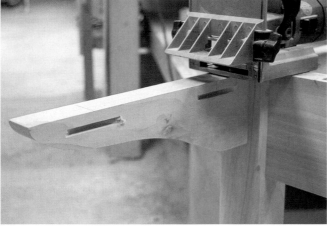

Double wide No.20 biscuit slots in the braces work well to hold the wooden top fasteners (shown above).

With the top milled to size, mark a $^5/_{16}$"-thick × 1"-wide tongue on each end with your marking gauge. Then use a straightedge and a $^3/_4$" pattern bit to shape the tongue on both sides of the top.

After marking and cutting the tenons on the breadboard tongue, use the finished tenons to locate the mortises in the already-grooved breadboard ends.

A simple coat of paint looks too new and shiny for a traditional Shaker piece of furniture.

Here I've wiped the piece with a very wet cloth as the paint dried, which removed some of the paint, creating an antique finish.

Greek Key Desk

BY JIM STACK

Got clamps? You'll need several to assemble this table. The building techniques used to make this table are completely different from any of the other tables in this book. All the parts are the same thickness and width — only the lengths vary. It could be called "stick furniture" if you like. All the joints are butted. I know what your thinking — will it really stay together? Yes, it will.

Even though the joinery is simple, it has to be as precise as you can make them. No gaps, no matter how small, are allowed. Yellow wood glue is what I used to assemble this desk.

This desk measures 40" long by 18" wide by 28½" high. The design encourages your eyes to follow the Greek key pattern around the entire desk; there is no beginning and no end. The use of contrasting colors of woods enhances the effect of the "movement" of this desk. This project is made of cherry and walnut with a clear finish.

The desk demands to have a glass top so it can show itself to the world. The glass should be at least ⅜" thick, ½" would be optimal. One other thing (this is very important) — the glass needs to be tempered — both for strength and safety. If it were to break, tempered glass would break into little pieces that look like gravel. If the glass wasn't tempered, it would break into shards that could cause serious personal injury.

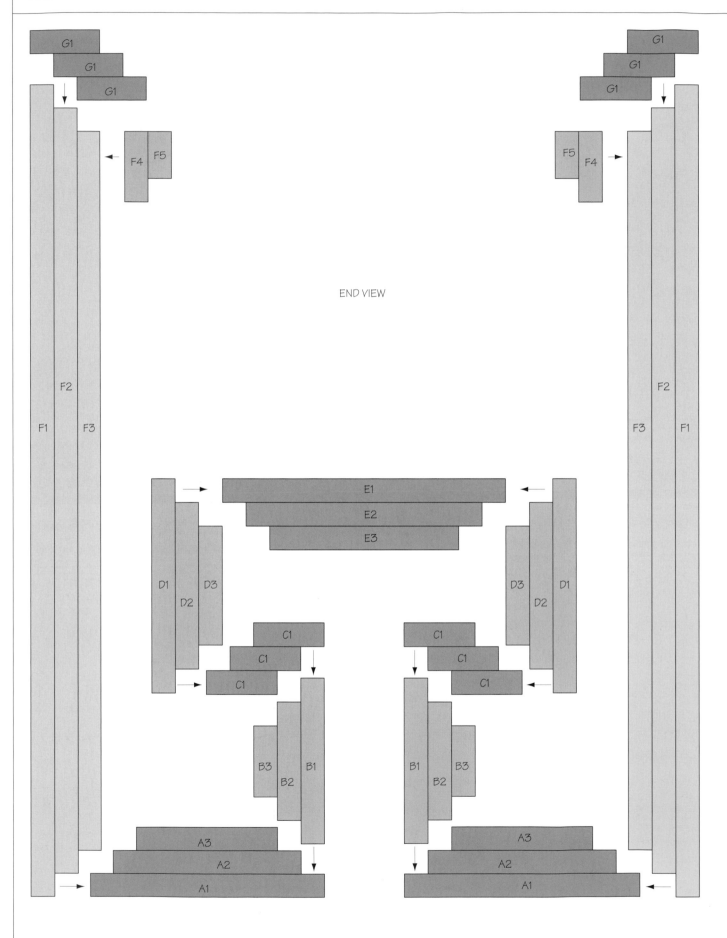

END VIEW

GREEK KEY DESK • INCHES (MILLIMETERS)

REFERENCE	QUANTITY	PART	STOCK	THICKNESS	(mm)	WIDTH	(mm)	LENGTH	(mm)	COMMENTS
A1	4	base	cherry	3/4	19	2 1/4	57	7 1/2	191	
A2	4	base	walnut	3/4	19	2 1/4	57	6	152	
A3	4	base	cherry	3/4	19	2 1/4	57	4 1/2	114	
B1	4	inner leg	cherry	3/4	19	2 1/4	57	5 1/4	133	
B2	4	inner leg	walnut	3/4	19	2 1/4	57	3 3/4	95	
B3	4	inner leg	cherry	3/4	19	2 1/4	57	2 1/4	57	
C1	12	Greek key bottom	*	3/4	19	2 1/4	57	2 1/4	57	*make 4 walnut, 8 cherry
D1	4	Greek key sides	Cherry	3/4	19	2 1/4	57	6 3/4	171	
D2	4	Greek key sides	walnut	3/4	19	2 1/4	57	5 1/4	133	
D3	4	Greek key sides	Cherry	3/4	19	2 1/4	57	3 3/4	95	
E1	2	Greek key top	Cherry	3/4	19	2 1/4	57	18	457	
E2	2	Greek key top	walnut	3/4	19	2 1/4	57	16 1/2	419	
E3	2	Greek key top	Cherry	3/4	19	2 1/4	57	15	381	
F1	4	outer legs	Cherry	3/4	19	2 1/4	57	27 3/4	705	
F2	4	outer legs	walnut	3/4	19	2 1/4	57	26 1/4	667	
F3	4	outer legs	Cherry	3/4	19	2 1/4	57	24 3/4	629	
F$	4	inner top brace	Cherry	3/4	19	2 1/4	57	2 1/4	57	
F5	4	outer top brace	walnut	3/4	19	2 1/4	57	1 1/2	38	
G1	6	top runners	*	3/4	19	2 1/4	57	48	1219	*2 walnut, 4 cherry

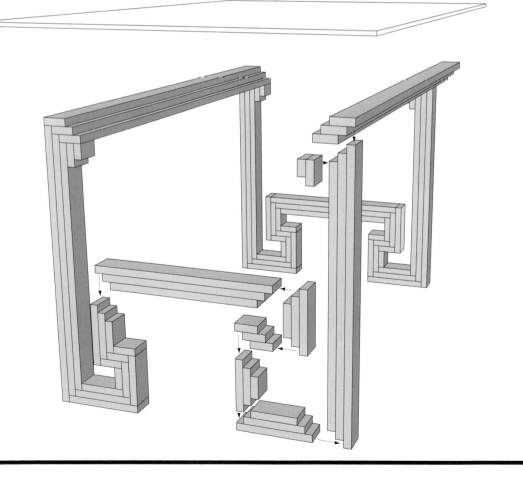

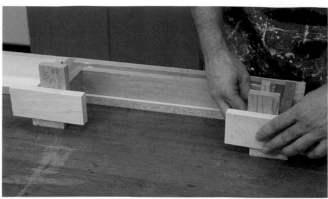

1 Setup for gluing subassembly E1E2E3 and two (2) D1D2D3. (Note the spacers to level the assembly with the jig.)

2 By using spacers at the ends of the D parts, clamp pressure is evened out.

3 Have clamps ready and begin glue-up.

4 **ABOVE:** All parts can have glue applied to them in just a few seconds.

5 **LEFT:** Put the spacers into place.

6 Clamp the length first.

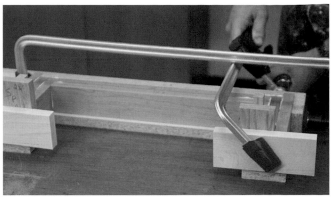

7 Then pull the D assemblies tight.

8 Use just enough clamping pressure to pull the joint tight.

9 Add clamps across the D assemblies.

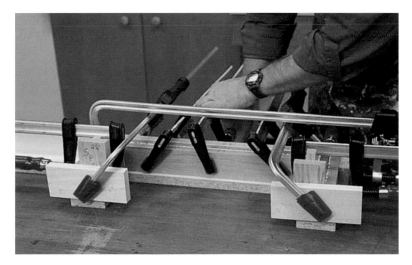

10 Finally, add clamps across the C assembly.

11 Setup for C1C1C1, B1B2B3, A1A2A3.

12 Glue and clamp the length of the assembly.

13 Add clamps across the B assembly.

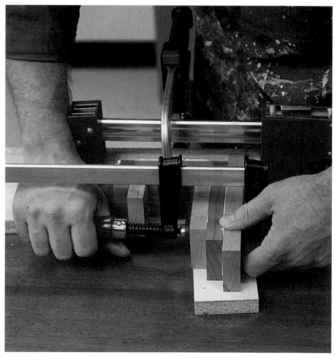

14 Add clamps across the A assembly.

15 Finally, put a clamp across the joint. Four (4) of these ABC assemblies are needed.

16 Setup for gluing up the three subassemblies.

17 Clamp the two ABC subassemblies into place on the straight jig. This will keep the whole assembly square.

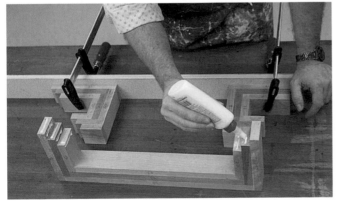

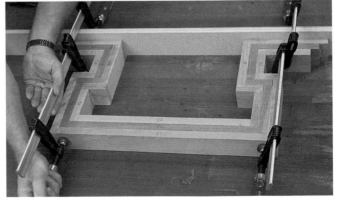

18 Apply glue to all surfaces of the step-miter joints.

19 Clamp the joint top to bottom.

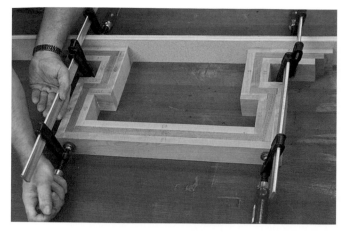

20 Clamp across the joint. Two (2) of these assemblies are needed.

21 Setup for gluing up the desk end assemblies. (Note the spacer at the tops of the legs.) Apply glue to the leg parts F1F2F3 and to the step-miter joint of the legs and the base subassembly.

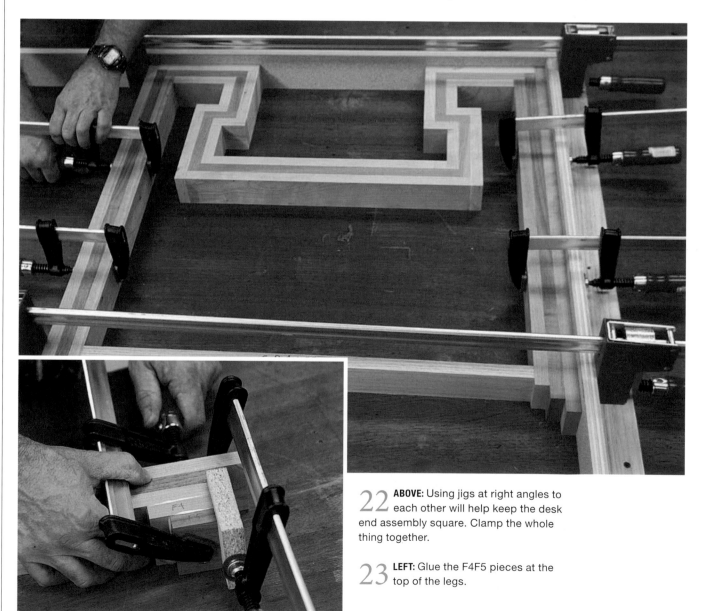

22 **ABOVE:** Using jigs at right angles to each other will help keep the desk end assembly square. Clamp the whole thing together.

23 **LEFT:** Glue the F4F5 pieces at the top of the legs.

  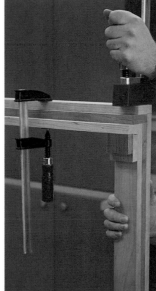 

24 Glue on the G1 rail pieces one at a time.

25 Make sure the joints at the tops of the legs and the G pieces are tight.

26 Attach the top G rail.

27 Clamp along the whole length of the G rail.

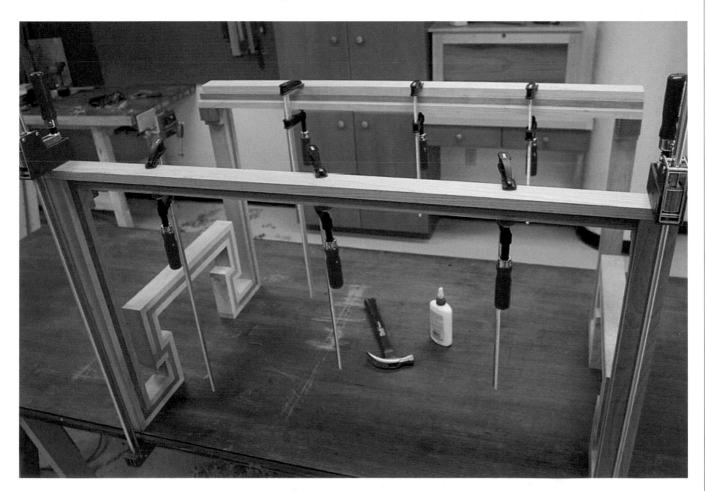

28 Final desk assembly clamped up. Let the glue cure overnight. Sand the table so all the strips are flush with each other and check for any dried glue. Then apply two or three coats of clear lacquer.

Suppliers

ADAMS & KENNEDY —
THE WOOD SOURCE
6178 Mitch Owen Rd.
P.O. Box 700
Manotick, ON
Canada K4M 1A6
613-822-6800
www.wood-source.com
Wood supply

B&Q
Portswood House
1 Hampshire Corporate Park
Chandlers Ford
Eastleigh
Hampshire, England SO53 3YX
0845 609 6688
www.diy.com
*Woodworking tools, supplies
and hardware*

BALL AND BALL
463 West Lincoln Hwyl.
Exton, PA 19341
800-257-3711
www.diy.com
*Antique hardware reproductions
and restoration*

BUSY BEE TOOLS
130 Great Gulf Dr.
Concord, ON
Canada L4K 5W1
1-800-461-2879
www.busybeetools.com
Woodworking tools and supplies

CONSTANTINE'S WOOD
CENTER OF FLORIDA
1040 E. Oakland Park Blvd.
Fort Lauderdale, FL 33334
800-443-9667
www.constantines.com
Tools, woods, veneers, hardware

DOVER DESIGNS, LLC
P.O. Box 3644
Hagerstown, MD 21742
301-733-0909
www.www.doverdesignsllc.com
*Suppliers of fine inlay, borders,
wood lines and marquetry designs*

FRANK PAXTON
LUMBER COMPANY
5701 W. 66th St.
Chicago, IL 60638
800-323-2203
www.paxtonwood.com
Wood, hardware, tools, books

HIGHLAND WOODWORKING
1045 North Highland Ave. NE
Atlanta, GA 30306
www.highlandwoodworking.com
*Tools, woodworking supplies,
books*

THE HOME DEPOT
2455 Paces Ferry Rd. NW
Atlanta, GA 30339
800-430-3376 (U.S.)
800-628-0525 (Canada)
www.homedepot.com
*Woodworking tools, supplies
and hardware*

HORTON BRASSES INC.
49 Nooks Hill Road
Cromwell, CT 06416
800-754-9127
www.horton-brasses.com
*Fine reproduction brass and iron
hardware*

KLINGSPOR ABRASIVES INC.
2555 Tate Blvd. SE
Hickory, N.C. 28602
800-645-5555
www.klingspor.com
Sandpaper of all kinds

LEE VALLEY TOOLS LTD.
P.O. Box 1780
Ogdensburg, NY 13669-6780
800-871-8158 (U.S.)
800-267-8767 (Canada)
www.leevalley.com
Woodworking tools and hardware

LONDONDERRY BRASSES LTD.
P.O. Box 415
Cochranville, PA 19330
610-593-6239
londonderry-brasses.com
Furniture hardware

LOWE'S COMPANIES, INC.
P.O. Box 1111
North Wilkesboro, NC 28656
800-445-6937
www.lowes.com
*Woodworking tools, supplies
and hardware*

ROCKLER WOODWORKING
AND HARDWARE
4365 Willow Dr.
Medina, MN 55340
800-279-4441
www.rockler.com
*Woodworking tools, hardware
and books*

TOOL TREND LTD.
140 Snow Blvd. Unit 1
Concord, ON
Canada L4K 4C1
416-663-8665
Woodworking tools and hardware

TREND MACHINERY &
CUTTING TOOLS LTD.
Odhams Trading Estate
St. Albans Rd.
Watford
Hertfordshire, U.K.
WD24 7TR
01923 224657
www.trendmachinery.co.uk
Woodworking tools and hardware

WATERLOX COATINGS
908 Meech Ave.
Cleveland, OH 44105
800-321-0377
www.waterlox.com
Finishing supplies

W.D. LOCKWOOD & CO., INC.
49 Walker St. 1st floor
New York, NY, 10013
866-293-8913
www.wdlockwood.com
Wood stains

WOODCRAFT SUPPLY LLC
1177 Rosemar Rd.
P.O. Box 1686
Parkersburg, WV 26102
800-535-4482
www.woodcraft.com
Woodworking hardware

WOODWORKER'S HARDWARE
P.O. Box 180
Sauk Rapids, MN 56379-0180
800-383-0130
www.wwhardware.com
Woodworking hardware

WOODWORKER'S SUPPLY
1108 N. Glenn Rd.
Casper, WY 82601
800-645-9292
http://woodworker.com
*Woodworking tools and
accessories, finishing supplies,
books and plans*

Index

Ideas. Instruction. Inspiration.

These and other great **Popular Woodworking** products are available at your local bookstore, woodworking store or online supplier.

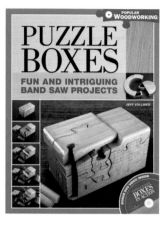

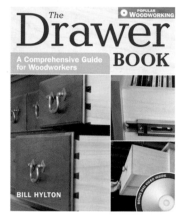

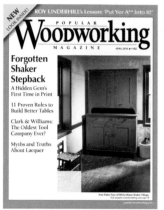

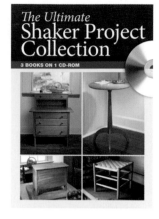

PUZZLE BOXES
BY JEFF VOLLMER

Have you ever thought *inside* the box? *Puzzle Boxes* includes a DVD where Jeff shows you how to set up your band saw and cutout, glue up, sand and fit and finish these amazing boxes.

ISBN 13: 978-1-55870-847-1
hardcover w/DVD • 144 pages • Z2116

THE DRAWER BOOK
BY BILL HYLTON

This is the best instruction manual you'll ever find that teaches you how to make, fit and finish drawers. Pick a drawer style that will work for any woodworking project you build needing drawers.

ISBN 13: 978-1-55870-842-6
hardcover w/DVD • 160 pages • Z2007

POPULAR WOODWORKING MAGAZINE

Whether learning a new hobby or perfecting your craft, *Popular Woodworking Magazine* has expert information to teach the skill, not just the project. Find the latest issue on newsstands, or order online at www.popularwoodworking.com.

THE ULTIMATE SHAKER PROJECT COLLECTION
CD-ROM, BOOKS BY KERRY PIERCE

If you want to build Shaker furniture, these books provide you with all the details and step-by-step instructions you'll need.

ISBN 13: 978-1-4403-0239-8

This disc includes the full book content from: *Storage & Shelving the Shaker Way*, *Chairmaking Simplified* and *Authentic Shaker Furniture*.
CD-ROM • Z4824

Visit **www.popularwoodworking.com** to see more woodworking information by the experts.

Recent Articles

Read the five most recent articles from Popular Woodworking Books.

• Kitchen Makeovers - Pull-Out Pantry Design & Construction
• Woodshop Lust Tom Rosati's Woodshop
• Woodshop Lust David Thiel's Woodshop
• Wood Finishing Simplified Strictly, Stickley Oak
• Wood Finishing Simplified In a Pickle (Whitewash on Oak or Pine)

Featured Product

Made By Hand
$21.95

Made By Hand takes you right to the bench and shows you how to start building furniture using hand tools. By working through the six projects in this book, you'll learn the basics of hand-tool woodworking and how to use the tools effectively and efficiently, then add joinery skills and design complexity. The accompanying DVD includes valuable insight into the tools themselves and a look at the techniques that make these tools work so well.

Note from the Editor

Welcome to Books & More
We've got the latest reviews and free sample excerpts from our favorite woodworking books, plus news on the newest releases. Check out the savings at our **Woodworker's Book Shop**, and don't miss out on building your Wish List for the holidays. If you missed our newsletter's **"Print Is Dead"** poll results, check them here, and subscribe (below) to our newsletter to receive special sale items and book reviews not found anywhere else.

– *David Baker-Thiel, Executive Editor*
Popular Woodworking Books

A woodworking education can come in many forms, including books, magazines, videos and community feedback. At Popular Woodworking we've got them all. Visit our website at www.popularwoodworking.com to follow our blogs, read about the newest tools and books and join our community. We want to know what you're building.

Sign up to receive our weekly newsletter at http://popularwoodworking.com/newsletters/